C000172420

Clinical Applications of Learning Theory

Clinical Applications of Learning Theory

Edited by Mark Haselgrove
and Lee Hogarth

Psychology Press
Taylor & Francis Group
HOVE AND NEW YORK

First published 2012
by Psychology Press
27 Church Road, Hove, East Sussex BN3 2FA

Simultaneously published in the USA and Canada
by Psychology Press
711 Third Avenue, New York, NY 10017

www.psypress.com

*Psychology Press is an imprint of the Taylor & Francis Group, an
Informa business*

Copyright © 2012 Psychology Press

All rights reserved. No part of this book may be reprinted or
reproduced or utilised in any form or by any electronic, mechanical,
or other means, now known or hereafter invented, including
photocopying and recording, or in any information storage or
retrieval system, without permission in writing from the publishers.

Trademark notice: Product or corporate names may be trademarks or
registered trademarks, and are used only for identification and
explanation without intent to infringe.

British Library Cataloguing in Publication Data
A catalogue record for this book is available from the British Library

Library of Congress Cataloging-in-Publication Data
Clinical applications of learning theory / Edited by Mark Haselgrove
and Lee Hogarth.
     p. cm.
  Includes bibliographical references and index.
  ISBN 978-1-84872-008-4 (hb)
  1. Learning, Psychology of. 2. Psychoses. 3. Neuroses. 4. Mental
Illness. I. Haselgrove, Mark, 1974–. II. Hogarth, Lee, 1973–. III.
Title.
  BF318.C55 2011
  153.1'5–dc22

ISBN: 978-1-84872-008-4 (hbk)
ISBN: 978-0-203-80350-9 (ebk)

Typeset in Times by Garfield Morgan, Swansea, West Glamorgan
Cover design by Sandra Heath
Printed and bound in Great Britain by TJ International Ltd, Padstow,
Cornwall

Contents

List of tables

List of figures

Contributors

Andrew G. Baker is at Department of Psychology, McGill University, Montreal, Canada.

Mark E. Bouton is at Department of Psychology, University of Vermont, Burlington, USA.

Helen J. Cassaday is at School of Psychology, The University of Nottingham, Nottingham, UK.

Henry W. Chase is at School of Psychology, The University of Nottingham, Nottingham, UK.

Paul Enck is at Department of Internal Medicine IV: Psychosomatic Medicine and Psychotherapy, University Hospital, Tübingen, Germany.

Andy P. Field is at School of Psychology, University of Sussex, Brighton, UK.

Geoffrey Hall is at Department of Psychology, University of York, York, UK.

Neil Hanley is at Department of Psychology, McGill University, Montreal, Canada.

Mark Haselgrove is at School of Psychology, The University of Nottingham, Nottingham, UK.

Lee Hogarth is at School of Psychology, The University of Nottingham, Nottingham, UK.

Ebrahim Kantini is at School of Psychology, The University of Nottingham, Nottingham, UK.

Sibylle Klosterhalfen is at Institute for Clinical Neurobiology and Medical Psychology, University of Düsseldorf, Germany.

Paula M. Moran is at School of Psychology, The University of Nottingham, Nottingham, UK.

Rachel M. Msetfi is at Department of Psychology, University of Limerick, Limerick, Ireland.

Robin A. Murphy is at Department of Experimental Psychology, University of Oxford, Oxford, UK.

Andrew J. D. Nelson is at School of Psychology, The University of Nottingham, Nottingham, UK.

Helena M. Purkis is at School of Psychology, University of Queensland, Australia.

Jenny L. Rouse is at School of Psychology, The University of Nottingham, Nottingham, UK.

Michelle Symonds is at Department of Psychology, University of York, York, UK.

Drina Vurbic is at Department of Psychology, University of Vermont, Burlington, USA.

Neil E. Winterbauer is at Department of Psychology, University of Vermont, Burlington, USA.

Introduction

Mark Haselgrove and Lee Hogarth

Broadly speaking, learning theorists concern themselves studying the mechanisms by which animals, including humans, acquire and utilize information about relationships between events. This endeavour includes the study of classical conditioning, instrumental conditioning, and the neural substrates that underlie these phenomena. The most enduring models that have emerged from this research argue that learning can be understood in terms of the formation of Pavlovian associations between events in the world (such as the sight of a dark alleyway and the witnessing of an assault) or instrumental associations between the agent's own actions and their consequences (such as choosing a restaurant and eating a delicious supper). Such associations are thought to provide the agent with the opportunity to anticipate the future and by dint of this knowledge behave adaptively on the basis of these predictions. However, the mechanisms of learning can sometimes go wrong, be undermined, or express themselves in an inappropriate manner, resulting in maladaptive behaviour. For example, individuals who are undergoing treatment for cancer will frequently experience unpleasant side effects of the cancer treatment (such as nausea and vomiting) that, with repeated treatment, may be elicited upon entering the clinic prior to the administration of the cytotoxic drugs themselves. To take another example, people who choose to inject themselves with heroin quickly report experiencing a rewarding sense of euphoria. However, long-term use of the drug can ultimately lead to chronic dysphoria. Both of these cases provide examples of a learning mechanism that enables the person to form associative connections between events (in one case the sight of a clinic and nausea, in the other injection of a drug and euphoria). Unfortunately, the consequences of this learning are far from desirable or adaptive and have significant clinical implications. The goal of this book is to introduce the reader to a selection of clinical problems that are thought to be influenced by the process of learning. In some cases it will be argued that the clinical problem itself is caused by a normally working learning mechanism (see, for example, the chapters by Symonds and Hall, and Field and Purkis). In other cases the clinical problem may be partially linked with aberrant learning (see, for example, the chapter by Moran and Rouse). In either case, the study of learning in both animals and people has provided us with an understanding of the conditions in which associative connections will, and will not, be formed between events. Armed with this knowledge, the clinician can apply the principles of learning theory to the clinical setting in order to either maximize the impact of a clinical intervention, or to better understand the conditions under which the clinical problem can emerge, and therefore prevent it.

In Chapter 1, Moran and Rouse provide a novel historical perspective on the influence of learning theory on the understanding of schizophrenia. The contributions of Clark Hull, Kenneth Spence, Ivan Pavlov, and B. F. Skinner are described, and in a number of cases, the proposals of these founders of learning theory are remarkably prophetic in anticipating contemporary issues in schizophrenia research. They then describe more recent research demonstrating that individuals with schizophrenia have deficits in learning phenomena such as latent inhibition and blocking, and the emerging correspondence between the neural mechanisms involved in blocking, and those that are disturbed in schizophrenia.

In Chapter 2 by Symonds and Hall, the acquisition of anxiety and aversion to the clinical context is described which can, ultimately, result in patients avoiding treatment. In particular, they provide an analysis in terms of classical conditioning for the phenomenon of anticipatory nausea and vomiting (ANV), in which patients (normally undergoing chemotherapy) come to acquire an aversion to the clinical context in which they receive treatment. This aversion can be so strong that it can evoke vomiting prior to the administration of cytotoxic drugs. Symonds and Hall describe a variety of animal models used to investigate this problem, and suggest a series of interventions (scape-goating and clinical pre-exposure) that are based upon the principles of associative learning that have the potential to attenuate the development of clinical aversions. Applications to the human clinical population are described that show some promising results; indeed some applications have been shown to reduce not only the magnitude of ANV but also post-treatment nausea.

Field and Purkis (Chapter 3) echo the perspective of Symonds and Hall, and begin their chapter on associative learning by outlining how the many routes by which a stimulus may come to evoke fear may all have associative learning as their basis. The authors then go on to provide a wide-ranging summary of the fundamental properties of conditioning and consider how these properties add to our understanding of the conditions under which fears and phobias may (or may not) be acquired, and subsequently treated. They conclude with a discussion of the role of attentional biases towards fear-inducing stimuli. In particular the possibility that attention to threat stimuli may be acquired through either an instrumentally conditioned habit, or vicarious conditioning.

In the chapter by Hogarth and Chase (Chapter 4), the paradoxical claims of contemporary theories of addiction are considered with regard to the vulnerabilities underlying drug dependence. On the one hand, hypersensitivity to the rewarding effects of drugs is thought to give rise to greater intentions, expectations, craving, and desire for drugs. But on the other hand, accelerated habit learning is thought to reduce intentional control over drug use behaviour, in favour of direct habitual control by antecedent Pavlovian stimuli. These claims are paradoxical inasmuch as drug use behaviour apparently cannot be both intentional and habitual at the same time. The chapter addresses these issues by describing a set of outcome devaluation and Pavlovian-to-instrumental transfer procedures conducted with smokers to probe the intentional versus habitual status of drug-seeking and -taking behaviour across levels of dependence and impulsivity. These studies suggest that whereas variation in dependence is associated with hypervaluation of the drug as a goal of intentional drug seeking, the partially orthogonal trait of impulsivity is associated with habitual control of drug use behaviour. These distinct vulnerabilities may differentially influence the uptake and perseveration of drug use across the life-course of addiction.

In Chapter 5, Bouton, Winterbauer, and Vurbic examine the role of context in the extinction of conditioned responding and use this as an explanation for instances of relapse following treatment for drug addiction. Bouton et al. describe a number of phenomena that show that the extinction of both Pavlovian and instrumental conditioned responding is particularly context specific. The implication for treatment is obvious: any behavioural therapy that has as its basis the extinction of an unwanted behaviour will be undermined once the client leaves the clinical (extinction) context. Examples are drawn from both animal and human studies, but conditioning established to drug stimuli in animals is considered in particular. Interestingly, contextual specificity does not have to be established by extroceptive stimuli, such as rooms or buildings, but can also be established by drugs (such as anxiolitics) or indeed the presence of emotional states themselves. The chapter concludes with a series of interventions that can be shown to reduce the impact of the contextual specificity of extinction, through behavioural and pharmacological means.

The placebo response is well known both in and outside the clinical setting, and refers to the beneficial effect of a clinical treatment that is not specific to that treatment. Less well known is the nocebo response that refers to the worsening of patient symptoms due to treatment that is, again, not specific to the treatment. Klosterhalfen and Enck (Chapter 6) consider these two responses in terms of learning theory, suggesting that placebo and nocebo responses are generated by Pavlovian and instrumental conditioning. This chapter reviews a number of effects noting the role of reward systems in the placebo response and anxiety systems in the nocebo response. Gaps in the literature are identified, for example, no demonstration yet exists of a dose–response curve [i.e. increasing the number of CS–US (conditioned stimulus–unconditioned stimulus) pairings] for the placebo effect, and the extent to which placebo responses generalize between clinical settings is, as yet, unknown. Despite this, a variety of physiological responses can come under the control of conditioning, including immune, endocrine, and allergic responses. Finally, the methodology of conditioning experiments has assisted clinicians in designing trials to determine the efficacy of a drug treatment under conditions in which placebo responses are minimized.

Baker, Msetfi, Hanley, and Murphy in Chapter 7 provide an experimental analysis of the depressive realism effect – the finding that depressed individuals are more accurate than nondepressed individuals at reporting zero contingencies between events. The authors question the paradoxical assertion that this effect reflects superior judgement on the part of depressed individuals, when the standard view is that depression is linked to less than optimal cognitive performance. From a series of experimental tests, the authors conclude that depression is not in fact linked to superior contingency judgement, but rather, the depressive realism effect arises from the absence in depressed individuals for a need to maintain self-esteem by overestimating the causal relationship between their actions and the consequences.

Tourette syndrome (TS) is characterized by involuntary chronic muscular and vocal tics. In Chapter 8, Nelson, Kantini, and Cassaday outline the behavioural neurological properties of TS, with particular emphasis placed on the role of a dysfunctional habit [S–R (stimulus–response)] learning system. It is notable that a significant overlap exists between the neural substrates of habit learning and tics. Nelson et al. go on to consider the potential role of Pavlovian [S–S (stimulus–stimulus)] associations in TS, and describe the outcome of an experiment examining conditioned inhibition in patients on and off medication for TS. Finally the implications of co-morbidity of TS with other related disorders such as obsessive-compulsive disorder and ADHD (attention deficit hyperactivity disorder) are considered.

1 Integrative theories of schizophrenia and learning

A historical perspective

Paula M. Moran and Jenny L. Rouse

Schizophrenia is a disease, or more accurately a cluster of psychiatric symptoms, characterized by bizarre perceptual experiences in sufferers. It is surprisingly common, with a prevalence of 1 in a 100, meaning that that 1 person in a 100 will suffer from schizophrenia at some time during their life, rising to 3 in a 100 when all psychotic disorders are considered (Peraala et al., 2007). From the earliest incarnations of modern psychiatry and experimental psychology there have been attempts to understand and ascertain the origins of the symptoms of schizophrenia. This is partly because schizophrenia has always been a significant societal burden, particularly prior to the discovery of antipsychotic medication in the 1950s. However, a more likely reason is that an interest in the mind and behaviour is naturally accompanied by an interest in what happens when perceptual processes and behaviour go awry in such a dramatic fashion. To the student of human behaviour there is something inherently fascinating about extremes of behaviour and experience such as hallucinations and delusions. This fascination crystallized in the 19th century as the search for the origin of schizophrenia symptoms moved from the hands of religion into those of science.

In this chapter we will first show that the collaboration between learning theory and schizophrenia research goes back much earlier than is commonly acknowledged to the earliest days of both experimental psychology and psychiatry, in some cases foreshadowing the most recent advances in the field today. Second we will indicate how current theoretical approaches to schizophrenia continue to reflect the applications of learning theory.

What is schizophrenia?

Symptoms of schizophrenia are typically classified as positive (reality distortions such as hallucinations, delusions), negative (flattened affect, social withdrawal), or cognitive (working memory/executive problems, thought disorder). The class of symptoms that characterize schizophrenia most effectively are distortions in reality. Although there are certainly individual differences in the presentation of reality distortions, there are two principal symptom types: delusions and hallucinations.

Delusions can be defined as false beliefs that are at the least unlikely to be true, or may defy logic to such a degree they are impossible. Although an abundance of evidence is typically available to contradict the belief, delusions will remain relatively unaltered (Butler & Braff, 1991). Delusions of persecution are the most common form of delusion and these are culturally specific (Bentall, Corcoran, Howard, Blackwood, & Kinderman, 2001). An American is more likely to believe he/she is being spied on by the CIA than an individual in a village in India, where beliefs in magic may lead an individual to believe he or she is being persecuted by an evil spirit (Kulhara, Avasthi, & Sharma, 2000).

The other common group of reality distortions are hallucinations. Hallucinations are perceptual experiences in the absence of external stimulation (Silbersweig et al., 1995) and can occur in any sensory modality. Auditory hallucinations are commonly voices. The nature of these voices varies between patients, with some individuals reporting friendly and encouraging voices, although most are critical and angry.

Formal thought disorder is the general term used to describe disturbances in thinking. Thought disorder is considered an overt sign as it can be observed as confused speech that is difficult for the listener to understand. Specific disruptions include loosely connected thought patterns and a general lack of awareness of the listener's needs (Docherty, Hall, Gordinier, & Cutting, 2000). Thought disorder is prominent in both descriptions and conceptualizations of schizophrenia (Kerns & Berenbaum, 2002).

The final major group of symptoms can be loosely defined as disruptions in emotionality. Sometimes these disruptions can appear to be over-emotional responses such as inappropriate laughter. However, the majority of emotional disorder is impoverished, leading many to liken the symptoms to those seen in major depression (Winograd-Gurvich, Fitzgerald, Georgiou-Karistianis, Bradshaw, & White, 2006). Patients withdraw from society and appear emotionally detached. Many individuals will also show a reduction in their emotional responses, not smiling or producing necessary gestures to allow normal conversation.

All the symptoms above are considered cardinal to diagnosis of schizophrenia, though not all patients will show evidence of all the groups. Specific diagnosis is made according to one of two major classification systems: The *Diagnostic and Statistical Manual of Mental Disorders* (DSM-IV-TR), or the *International Classification of Diseases and Related Health Problems* (ICD-10). It is notable that neither DSM-IV-TR nor ICD-10 include cognitive symptoms specifically, however this is likely to change in the forthcoming DSM-V and ICD-11 due to be published in 2013 (Keefe & Fenton, 2007). Given the complexity of the symptom profile and overlap with other disorders such as bipolar disorder, many have claimed that a single syndrome of schizophrenia does not exist and it is more accurate to consider the individual symptoms (Bentall, 2006).

It is important to note that there are demonstrated cultural differences not only in the manifestation of symptoms, but also in the diagnosis and clinical outcomes of schizophrenia. Patients in Western, developed countries show a higher frequency of depressive symptoms, thought insertion, and thought broadcasting and a less favourable progression and outcome than in developing countries (Sartorius et al., 1986). The specific cultural factors that contribute to these differences are not clear but may comprise social and kinship factors (Jablensky et al., 1992; Jablensky & Sartorious, 2008).

Biological theories of schizophrenia

A full treatment of the biological theories of schizophrenia are beyond the scope of this chapter but have been covered elsewhere in great detail (for recent comprehensive reviews see Van Os & Kapur, 2009; Keshavan, Tandon, Boutros, & Nasrallah, 2008). They can be considered under the rubrics of neurochemical, neurodevelopmental, and genetic hypotheses and most would agree that it is likely that abnormalities in all of these dimensions interact to produce the range of behavioural symptoms associated with the disease (Maynard, Sikich, Lieberman, & LaMantia, 2001; Wong & Van Tol, 2003).

There are a number of biological theories that have particular import for how the theoretical understanding of learning has been applied to understanding schizophrenia symptoms. The neurotransmitters dopamine and glutamate both have specific roles in learning and have been suggested to be abnormal in schizophrenia. The dopamine hypothesis of schizophrenia essentially suggests that overactivity in subcortical dopamine neural circuitry, including the ventral striatum, engenders the positive symptoms of schizophrenia while a later revision suggested that a consequent underactivity in meso-cortical regions gives rise to negative and cognitive symptoms (Toda & Abi-Dargham, 2007). This revision allowed the hypothesis to simultaneously explain hallucinations and delusions (overactivity in subcortical dopamine) and flat affect and executive dysfunction (underactivity in prefrontal dopamine) (Howes & Kapur, 2009). The glutamate hypothesis suggests that dysfunction in glutamatergic transmission in cortico-limbic brain regions is primarily responsible for the symptoms of schizophrenia, particularly the negative and cognitive symptoms (Coyle, 1996; Javitt, 2007; Belforte et al., 2010).

The role of dopamine in learning is complex and there are many hypotheses suggesting that dopamine and in particular the phasic signal mediates a number of aspects of the learning process; prediction error (a mismatch between actual and expected outcomes to stimuli that initiate learning) (Waelti, Dickinson, & Schultz, 2001), the gating of new information to the frontal cortex (Cohen, Braver, & Brown, 2002), and the assignation of **incentive value** to environmental stimuli (Berridge &

Robinson, 1998). Glutamate plays an important role in long-term memory formation and there is strong evidence for modulatory actions on memory consolidation (for review see Riedel, Platt, & Micheau, 2003).

We will see how modern integrative theories of schizophrenia make explicit reference to these processes that are underpinned by dopamine and glutamate circuitry and hypothesized to be abnormally regulated in schizophrenia.

Applications of learning theory to schizophrenia: A long history

The first systematic attempts to describe schizophrenia in experimental terms was in the work of Kraepelin and Bleuler in the late 1800s and early 1900s, considered to be the founding fathers of modern Psychiatry. Emile Kraepelin (influenced by working closely with Alois Alzheimer who identified the first neuropathological hallmarks of what is now called Alzheimer's Disease) suggested in 1896 that the disease was not a single psychotic entity but could be divided into "dementia praecox" and "manic depressive insanity". He originally classified the disorder into three subtypes (catatonic, hebephrenic, and paranoid) but later added a fourth type (simple) and was one of the first to identify the progressive nature of the disease. It was Eugene Bleuler, a Swiss psychiatrist, who suggested the name "Schizophrenia" in 1911, to denote a splitting of psychic functions, "schiz" meaning split and "phren" meaning mind. Bleuler proposed that the fundamental symptoms were incongruity of affect, ambivalences, autism, and loosening of associations (the Four As). The loosening of associations he described as follows:

> Contradictory, competing, and more or less
> irrelevant responses can no longer be excluded.
> . . . Schizophrenic patients themselves often
> complain about the confusion in their talk and
> thinking, saying that everything seems mixed
> up, the words do not come as they once did,
> thoughts rush in and are jumbled . . . .
> "There are a million words," one patient said,
> "I can't make sentences; everything is disconnected."
> Another patient made several attempts
> to speak and then gave up; the next
> day she complained her thoughts had been
> rushing through her mind so that she could say nothing.
>
> (1911, p. 511)

While the Kraepelinian view is considered to be the most influential, it was Bleuler's ideas that disordered thought processes in schizophrenia represent a loosening of associations that were crucial in the development of the idea that a disruption in learning might be of relevance to understanding the fragmented thinking and delusions that characterize schizophrenia. While documentary evidence is scarce, it is highly likely that psychiatrists such as Bleuler were influenced by the concurrent developments in experimental psychology in the late 19th and early 20th century, particularly the work of stimulus-response theorists Pavlov and Watson. In 1913 Watson published his behaviourist manifesto, marking a period in history when focus in Psychology began to shift away from the mind and towards behaviour. This is exemplified by a quote from Watson on mental illness "When the psychopathologist tries to tell me about a 'schiz' . . . I have the feeling that he doesn't know what he is talking about. And the reason I think he doesn't know what he is talking about is that he has always approached his patients from the point of view of the mind" (Watson, 1924). In the early 20th century experimental psychology was dominated by stimulus-response learning theory with the work of Watson, Pavlov, Hull, Spence, and later Skinner dominating accounts of learning and human behaviour. The influence of these theoretical advances was evident in psychiatric studies in patients and in particular schizophrenia from their earliest inception.[1]

Clark Hull and Kenneth Spence

One of the first examples of the convergence of learning theory and schizophrenia research was in the work of Hull (1884–1952) who proposed a highly influential theory on the importance of drive state on behaviour (Hull, 1943). Hull turned his attention to schizophrenia in an early paper that investigated associations in the insane (Hull, 1917). His theory broadly proposed that the effect of increased drive in an individual (e.g. hunger, anxiety, fear) is to augment the response strength of any habitual behaviours elicited by environmental stimuli. Thus in general the hungrier or more anxious or more fearful the organism, the greater the drive and the greater the speed and amplitude of its response. In a simple **conditioning** situation where the number of response alternatives is limited, high drive should augment the response strength of the **conditioned response**. Thus he predicted correctly that schizophrenia patients who by virtue of their illness display high drive and anxiety should show faster conditioning than a low drive group (Mednick, 1958). These findings were later replicated in larger cohorts of patients and it was suggested that specific patient subgroups may be associated with different arousal/anxiety levels, thereby affecting learning rates (Howe, 1958).

A number of early studies addressed the question whether patients with schizophrenia could be conditioned effectively. Pfaffman and Schlosberg (1936) investigated the conditioned knee-jerk response in 25 schizophrenics and 25 controls. The patients were found to condition more quickly than controls. Studies by Mays (1934) and Shipley (1934) indicated that schizophrenics show faster conditioning of the psychogalvanic response than do controls. Taylor and Spence (1954) found that schizophrenics showed faster eyeblink conditioning than controls or anxiety neurotics. Eyeblink conditioning is where a neutral **conditioned stimulus** (CS), such as a tone, is followed by an **unconditioned stimulus** (US), such as an air puff across the eye that evokes an **unconditioned response** (UR), which is the eyeblink. With repeated CS–US paired presentations the subject "learns" to blink prior to the US. The results of several eyeblink conditioning studies support the prediction that schizophrenics show faster conditioning than controls (Mednick, 1958). There are many more recent studies that have shown abnormal eyeblink conditioning in schizophrenia (Lubow, 2009) that is suggested to result from abnormally high cerebellar activity conse-quent to cortico–cerebellar–thalamic–cortical circuit dysfunction (Sears, Andreasen, & O'Leary, 2000). Recently it has been noted that deficits are seen mainly in studies with medicated patients, suggesting that effects may be consequent to long-term treatment with antipsychotic drugs. Unmedi-cated patient studies show either no effect or faster conditioning (Lubow, 2009). This concurs with the (necessarily unmedicated) early studies of Hull, Spence, and Taylor that there is faster conditioning in schizophrenia. There are further instances of faster conditioning in schizophrenia such as in disrupted **latent inhibition**, which is faster conditioning to an irrelevant stimulus (Lubow, 2005); this has theoretical implications for how abnormal associations are formed in the disease and will be discussed in detail below.

It may be possible to interpret a patient's inability to perform complex learning tasks in Hullian terms. A complex task will necessarily involve incorrect and irrelevant habit tendencies that compete with the correct ones while high drive will tend to push irrelevant responses above the evocation threshold (Mednick, 1958). Such interpretation has some clear common-alities with later theoretical proposals (discussed in more detail later) such as that of Gray, Feldon, Rawlins, Smith, and Hemsley (1991), who suggested that in schizophrenia there is a fundamental problem in integrating past experience with current perception and with the switching hypothesis suggesting that patients have an impairment in the tendency to change a learned response although it continues to be relevant (Yogev, Hadar, Gutman, & Sirota, 2003; Weiner, 1990).

The influence of emotional processing and anxiety on cognitive and other symptoms in schizophrenia is also now an important research area in schizophrenia driven by increasing knowledge of its biological under-pinnings using new brain-imaging technology (Kerr & Neale, 1993; Hooker & Park, 2002).

Ivan Pavlov

Pavlov (1849–1936) discovered classical conditioning and it is through this discovery, and the broad theoretical understanding that followed the formalization of the laws of associative learning, that he had greatest influence on schizophrenia research. It is not widely documented but towards the end of his life Pavlov turned his attention to the study of schizophrenia, and observed a number of schizophrenic patients at the Balinskii Hospital in Leningrad (Windholz, 1993). He described the aetiology of the disorder as occurring in people of the weak temperament type who during childhood developed improperly and suffered severe traumatic life experiences (Windholz, 1993). This foreshadows modern ideas about the neurodevelopmental aspects of the disorder and indeed the concept of a psychosis-proneness personality (Meehl, 1962; Van Os, Linscott, Myin-Germeys, Delespaul, & Krabbendam, 2009). Currently held views on the biological origin of schizophrenia include the "two hit hypothesis". This suggests that genetic or environmental factors disrupt early central nervous system (CNS) development and that these early disruptions produce long-term vulnerability to a "second hit" in the form of an environmental insult that then leads to the onset of schizophrenia symptoms (Maynard et al., 2001). It has been widely demonstrated that relatives of people with schizophrenia are more prone to develop schizophrenia and show a number of abnormalities in information processing such as sensory gating and attention (Cornblatt & Keilp, 1994; O'Connor et al., 2009). While we would not describe them as being of weak temperament today, there are individuals who score highly on psychometric schizotypy scales or are identified clinically as being at high risk who show early information processing and social difficulties that can serve as useful early indicators of future disease (Raine, 2006).

Pavlov explained the behaviour of schizophrenics in terms of his theory of higher nervous activity, which focused on the function of the brain of higher animals and emphasized their interaction with the external environment. If we consider that the origin of what Pavlov termed "weak" temperament as being genetic, then his proposed interaction between "weak" temperament and traumatic environmental events has foreshadowed the most current thinking about the aetiology of schizophrenia as the likely interaction between genes and environment (Agid et al., 1999; Caspi & Moffitt, 2006). This conclusion in relation to schizophrenia is all the more perspicacious when it is considered that this idea pre-dates the major 20th-century discoveries of the nature of genetic material and the identification of developmental and environmental risk factors for the disorder such as urban environment and perinatal complications (Pederson & Mortensen, 2001; Hare, 1956; Jones, Rantakallio, Hartikainen, Ischanni, & Sipila, 1998).

According to Pavlov, the cortex of schizophrenics was overwhelmed by neural excitation that resulted in irrational or nonadaptive activity (Lynn, 1963). "[S]ymptoms can be looked on as beginning inhibition of the cortex so that the subcortical areas not only are released from the constant inhibition exercised on them by the cortex but get into a state of chaotic excitation" (Pavlov, 1930, translated by Kasanin, in Putnam & Myerson, 1932). Many recent theories of the origin of neurochemical abnormalities in schizophrenia are based on electrophysiological recording in cortical and hippocampal regions. One important view currently is that dopamine neuronal overactivity in subcortical brain regions gives rise to hallucinations and delusions (Toda & Abi-Dargham, 2007). Such activity is reminiscent of Pavlov's idea of impairment of cortical inhibition, though it is the hippo-campus rather than the cortex itself that current theorists consider to be the origin of the overactivity (Grace, Lodge, & Behrens, 2009). A possible neurochemical correlate of Pavlov's faulty inhibitory process may be the glutamate system. It has been suggested that brain glutamate systems (thought to be dysfunctional in schizophrenia) are inhibitory on dopamine systems (thought to be overactive in schizophrenia) (Toda & Abi-Dargham, 2007; Javitt, 2007). If there is loss of glutamate receptor function in prefrontal cortical regions, as has been proposed in schizophrenia, this disinhibits dopamine function in subcortical brain regions thereby leading to overactivity. This subcortical dopamine overactivity then leads to symptoms as has been suggested by the dopamine hypothesis (e.g. prior to Laruelle, Kegeles, & Abi-Dargham, 2003).

Pavlov additionally suggested that acquired manic-depressive and schizophrenic disorders may become hereditary (i.e., acquired and then passed down through the families) and that psychiatrists failed to study patients adequately across the generations (Windholz, 1996, 1999). Such insight could be considered to foreshadow the newest developments in the field of epigenetics. Epigenetics is the study of how environment can elicit modifications in chromatin, non-DNA heritable genetic material contained in the nucleus of the cell. There is evidence that modifications in chromatin structure that occur in response to early stressful events may be inherited (Zhang & Meaney, 2010). This may suggest a potential mechanism through which acquired schizophrenia might become heritable, though this awaits empirical verification. Perhaps to identify the next breakthrough in schizo-phrenia research one needs to look no further than the early 20th-century writings of Pavlov.

Burrhus Frederic Skinner

B. F. Skinner (1904–1990) formulated the principles of **instrumental** or **operant conditioning** (Skinner, 1938; Ferster & Skinner, 1957) and was considered to be the father of modern behaviourism. It is a little-known fact that in common with his illustrious predecessors Hull, Spence, and Pavlov he too turned his attention briefly to the study of patients with chronic schizophrenia (Skinner, 1954). He investigated whether, in common with rats and children, patients showed operant conditioning. Patients were required to pull levers to acquire candy or cigarettes as reinforcement. Unsurprisingly for modern scholars, he found that indeed they did show similar patterns of conditioning. He concluded that "the similarity of the performance between psychotic patients and the performance of 'normal' rats, pigeons and children on two intermittent schedules of reinforcement suggest that psychotic behaviour is controlled to some extent by the reinforcing properties of the immediate physical environment . . ." (Lindsley & Skinner, 1954, p. 419).

Thus the association between schizophrenia research and the pioneers of learning theory has a longer history than is commonly acknowledged and set the foundations for modern theoretical approaches to integrating what is known about the disorder.

Abnormal learning as an explanatory framework to understand the symptoms of schizophrenia

A number of modern theoretical frameworks have suggested how abnormal learning might lead to the characteristic symptoms associated with schizophrenia. Gray, Hemsley, and colleagues (1991) in "The neuropsychology of schizophrenia" proposed a theory that attempted to explain schizophrenia comprehensively from brain malfunction to psychological symptoms across a number of levels of description. It was suggested that structural abnormality in the brain in hippocampal, amygdalar, and temporal neocortical regions gives rise to neurochemical abnormality, namely hyperactivity in dopamine circuitry, that in turn dysregulates the cognitive process of integration of past experience with current learning about environmental stimuli. It is this dysregulation that then forms the basis of the positive symptoms of psychosis. Delusions have long been interpreted as resulting from unusual and inappropriate associations (Chapman & McGhie, 1962; Chapman, 1966). These ideas have been recently updated and expanded (Kapur, 2003; Kapur, Mizrahi, & Li, 2005). Kapur has suggested that the dysregulated, hyperdopaminergic state that characterizes schizophrenia leads to an aberrant assignment of salience (or associability) to the elements of experience. Symptoms such as delusions arise as a patient tries to make sense of these aberrantly salient experiences, whereas hallucinations reflect a direct experience of the aberrant salience of internal representations. Antipsychotic drugs through their actions on dopamine D2 receptors have been proposed to "dampen the salience" of these abnormal experiences, thus alleviating symptoms. Negative symptoms may be a consequence of a "drowning out" of stimuli indicating reward (the stimuli that should be labelled as salient). This could lead to negative symptoms such as social withdrawal and neglect of interests.

The early difficulty in testing these predictions at the cognitive level in patients was that they show generally poor performance on most learning tasks, these abilities being related more to performance variables and difficult to ascribe impairment to a specific process. However, drawing on established procedures from animal learning theory proved to be a way of circumventing this confound.

Latent inhibition and schizophrenia

Latent inhibition is the phenomenon whereby prior exposure to a stimulus without consequence slows down subsequent learning about that stimulus. If a stimulus is presented without consequence and later serves as the CS in a standard Pavlovian conditioning paradigm, the pre-exposed CS is associated less strongly with the US as measured by the strength of a condition response (CR) than a CS that has not been pre-exposed without consequence. It was first described by Lubow and Moore (1959) in sheep and goats and since then has been replicated in a wide variety of mammalian species including humans, rats, dogs, and rabbits (Lubow, 1973). A number of explanations of the latent inhibition effect ensued that included habituation of the orienting response (Wolf & Maltzman, 1968), **conditioned inhibition** or stimulus salience reduction (Reiss & Wagner, 1972; Rescorla, 1971). Most theories of learning have provided an explanation of the phenomenon (Pearce & Hall, 1980; Rescorla-Wagner, 1972; Mackintosh, 1975; McLaren & Mackintosh, 2000, 2002). However, it was the idea that it represented an attentional phenomenon that brought it into the domain of schizophrenia research (for reviews see Weiner, 1990; Lubow & Gewirtz, 1995; Gray, 1998; Weiner, 2003; Weiner, Schiller, & Gaisler-Salomon, 2003; Arad & Weiner, 2009; Weiner & Arad, 2009; Lubow & Weiner, 2010). Conditioned attention theory proposed that attention is a hypothetical construct (R_A) with the properties of a Pavlovian response except in one important regard. While a CR is elicited by a CS after repeated presentations, R_A elicits a CR immediately and the function of the US is to prevent the CS from declining (Lubow, Schnur, & Rifkin, 1976; Lubow, 1989). According to this view latent inhibition may serve as a system for determining how limited attentional resources are allocated, moving attention away from the irrelevant and providing protection against information processing overload (Lubow, 2005). It is possible that people with schizophrenia may have diminished protection of this kind. Solomon et al. (1981) and Weiner et al. (Weiner, Lubow, & Feldon, 1981, 1984) were the first to suggest that latent inhibition may be of relevance to schizophrenia. They reported that in rats, amphetamine, an indirect dopamine agonist that induces psychosis, disrupts latent inhibition and this disruption was subsequently shown to be reversed by antipsychotic drugs (Moser, Hitchcock, Lister, & Moran, 2000; Arad & Weiner, 2009). Baruch, Hemsley, and Gray (1988) later demonstrated that latent inhibition (LI) was impaired in acute schizophrenia patients (within the first two weeks of their psychotic episode) but not in chronic patients (who were stable and free of hallucinations or delusions). These findings have since been replicated a number of times and further extended to show that under certain experimental conditions enhanced LI can be seen in chronic schizophrenia patients (Gray, Pilowsky, Grey, & Kerwin, 1995; Swerdlow, Braff, Hartston, Perry, & Geyer, 1996; Vaitl & Lipp, 1997; Rascle et al., 2001; Gal et al., 2009). This move from disrupted to enhanced LI is thought to reflect the increasing influence of antipsychotic medication. There are however some studies that have failed to find reduced LI in patients (Swerdlow et al., 1996; Williams et al., 1998).

Latent inhibition disruption in schizophrenia, in addition to studies showing similar sensitivity to the effects of psychosis-inducing and anti-psychotic drugs between rodents and humans (Moser et al., 2000), provided powerful evidence that patients have problems in allocating salience appropriately and that these problems could be linked to neurochemical abnormalities purported to exist in the disorder, the central idea running through current theories (Gray et al., 1991; Kapur, 2003; Kapur et al., 2005; Corlett et al., 2009).

Kamin blocking prediction error and schizophrenia

Learning theories propose that reward-dependent learning is driven by the degree of surprise or unpredictability of a rewarding outcome, or more specifically, errors in predictions of reward. Hebb (1949) suggested that the pairing of a CS with an US was sufficient for learning to take place; however, instances were identified where this is not necessarily the case, as in for example the Kamin **blocking** effect (Kamin, 1968). In certain conditions a full association between CS and US will not be formed. Rescorla and Wagner's (1972) theory was the first model to mathematically represent the conditions necessary for the relationship to form. The theory centres round an equation that captures all the factors that determine the amount of learning about the CS–US association. Rescorla and Wagner proposed the strength of CS–US association depended on three crucial elements: the intensity/salience of the CS, the intensity/salience of the US, and the difference between the maximum level of associative strength possible between the CS and US and the current associative strength experienced on the specified trial. The most crucial element of the Rescorla and Wagner model is the difference between the maximal possible level of associative strength (λ) and the sum of the associative strength of all stimuli present on a particular trial (ΣV). Learning will not occur unless there is a difference between λ and ΣV. This part of the formula can be considered the element of surprise. If the US is fully predicted, it is not surprising and there is no further learning possible about the CS–US association. The difference between λ and ΣV can be referred to as the "prediction error". The defining paradigm that demonstrates the use of prediction error is the Kamin blocking effect. Kamin blocking was identified by Leon Kamin in rats (1968) and is where prior learning about a stimulus blocks future learning about that stimulus when it is later paired with a second stimulus.

In Phase 1 of the experiment an association between an initial conditioned stimulus (CS 1) and an outcome (the US) is learnt. In Phase 2 a second conditioned stimulus (CS 2) is then presented in conjunction with CS 1, and both CS 1 and CS 2 predict the US. When tested, the response to CS 2 is found to be reduced in comparison with the response of a control group, who were conditioned with CS 1 and CS 2 together in compound without the initial training to CS 1 alone. In Kamin blocking no prediction error is generated in the blocking group in Phase 2 of a typical experiment, as there is no mismatch between expectation and outcome, the outcome being fully predicted by stimulus CS 1 from Phase 1.

Because Kamin blocking taps into formally similar processes to latent inhibition it was investigated in schizophrenia to test the generality of the hypothesis that the core deficit in schizophrenia is the inability to correctly allocate salience, i.e., an inability to ignore irrelevant or redundant information (Gray et al., 1991).

There are a number of different tasks used to measure Kamin blocking in humans but broadly they can be divided into **contingency** judgement tasks (where learning certainty is self rated), physiological tasks (using autonomic measures such as galvanic skin response), or behavioural tasks (measuring for example reaction time). Jones et al. (Jones, Gray, & Hemsley, 1992; Jones, Hemsley, Ball, & Serra, 1997) showed disrupted Kamin blocking in acute but not chronic schizophrenia using a contingency judgement task, where participants were asked to rate their predictions about how successful a fictitious film would be based on the inclusion of film stars who had been previously associated with high or low success. Using a different task involving coloured shapes and prediction of correct sequences of shapes, the same group confirmed significant reduction in Kamin blocking in schizophrenia (Serra, Jones, Toone, & Gray, 2001), though this study did not find a relationship between stage of illness and Kamin blocking reduction. Oades and colleagues (Oades, Zimmermann, & Eggers, 1996; Bender, Muller, Oades, & Sartory, 2001), using a computer-based behavioural task measuring reaction times to correctly locate a hidden spatial location cued by colour combinations, showed dramatic reduction in Kamin blocking performance in patients. In these studies Oades, Muller, Bender, and Sartory (2000) showed that this reduction in Kamin blocking is seen in nonparanoid but not in paranoid patients, suggesting some specificity in the pattern of reduction in patients. Using the same task we have shown reduction in Kamin blocking in patients and crucially we have also shown that this is specific to nonparanoid but not to paranoid subgroups of patients (Moran, Al-Uzri, Watson, & Reveley, 2003). We have recently investigated Kamin blocking in a larger community-based sample of patients. This study used patients that were relatively young and free from psychotic symptoms, living in the community and with no documented comorbidity who were matched for premorbid IQ (Moran, Owen, Crookes, Al-Uzri, & Reveley, 2008). We found that Kamin blocking performance was significantly associated with negative and depressive rather than positive symptoms in this high functioning group.

An association between Kamin blocking impairment and dopamine neuronal firing was demonstrated in electrophysiological studies that connected behavioural and neural levels of enquiry. In primates the development of Kamin blocking is mirrored by reduced dopaminergic neuronal firing in the Ventral Tegmental Area in Kamin blocking versus control groups (Waelti et al., 2001; Schultz, 2006). It is therefore unsurprising to find Kamin blocking disrupted in a disease associated with abnormally regulated dopamine. It should be noted that disrupted Kamin blocking does not indicate a failure of prediction error as this would produce a generalized failure to learn. Rather, disrupted Kamin blocking is an example of the inappropriate generation of a prediction error (Haselgrove & Evans, 2010; Moran et al., 2007), which is consistent with inappropriate attention to stimuli that are redundant and should be ignored. A number of behavioural paradigms specifically designed to measure prediction error particularly in the context of fMRI (functional magnetic resonance imaging) studies using paradigms have been investigated, such as unovershadowing and retrospective revaluation (Corlett, Honey, & Fletcher, 2007). These studies concur that patients have impairments and that drugs that induce psychosis induce abnormal responses.

In psychopharmacological studies in rats we and others have demonstrated that amphetamine, the indirect dopaminergic agonist, which is psychotomimetic, disrupts Kamin blocking (Crider, Solomon, & McMahon, 1982; Ohad, Lubow, Weiner, & Feldon, 1987; O'Tuathaigh et al., 2003). We examined at which stage of the procedure this disruption occurs and have established that disruption occurs critically when drug is administered prior to learning the **compound stimulus** of the blocking paradigm. These studies suggest that hyperdopaminergia induces abnormal use of prediction error and, consistent with theoretical predictions, this may occur at the stage of the experiment, i.e., the conditioning phase, crucial for the integration of past learned contingencies with current perception.

Recent studies show that performance on tasks explicitly manipulating prediction error is associated with activation of the ventral striatum/nucleus accumbens, a region that contains significant dopaminergic innervation and part of the neural circuitry proposed to be abnormal in schizophrenia (Rodriguez, Aron, & Poldrack, 2006). In patients with schizophrenia, ventral striatal activation is reduced compared with that in controls during performance of a reward prediction task (Juckel et al., 2006). Roiser et al. (2009) using a probabilistic monetary task showed impaired adaptive salience in patients. Corlett et al. (2007) using unovershadowing and revaluation tasks to address prediction error have shown reductions in patients that are associated with delusions and right prefrontal cortical activation. Murray et al. (2008) showed similar changes in the ventral striatal region. One of the most recent theoretical formulations has been by Corlett et al.

(2009), who have suggested a Bayesian approach to explaining psychosis that emphasizes the influence of prior expectancies and current inputs and suggest a possible extension to explain the effects of psychotomimetic drugs.

A testament to the influence of these integrative theories has been that recently there has been a call to establish a separate category of psychiatric disorder based on salience (associability) irregularities (Van Os, 2009a, 2009b).

Conclusions

It is concluded that recent integrative neuropsychological theories of schizophrenia have their origins in and are dependent upon concepts drawn from learning theory. Evidence of collaboration between schizophrenia and learning theorists dates back to the pioneers of experimental psychology and there is clear continuity between early ideas and modern explanatory frameworks.

Note

1 It should be noted that there are caveats that must be applied in retrospective analyses of early studies in schizophrenia patients. Retrospective studies may be limited by imprecise definitions of schizophrenia and imposition of current concepts of schizophrenia onto the past (Fraguas & Breathnach, 2009). One inadvertent advantage is that by definition they were mainly carried out on unmedicated patients (a ubiquitous and unwanted confound in many modern psychiatric studies). Antipsychotic drugs produce severe motor and motivational effects on individuals independently of their therapeutic effects, making it difficult to distinguish disease and treatment effects; these were not widely used until the 1950s.

References

Agid, O., Shapira, B., Zislin, J., Ritsner, M., Hanin, B., Murad, H., et al. (1999). Environment and vulnerability to major psychiatric illness: A case control study of early parental loss in major depression, bipolar disorder and schizophrenia. *Molecular Psychiatry*, *4*(2), 163–172.

Arad, M., & Weiner, I. (2009). Disruption of latent inhibition induced by ovariectomy can be reversed by estradiol and clozapine as well as by co-administration of haloperidol with estradiol but not by haloperidol alone. *Psychopharmacology*, *206*(4), 731–740.

Baruch, I., Hemsley, D. R., & Gray, J. A. (1988). Latent inhibition and psychotic proneness in normal subjects. *Personality and Individual Differences*, *9*(4), 777–783.

Belforte, J. E., Zsiros, V., Sklar, E. R., Jiang, Z. H., Yu, G., Li, Y. Q., et al. (2010). Postnatal NMDA receptor ablation in corticolimbic interneurons confers schizophrenia-like phenotypes. *Nature Neuroscience*, *13*(1), 76–83.

Bender, S., Muller, B., Oades, R. D., & Sartory, G. (2001). Conditioned blocking and schizophrenia: A replication and study of the role of symptoms, age, onset-age of psychosis and illness-duration. *Schizophrenia Research*, *49*(1–2), 157–170.

Bentall, R. (2006). Madness explained: Why we must reject the Kraepelinian paradigm and replace it with a 'complaint-orientated' approach to understanding mental illness. *Medical Hypotheses*, *66*(2), 220–233.

Bentall, R. P., Corcoran, R., Howard, R., Blackwood, N., & Kinderman, P. (2001). Persecutory delusions: A review and theoretical integration. *Clinical Psychology Review*, *21*(8), 1143–1192.

Berridge, K. C., & Robinson, T. E. (1998). What is the role of dopamine in reward: Hedonic impact, reward learning, or incentive salience? *Brain Research Reviews*, *28*(3), 309–369.

Bleuler, E. (1911). *Dementia praecox or the group of schizophrenias* (trans. by J. Zinkin; with a Foreword by Nolan D. C. Lewis added 1951). London: George Allen & Unwin.

Butler, R. W., & Braff, D. L. (1991). Delusions: A review and integration. *Schizophrenia Bulletin*, *17*(4), 633–647.

Caspi, A., & Moffitt, T. E. (2006). Opinion: Gene–environment interactions in psychiatry: Joining forces with neuroscience. *Nature Reviews Neuroscience*, *7*(7), 583–590.

Chapman, J. (1966). The early symptoms of schizophrenia. *British Journal of Psychiatry*, *112*(484), 225–251.

Chapman, J., & McGhie, A. (1962). A comparative study of disordered attention in schizophrenia. *Journal of Mental Science*, *108*(455), 487–500.

Cohen, J., Braver, T. S., & Brown, J. W. (2002). Computational perspectives on dopamine function in prefrontal cortex: Commentary. *Current Opinion in Neurobiology*, *12*(2), 223–229.

Corlett, P. R., Frith, C. D., & Fletcher, P. C. (2009). From drugs to deprivation: A Bayesian framework for understanding models of psychosis. *Psychopharmacology*, *206*(4), 515–530.

Corlett, P. R., Honey, G. D., & Fletcher, P. C. (2007). From prediction error to psychosis: Ketamine as a pharmacological model of delusions. *Journal of Psychopharmacology*, *21*(3), 238–252.

Cornblatt, B. A., & Keilp, J. G. (1994). Impaired attention, genetics, and the pathophysiology of schizophrenia. *Schizophrenia Bulletin*, *20*(1), 31–46.

Coyle, J. T. (1996). The glutamatergic dysfunction hypothesis for schizophrenia. *Harvard Review of Psychiatry*, *3*(5), 241–253.

Crider, A., Solomon, P. R., & McMahon, M. A. (1982). Disruption of selective attention in the rat following chronic D-amphetamine administration: Relationship to Schizophrenic Attention Disorder. *Biological Psychiatry*, *17*(3), 351–361.

Docherty, N. M., Hall, M. J., Gordinier, S. W., & Cutting, L. P. (2000). Conceptual sequencing and disordered speech in schizophrenia. *Schizophrenia Bulletin*, *26*(3), 723–735.

Ferster, C. B., & Skinner, B. F. (1957). Schedules of reinforcement. *Psychological Reports*, *3*(4), 695–695.

Fraguas, D., & Breathnach, C. S. (2009). Problems with retrospective studies of the presence of schizophrenia. *History of Psychiatry*, *20*(1), 61–71.

Gal, G., Barnea, Y., Biran, L., Mendlovic, S., Gedi, T., Halavy, M., et al. (2009). Enhancement of latent inhibition in patients with chronic schizophrenia. *Behavioural Brain Research*, *197*(1), 1–8.

Grace, A. A., Lodge, D. J., & Behrens, M. M. (2009). Hippocampal hyperactivity due to inter neuron loss accounts for dopamine hyper-responsivity and diminished oscillatory activity in mam model of schizophrenia. *Schizophrenia Bulletin, 35*, 142–142.

Gray, J. A. (1998). Integrating schizophrenia. *Schizophrenia Bulletin, 24*(2), 249–266.

Gray, J. A., Feldon, J., Rawlins, J. N. P., Smith, A. D., & Hemsley, D. R. (1991). The neuropsychology of schizophrenia. *Behavioral and Brain Sciences, 14*(1), 1–19.

Gray, N. S., Pilowsky, L. S., Gray, J. A., & Kerwin, R. W. (1995). Latent inhibition in drug-naive schizophrenics: Relationship to duration of illness and dopamine D2 binding using SPET. *Schizophrenia Research, 17*(1), 95–107.

Hare, E. H. (1956). Family setting and the urban distribution of schizophrenia. *Journal of Mental Science, 102*(429), 753–760.

Haselgrove, M., & Evans, L. H. (2010). Variations in selective and non-selective prediction error with the negative dimension of schizotypy. *Quarterly Journal of Experimental Psychology, 63*, 1127–1149.

Hebb, D. O. (1949). *The organization of behavior: A neuropsychological theory.* New York, NY: Wiley.

Hooker, C., & Park, S. (2002). Emotion processing and its relationship to social functioning in schizophrenia patients. *Psychiatry Research, 112*(1), 41–50.

Howe, E. S. (1958). Gsr conditioning in anxiety-states, normals, and chronic functional schizophrenic subjects. *Journal of Abnormal and Social Psychology, 56*(2), 183–189.

Howes, O. D., & Kapur, S. (2009). The dopamine hypothesis of schizophrenia: Version III: The final common pathway. *Schizophrenia Bulletin, 35*(3), 549–562.

Hull, C. L. (1917). The formation and retention of associations among the insane. *American Journal of Psychology, 28*, 419–435.

Hull, C. L. (1943). *Principles of behaviour.* New York and London: D. Appleton Century Company.

Jablensky, A., & Sartorious, N. (2008). What did the WHO studies really find? *Schizophrenia Bulletin, 34*(2), 253–255.

Jablensky, A., Sartorius, N., Ernberg, G., Anker, M., Korten, A., Cooper J. E., et al. (1992). Schizophrenia: Manifestations, incidence and course in different countries: A World Health Organization ten country study. *Psychological Medicine, Monograph Supplement 20.* Cambridge, UK: Cambridge University Press.

Javitt, D. C. (2007). Glutamate and schizophrenia: Phencyclidine, N-methyl-D-aspartate receptors, and dopamine-glutamate interactions. In A. Abi-Dargham & O. Guillin (Eds.), *International review of neurobiology: Vol. 78. Integrating the neurobiology of schizophrenia.* San Diego, CA: Elsevier/Academic Press.

Jones, P. B., Rantakallio, P., Hartikainen, A. L., Isohanni, M., & Sipila, P. (1998). Schizophrenia as a long-term outcome of pregnancy, delivery, and perinatal complications: A 28-year follow-up of the 1966 North Finland general population birth cohort. *American Journal of Psychiatry, 155*(3), 355–364.

Jones, S. H., Gray, J. A., Hemsley, D. R. (1992). Loss of Kamin blocking effect in acute but not chronic schizophrenics. *Biological Psychiatry, 32*(9), 739–755.

Jones, S. H., Hemsley, D., Ball, S., & Serra, A. (1997). Disruption of the Kamin blocking effect in schizophrenia and in normal subjects following amphetamine. *Behavioural Brain Research, 88*(1), 103–114.

Juckel, G., Schlagenhauf, F., Koslowski, M., Wustenberg, T., Villringer, A., Knutson, B., et al. (2006). Dysfunction of ventral striatal reward prediction in schizophrenia. *Neuroimage, 29*(2), 409–416.

Kamin, L. J. (1968). Attention-like processes in classical conditioning. In M. Jones (Ed.), *Miami symposium on the prediction of behavior: Aversive stimulation* (pp. 9–33). Miami, FL: University of Miami Press.

Kapur, S. (2003). Psychosis as a state of aberrant salience: A framework linking biology, phenomenology, and pharmacology in schizophrenia. *American Journal of Psychiatry, 160*(1), 13–23.

Kapur, S., Mizrahi, R., & Li, M. (2005). From dopamine to salience to psychosis: Linking biology, pharmacology and phenomenology of psychosis. *Schizophrenia Research, 79*(1), 59–68.

Keefe, R. S. E., & Fenton, W. S. (2007). How should DSM-V criteria for schizophrenia include cognitive impairment? *Schizophrenia Bulletin, 33*(4), 912–920.

Kerns, J. G., & Berenbaum, H. (2002). Cognitive impairments associated with formal thought disorder in people with schizophrenia. *Journal of Abnormal Psychology, 111*(2), 211–224.

Kerr, S. L., & Neale, J. M. (1993). Emotion perception in schizophrenia: Specific deficit or further evidence of generalized poor performance. *Journal of Abnormal Psychology, 102*(2), 312–318.

Keshavan, M. S., Tandon, R., Boutros, N. N., & Nasrallah, H. A. (2008). Schizophrenia, "just the facts": What we know in 2008 part 3: Neurobiology. *Schizophrenia Research, 106*(2–3), 89–107.

Kraepelin, E. (1896). *Psychiatrie.* Leipzig: Barth.

Kulhara, P., Avasthi, A., & Sharma, A. (2000). Magico-religious beliefs in schizophrenia: A study from North India. *Psychopathology, 33*(2), 62–68.

Laruelle, M., Kegeles, L. S., & Abi-Dargham, A. (2003). Glutamate, dopamine, and schizophrenia: From pathophysiology to treatment. *Glutamate and Disorders of Cognition and Motivation, 1003*, 138–158.

Lindsley, O. R., & Skinner, B. F. (1954). A method for the experimental analysis of the behaviour of psychotic patients. *Program of the Sixty-Second Annual Convention of the American Psychological Association. The American Psychologist, 9*(8), 419.

Lubow, R. E. (1973). Latent inhibition. *Psychological Bulletin, 79*(6), 398–407.

Lubow, R. E. (1989). *Latent inhibition and conditioned attention theory.* New York, NY: Cambridge University Press.

Lubow, R. E. (2005). Construct validity of the animal latent inhibition model of selective attention deficits in schizophrenia. *Schizophrenia Bulletin, 31*(1), 139–153.

Lubow, R. E. (2009). Classical eyeblink conditioning and schizophrenia: A short review. *Behavioural Brain Research, 202*(1), 1–4.

Lubow, R. E., & Gewirtz, J. C. (1995). Latent inhibition in humans: Data, theory, and implications for schizophrenia. *Psychological Bulletin, 117*(1), 87–103.

Lubow, R. E., & Moore, A. U. (1959). Latent inhibition: The effect of non-reinforced pre-exposure to the conditional stimulus. *Journal of Comparative and Physiological Psychology, 52*(4), 415–419.

Lubow, R. E., Schnur, P., & Rifkin, B. (1976). Latent inhibition and conditioned attention theory. *Journal of Experimental Psychology: Animal Behavior Processes*, *2*(2), 163–174.

Lubow, R. E., & Weiner, I. (2010). *Latent inhibition: Cognition, neuroscience and applications to schizophrenia*. Cambridge, UK: Cambridge University Press.

Lynn, R. (1963). Russian theory and research on schizophrenia. *Psychological Bulletin*, *60*(5), 486–498.

Mackintosh, N. J. (1975). Theory of attention: Variations in associability of stimuli with reinforcement. *Psychological Review*, *82*(4), 276–298.

Maynard, T. M., Sikich, L., Lieberman, J. A., & LaMantia, A. S. (2001). Neural development, cell–cell signaling, and the "two-hit" hypothesis of schizophrenia. *Schizophrenia Bulletin*, *27*(3), 457–476.

Mays, L. L. (1934). Studies of catatonia V: Perseverational tendencies in catatonic patients. *Psychiatric Quarterly*, *8*, 728–735.

McLaren, I. P. L., & Mackintosh, N. J. (2000). An elemental model of associative learning: I. Latent inhibition and perceptual learning. *Animal Learning & Behavior*, *28*(3), 211–246.

McLaren, I. P. L., & Mackintosh, N. J. (2002). Associative learning and elemental representation: II. Generalization and discrimination. *Animal Learning & Behavior*, *30*(3), 177–200.

Mednick, S. A. (1958). A learning-theory approach to research in schizophrenia. *Psychological Bulletin*, *55*(5), 316–327.

Meehl, P. E. (1962). Schizotaxia, schizotypy, schizophrenia. *American Psychologist*, *17*(12), 827–838.

Moran, P. M., Al-Uzri, M. M., Watson, J., & Reveley, M. A. (2003). Reduced Kamin blocking in non paranoid schizophrenia: Associations with schizotypy. *Journal of Psychiatric Research*, *37*(2), 155–163.

Moran, P. M., Owen, L., Crookes, A. E., Al-Uzri, M. M., & Reveley, M. A. (2008). Abnormal prediction error is associated with negative and depressive symptoms in schizophrenia. *Progress in Neuro-psychopharmacology and Biological Psychiatry*, *32*(1), 116–123.

Moser, P. C., Hitchcock, J. M., Lister, S., & Moran, P. M. (2000). The pharmacology of latent inhibition as an animal model of schizophrenia. *Brain Research Reviews*, *33*(2–3), 275–307.

Murray, G. K., Corlett, P. R., Clark, L., Pessiglione, M., Blackwell, A. D., Honey, G., et al. (2008). Substantia nigra/ventral tegmental reward prediction error disruption in psychosis. *Molecular Psychiatry*, *13*(3), 267–276.

Oades, R. D., Zimmerman, B., & Eggers, C. (1996). Conditioned blocking in patients with paranoid, non-paranoid psychosis or obsessive compulsive disorder: Associations with symptoms, personality and monoamine metabolism. *Journal of Psychiatric Research*, *30*(5), 369–390.

O'Connor, M., Harris, J. M., McIntosh, A. M., Owens, D. G. C., Lawrie, S. M., & Johnstone, E. C. (2009). Specific cognitive deficits in a group at genetic high risk of schizophrenia. *Psychological Medicine*, *39*(10), 1649–1655.

Ohad, D., Lubow, R. E., Weiner, I., & Feldon, J. (1987). The effects of amphetamine on blocking. *Psychobiology*, *15*(2), 137–143.

O'Tuathaigh, C. M. P., Salum, C., Young, A. M. J., Pickering, A. D., Joseph, M. H., & Moran, P. M. (2003). The effect of amphetamine on Kamin blocking and overshadowing. *Behavioural Pharmacology*, *14*(4), 315–322.

Pearce, J. M., & Hall, G. (1980). A model for Pavlovian learning: Variations in the effectiveness of conditioned but not of unconditioned stimuli. *Psychological Review, 87*(6), 532–552.

Pedersen, C. B., & Mortensen, P. B. (2001). Evidence of a dose–response relationship between urbanicity during upbringing and schizophrenia risk. *Archives of General Psychiatry, 58*(11), 1039–1046.

Peraala, J., Suvisaari, J., Saarni, S. I., Kuoppasalmi, K., Isometsa, E., Pirkola, S., et al. (2007). Lifetime prevalence of psychotic and bipolar I disorders in a general population. *Archives of General Psychiatry, 64*(1), 19–28.

Pfaffman, C., & Schlosberg, H. (1936). The conditioned knee jerk in psychotic and normal individuals. *Journal of Psychology, 1*, 201–206.

Putnam, T. J., & Myerson, A. (1932). Boston Society of Psychiatry and Neurology. *Archives of Neurology & Psychiatry, 28*(1), 203–218.

Raine, A. (2006). Schizotypal personality: Neurodevelopmental and psychosocial trajectories. *Annual Review of Clinical Psychology, 2*, 291–326.

Rascle, C., Mazas, O., Vaiva, G., Tournant, M., Raybois, O., Goudemand, M., et al. (2001). Clinical features of latent inhibition in schizophrenia. *Schizophrenia Research, 51*(2–3), 149–161.

Reiss, S., & Wagner, A. R. (1972). CS habituation produces a "latent inhibition" effect but no active "conditioned inhibition". *Learning and Motivation, 3*, 237–245.

Rescorla, R. A. (1971). Summation and retardation tests of latent inhibition. *Journal of Comparative and Physiological Psychology, 75*(1), 77–81.

Rescorla, R. A., & Wagner, A. R. (1972). A theory of Pavlovian conditioning: Variations in the effectiveness of reinforcement and nonreinforcement. In A. H. Black & W. F. Prokasy (Eds.), *Classical conditioning II* (pp. 64–99). New York, NY: Appleton-Century-Crofts.

Riedel, G., Platt, B., & Micheau, J. (2003). Glutamate receptor function in learning and memory. *Behavioural Brain Research, 140*(1–2), 1–47.

Rodriguez, P. F., Aron, A. R., & Poldrack, R. A. (2006). Ventral-striatal/nucleus-accumbens sensitivity to prediction errors during classification learning. *Human Brain Mapping, 27*(4), 306–313.

Roiser, J. P., Stephan, K. E., den Ouden, H. E. M., Barnes, T. R. E., Friston, K. J., & Joyce, E. M. (2009). Do patients with schizophrenia exhibit aberrant salience? *Psychological Medicine, 39*(2), 199–209.

Sartorius, N., Jablensky, A., Korten, A., Ernberg, G., Anker, M., Cooper, J. E., et al. (1986). Early manifestations and first-contact incidence of schizophrenia in different cultures. *Psychological Medicine, 16*, 909–928.

Schultz, W. (2006). Behavioral theories and the neurophysiology of reward. *Annual Review of Psychology, 57*, 87–115.

Sears, L. L., Andreasen, N. C., & O'Leary, D. S. (2000). Cerebellar functional abnormalities in schizophrenia are suggested by classical eyeblink conditioning. *Biological Psychiatry, 48*(3), 204–209.

Serra, A. M., Jones, S. H., Toone, B., & Gray, J. A. (2001). Impaired associative learning in chronic schizophrenics and their first-degree relatives: A study of latent inhibition and the Kamin blocking effect. *Schizophrenia Research, 48*(2–3), 273–289.

Shipley, W. C. (1934). Studies of catatonia VI: Further investigation of the perseverative tendency. *Psychiatric Quarterly, 8*, 736–744.

Silbersweig, D. A., Stern, E., Frith, C., Cahill, C., Holmes, A., Grootoonk, S., et al.

(1995). A functional neuroanatomy of hallucinations in schizophrenia. *Nature*, *378*(6553), 176–179.

Skinner, B. F. (1954). A new method for the experimental analysis of the behavior of psychotic patients. *Journal of Nervous and Mental Disease*, *120*(5–6), 403–406.

Skinner, B. F. (1938). *The behavior of organisms: An experimental analysis*. Oxford, UK: Appleton-Century.

Solomon, P. R., Crider, A., Winkelman, J. W., Turi, A., Kamer, R. M., & Kaplan, L. J. (1981). Disrupted latent inhibition in the rat with chronic amphetamine or haloperidol-induced super-sensitivity: Relationship to Schizophrenic Attention Disorder. *Biological Psychiatry*, *16*(6), 519–537.

Swerdlow, N. R., Braff, D. L., Hartston, H., Perry, W., & Geyer, M. A. (1996). Latent inhibition in schizophrenia. *Schizophrenia Research*, *20*(1–2), 91–103.

Taylor, J. A., & Spence, K. W. (1954). Conditioning level in the behavior disorders. *Journal of Abnormal and Social Psychology*, *49*(4), 497–502.

Toda, M., & Abi-Dargham, A. (2007). Dopamine hypothesis of schizophrenia: Making sense of it all. *Current Psychiatry Reports*, *9*(4), 329–336.

Vaitl, D., & Lipp, O. V. (1997). Latent inhibition and autonomic responses: A psychophysiological approach. *Behavioural Brain Research*, *88*(1), 85–93.

Vaitl, D., Lipp, O. V., Bauer, U., Schuler, G., & Stark, R. (1999). Latent inhibition and schizophrenia. *Psychophysiology*, *36*, S117–S117.

Van Os, J. (2009a). A salience dysregulation syndrome. *British Journal of Psychiatry*, *194*(2), 101–103.

Van Os, J. (2009b). 'Salience syndrome' replaces 'schizophrenia' in DSM-V and ICD-11: Psychiatry's evidence-based entry into the 21st century? *Acta Psychiatrica Scandinavica*, *120*(5), 363–372.

Van Os, J., & Kapur, S. (2009). Schizophrenia. *Lancet*, *374*(9690), 635–645.

Van Os, J., Linscott, R. J., Myin-Germeys, I., Delespaul, P., & Krabbendam, L. (2009). A systematic review and meta-analysis of the psychosis continuum: Evidence for a psychosis proneness–persistence–impairment model of psychotic disorder. *Psychological Medicine*, *39*(2), 179–195.

Waelti, P., Dickinson, A., & Schultz, W. (2001). Dopamine responses comply with basic assumptions of formal learning theory. *Nature*, *412*(6842), 43–48.

Watson, J. B. (1913). Psychology as the behaviorist views it. *Psychological Review*, *20*(2), 158–177.

Watson, J. B. (1924). *Behaviorism*. New York, NY: Peoples Institute.

Weiner, I. (1990). Neural substrates of latent inhibition: The switching model. *Psychological Bulletin*, *108*(3), 442–461.

Weiner, I. (2003). The 'two-headed' latent inhibition model of schizophrenia: Modeling positive and negative symptoms and their treatment. *Psychopharmacology*, *169*(3–4), 257–297.

Weiner, I., & Arad, M. (2009). Using the pharmacology of latent inhibition to model domains of pathology in schizophrenia and their treatment. *Behavioural Brain Research*, *204*(2), 369–386.

Weiner, I., Lubow, R. E., & Feldon, J. (1981). Chronic amphetamine and latent inhibition. *Behavioural Brain Research*, *2*(2), 285–286.

Weiner, I., Lubow, R. E., & Feldon, J. (1984). Abolition of the expression but not the acquisition of latent inhibition by chronic amphetamine in rats. *Psychopharmacology*, *83*(2), 194–199.

Weiner, I., Schiller, D., & Gaisler-Salomon, I. (2003). Disruption and potentiation of latent inhibition by risperidone: The latent inhibition model of atypical antipsychotic action. *Neuropsychopharmacology, 28*(3), 499–509.

Williams, J. H., Wellman, N. A., Geaney, D. P., Cowen, P. J., Feldon, J., & Rawlins, J. N. P. (1998). Reduced latent inhibition in people with schizophrenia: An effect of psychosis or of its treatment. *British Journal of Psychiatry, 172*, 243–249.

Windholz, G. (1996). Pavlov's conceptualization of paranoia within the theory of higher nervous activity. *History of Psychiatry, 7*(25), 159–166.

Windholz, G. (1999). Protopopov's ideas on habit formation and their relation to the Pavlovian theory of higher nervous activity. *American Journal of Psychology, 112*(3), 437–448.

Winograd-Gurvich, C., Fitzgerald, P. B., Georgiou-Karistianis, N., Bradshaw, J. L., & White, O. B. (2006). Negative symptoms: A review of schizophrenia, melancholic depression and Parkinson's disease. *Brain Research Bulletin, 70*(4–6), 312–321.

Wolf, C., & Maltzman, I. (1968). Conditioned orienting reflex and amount of preconditioning habitaution. *Proceedings of the 76th Annual Convention of the American Psychological Association, 3*, 129–130 (summary).

Wong, A. H. C., & Van Tol, H. H. M. (2003). Schizophrenia: From phenomenology to neurobiology. *Neuroscience and Biobehavioral Reviews, 27*(3), 269–306.

Yogev, H., Hadar, U., Gutman, Y., & Sirota, P. (2003). Perseveration and over-switching in schizophrenia. *Schizophrenia Research, 61*(2–3), 315–321.

Zhang, T.-Y., & Meaney, M. J. (2010). Epigenetics and the environmental regulation of the genome and its function. *Annual Review of Psychology, 61*, 439–466, C431–433.

2 Avoidance, anxiety, and aversion in the clinical setting

The role of classical conditioning

Michelle Symonds and Geoffrey Hall

In the classical conditioning procedure, so widely used in the learning laboratory, a neutral cue, otherwise known as a conditioned stimulus (CS), is paired with the occurrence of a motivationally significant event, known as an unconditioned stimulus (US). After a number of CS–US pairings, presentation of the CS alone is capable of producing a conditioned response (CR) that is often similar to that evoked by the US alone. Since the introduction of this experimental arrangement, reported by Pavlov (1927/1960), decades of experimental work have demonstrated that this form of learning can operate with a wide range of CSs (visual, auditory, gustatory, and so on) and with a range of USs (such as food, nausea, and electric shock). At a theoretical level, the favoured explanation of the classical conditioning phenomenon has been in terms of a process of association formation, by which the co-occurrence of a pair of events establishes a link between them (or rather, between their central representations). This link allows the presentation of one event (the CS) to evoke some aspects of the behaviour appropriate to the other event (the US). The simplicity of the procedure has ensured its popularity as a laboratory test-bed on which hypotheses about the principles governing associative learning can be examined. The principles established by such work (in particular those describing processes that determine the readiness with which associations can be formed) turn out to have direct relevance to the practical issues that form the bulk of this chapter.

There is no reason to think that this type of learning will be confined to the laboratory (as Pavlov himself insisted). In our everyday lives we are constantly presented with co-occurring events and contingencies, and the notion that we continually learn about the connections or associations between such events has a long history in empiricist philosophy. A much-cited example of classical conditioning in everyday life is the phenomenon of taste aversion learning. It is probably true that most people can describe an episode in which consumption of a particular food or drink (often a novel alcoholic drink) has been followed by an unpleasant consequence (usually illness), with the result that they have developed a tendency to shun that particular taste thereafter. In this case, the offending flavour acts as the

CS, and the illness acts as the US, and the resulting CR is the aversion acquired to the flavour. This example illustrates an adaptive aspect of associative learning; for humans, as for laboratory animals, the avoidance of illness-inducing foodstuffs can only be regarded as a positive outcome, and the advantages bestowed on the wild animal that can learn to avoid poisonous or harmful foodstuffs are obvious. We shall see, however, that there are circumstances in which the formation of such associations is not so advantageous. For these, information about the conditions that control associative learning, derived from experimental studies in the learning laboratory, suggests ways of reducing their occurrence. It is this application of these ideas to the clinical **context** that forms the focus of this chapter.

No sooner had classical conditioning been established and formalized than its application to clinical issues began to be advocated. Pavlov's famous 1927 book included several chapters on what he termed "pathological disturbances of the cortex", and in the West the equally famous study by Watson and Rayner (1920) was based on the assertion that conditioning was responsible for the development of irrational fears and phobias, and that conditioning principles might be applied in devising effective treatments. Our concern in this chapter is not (or, at least, not directly) with the analysis of specific phobias; rather we intend to take the notion of a *clinical context* quite literally and concentrate on conditions that can be described in terms of patients coming to show an aversion to that context itself. For these purposes, a clinical context will be defined as a place in which a patient receives a medical treatment of some sort (a treatment that may be construed by some as unpleasant). As our starting point, we will simply describe some phenomena that occur in the clinical setting, phenomena that we have a strong case for believing to be the product of a simple conditioning process. Next, we will explore what we think to be the closest parallels to these conditions in the animal learning laboratory, before suggesting (on the basis of the laws of association formation) ways in which we might set about developing appropriate intervention strategies that may be useful in the clinic.

Fear, aversion, and avoidance of the clinical context

Procedures carried out in the clinic that are necessary for our general health and well-being (and sometimes for our survival) often carry with them a number of unavoidable side-effects such as pain, nausea, and discomfort. If the cues that constitute the clinic can become associated with such unpleasant outcomes, then this contingency could lead to the context acquiring (by a process of classical conditioning) negative properties that might have a serious impact on both the psychological and physical well-being of the patient. (At its simplest, a patient who acquires an avoidance response to the clinical context may fail to return to complete the course of treatment he or she needs.) We will begin by describing two examples of phenomena that might potentially be explained in terms of classical conditioning generated by the unpleasant side-effects of a clinical procedure. In the first example, the acquired response appears to be fear (as in orthodox specific phobias); in the second example, the role of fear is more debatable and an aversion based on nausea seems a more likely interpretation.

Medical phobias

In the popular press, at least, the concept of a hospital phobia is well-established.

> Jonty Ricketts, who received national recognition for standing up to bullies, has died because of a fear of hospitals. The wheelchair-bound 25-year-old was found dead in his Richards Road home in Cheltenham the day after his doctor recommended hospital treatment. He spent much of his childhood in and out of medical centres, had a phobia of hospitals and doctors and had refused treatment, a Gloucester inquest was told.
>
> (*The Gloucestershire Echo*, 31 May 2008)

The final sentence of this report hints at the suspected aetiology, with its suggestion that his childhood experience in hospitals was responsible for Mr Ricketts's condition.

The scientific literature does not acknowledge this condition in its own right, but a place is found for related problems that might be described as medical phobias. The *Diagnostic and Statistical Manual* of the American Psychiatric Association (1994, *DSM-IV*) has a specific category of blood–injection–injury type phobia (needle phobia, being the popular name for one manifestation of this disorder). And standard textbooks (e.g., Barlow, 1988; Marks, 1987) treat dental phobia as an issue worthy of serious consideration (having a reported prevalence of 24 per 1000 population; Barlow, 1988).

Patients categorized as having a dental phobia show heightened avoidance of the dental clinic, or, if they do attend, show a high level of anxiety when faced with the treatment situation. In either case, the disadvantages are obvious; patients who avoid the dentist and repeatedly cancel their appointments will, as might be expected, exhibit a high degree of oral health problems. For those who do attend, the high level of anxiety is likely to make the treatment process a rather difficult and unpleasant experience (see, e.g., Weinstein, 1990, for a discussion of dental fear as a public health problem).

There is some agreement that the dental phobia is a learned fear that has its roots in a classical conditioning process (e.g., Davey, 1989; Townend, Dimigen, & Fung, 2000). In this case, the initially neutral CS could be any of a number of stimuli, including the dentist's chair, presentation of a hypodermic needle, the sound of the drill, or the sights and smells of the treatment room as a whole. The US in this situation will be a treatment that commonly gives rise to some degree of pain (De Jongh, Muris, Ter Horst, & Duyx, 1995). Even after one such pairing, further contact with the stimuli that constitute the dental clinic will evoke a fear response. Two obser-vations have been put forward as supporting a conditioning interpretation. First, the degree of dental phobia is directly related to the severity (or perceived severity) of the pain or anxiety experienced during treatment. Second, dental fear is more likely to occur in patients that have had little prior exposure to the treatment setting in the absence of any unpleasant effects (Davey, 1989). Both of these factors, the intensity or effectiveness of the US, and the extent to which the CS is familiar (an issue that we will explore later in this chapter), are well known for their ability to modulate the development of conditioning.

Whether fear of the dental clinic (and by extension hospital phobia, generally) really deserves to be treated as a distinct entity is debatable. If we allow the reality of, for example, needle phobia, avoidance of the clinic may just be an example of a phobia of the blood–injection–injury type; the clinic need not have acquired fear-provoking properties in itself – rather it may be avoided simply as being a place in which the feared procedure may occur. In the next example to be considered, however, it appears to be the clinic itself that acquires new and aversive properties.

Anticipatory nausea and vomiting (ANV)

The cytotoxic drugs used in chemotherapy regimes for the treatment of cancer are notorious for their tendency to evoke distressing side-effects – nausea and vomiting are common direct reactions to such drugs. Further-more, patients who experience nausea in the clinic may also develop another problem. In addition to the direct side-effects of chemotherapy, they may also begin to feel nauseous and even vomit in *anticipation* of their treatment sessions. In particular, mere exposure to the sights, smells, and sounds of the clinic may be enough to induce a feeling of sickness (e.g., Andrykowski & Redd, 1987). The problems posed by this condition are quite clear. Anticipatory nausea imposes an extra burden on individuals who may already be finding themselves in a potentially life-threatening situation. Patients who develop anticipatory symptoms of this sort experi-ence a reduced quality of life, and in some cases the onset of ANV can contribute to a decision to discontinue the required course of treatment (e.g., Boakes, Tarrier, Barnes, & Tattersall, 1993).

Although other factors may be involved (see, e.g., Aapro, Molassiotis, & Oliver, 2005) there appears to be general agreement that classical condi-tioning plays an important role in the development of ANV – that the problem arises from associative learning, with the cues of the clinical context providing the CS and drug-induced nausea the US. As a result of the co-occurrence of these stimuli, the context acquires the ability to evoke nausea as a CR (see Stockhorst, Klosterhalfen, & Steingruber, 1998, for a review). The case for ANV having its origins in a conditioning process is supported by the observation that it develops only in patients who have received at least one chemotherapy session (i.e., have experienced at least one pairing of the putative CS and US), and the severity of ANV is related to the intensity of the nausea and vomiting that is experienced as a consequence of the treatment (that is, the readiness with which conditioning occurs is related to the strength of the US).

The most obvious treatment for ANV would be to prevent the patients from experiencing nausea and vomiting in the first instance, but this is not always possible. Even with the application of modern anti-emetics, nausea during treatment cannot be totally eliminated, and prevalence rates for ANV of around 25 percent are not uncommon (Morrow & Rosenthal, 1996; Morrow, Roscoe, Kirshner, Hynes, & Rosenbluth, 1998). If pairings of the CS and the US cannot be avoided, then an alternative strategy might be to devise a procedure that prevents the formation of an association between them. This procedure could then be adopted by clinicians as a complement to drug-based interventions and other therapies as part of an overall strategy for the management of anticipatory symptoms. Modern learning theory has identified several procedures that will attenuate the formation of a CS–US association in the face of the contiguous occurrence of these events. A major concern of this chapter will be to assess the effectiveness of these procedures in an animal model of aversion to the clinic. The experimental work has been done with nausea-based conditioning, and thus is most directly relevant to the case of ANV. We hope, however, that the principles discovered have wider relevance to medical phobias more generally.

Developing the conditioning model of clinical aversions with studies of contextual learning in animals

Our hypothesis is that patients form an (unwanted) association between a set of environmental cues (the clinical context) and unpleasant events that occur in that context. The first step, therefore, is to assess the evidence that subjects can acquire an aversion to contextual cues under controlled laboratory conditions. Such procedures would then allow the possibility to develop an animal model that could be used to evaluate the effectiveness of treatments to alleviate the unwanted effects of context conditioning.

For the case in which the US is a painful event (perhaps paralleling what occurs in the dental clinic), contextual conditioning of fear is well established. In what is now a standard procedure for studying fear conditioning in rats, the animal is placed in a conditioning chamber (distinctively different from the home cage) for a specified period of time before receiving an electric footshock. When the animal is then removed from the chamber and later returned to that place, it will show almost complete immobility; it will freeze in a stereotyped crouching position, immobile except for movements necessary for breathing (see Fanselow, 1990; Kiernan & Westbrook, 1993). Whether we are justified in comparing this form of learning with the fear shown by humans to certain environments remains a matter for debate; none the less, this contextual learning preparation has revealed some important findings (to be discussed later) that have relevance to identifying factors that may be important in the development of clinical contextual fear.

Ironically (given our suggestion that ANV may be a more convincing case of context conditioning than dental phobia), it has proved more problematic to demonstrate that contextual cues can acquire the power to evoke conditioned nausea. Historically, the notion that an association can be formed between an **exteroceptive** cue such as a context, and an **interoceptive** event such as illness, has been often rejected. This argument has been advanced in particular by Garcia and his colleagues. For example, Garcia, Brett, and Rusiniak (1989) asserted that nausea-based learning obeys its own special laws, different from those governing orthodox Pavlovian conditioning. According to Garcia et al., a taste will readily acquire aversive properties if it is paired with nausea, but only in special circumstances will nontaste cues, such as those that make up a context, come to serve as CSs in illness-based conditioning. In the light of this scepticism a satisfactory experimental demonstration of context–nausea association becomes an essential first step.

The standard experimental procedure is very simple. Rat subjects are exposed to a novel environment (one that is distinctive from the home cage) in conjunction with an injection of the illness-inducing agent lithium chloride (LiCl). Sometimes the injection is given just after the rat is put in the experimental context (e.g., Symonds & Hall, 1997, 1999; Mitchell & Heyes, 1996), although a procedure in which the rats receive the injection of LiCl *prior* to being placed in the context is often used (e.g., Symonds & Hall, 2002; Hall, Symonds, & Rodriguez, 2009). The latter procedure constitutes a more direct parallel with clinical ANV, in that the rats are likely to experience the immediate effects of the illness-producing agent in the presence of the relevant contextual cues. Whichever procedure is used, the problem now becomes that of devising an appropriate test procedure, capable of revealing that this type of training will allow the context to evoke a CR of nausea (or something similar) in a way that parallels the ANV shown by chemotherapy patients. This task is made particularly problematic by the fact that the rodents routinely used as experimental subjects in the learning laboratory do not exhibit a vomiting reflex. We outline next three of the procedures that have been devised in an attempt to solve this problem.

The consumption test

In standard laboratory demonstrations of taste aversion learning, rats are allowed to consume a novel flavoured solution before receiving an injection of LiCl. In a subsequent test, it is found that when presented with the target flavour, the rat will show a tendency to refuse it. This is often taken to indicate that the animals have acquired an aversion to the taste based on its association with nausea. Moreover, it has been shown that one of the direct effects of an injection of LiCl is the refusal to consume a novel flavour during the time immediately following the injection (Domjan, 1977), and that this rejection could plausibly be taken to reflect the presence of nausea. Given these findings, it seems reasonable to suggest that one possible measure of context–illness conditioning would be to present the animal with a novel flavour in the illness-paired context. Rejection of the flavour would indicate that the contextual cues were capable of evoking a conditioned response that is akin to the state produced by the injection of LiCl itself. This consumption test procedure was investigated by Rodriguez, Lopez, Symonds, and Hall (2000), who gave rats training in which one context, A, was paired with an injection of LiCl, whereas a second (control) context, B, was paired with an injection of saline. In a subsequent test phase, rats were allowed to consume a novel sweet taste in either context A or context B. The subjects tested in context A showed more suppression of consumption than those tested in context B, a result consistent with the proposal that the contextual cues previously paired with LiCl had acquired aversive properties based on their association with nausea.

The blocking test

Converging evidence in support of this interpretation of the consumption test results has come from experiments using a different test procedure, based on the phenomenon known as **blocking**. An example of this procedure is found in an experiment by Symonds and Hall (1997). In this procedure, one group of rats received trials in which experience of a distinctive context was followed by an injection of LiCl; a second, control, group, experienced both the context and the injections but these events were not paired (they occurred several hours apart). In a second phase of training the subjects were given conditioning with a compound cue as the CS. Specifically, all subjects received trials in which they experienced the target context, and were allowed to consume a novel flavour before receiving an injection of LiCl (the compound cue was thus context plus flavour). It is well established that if a CS is trained as a signal for a particular US, and then presented in compound with a second CS as a signal for the same US, the initial training given to the first CS will *block* learning to the second CS (Kamin, 1969). Blocking provides a way of measuring the strength of the initial CS–US association. If the training

given to the experimental group resulted in a strong context–illness association, then this group should show blocked or retarded acquisition of an
aversion to the novel flavour, relative to the control group. This was the
result obtained by Symonds and Hall – in a final test, control animals
showed a strong aversion to the flavour whereas the experimental group did
not (see also Symonds et al., 1998). Although rather more complex, this test
procedure has certain advantages over the consumption test, as will become
apparent later in this chapter; for the time being, it is enough to note that
its outcome is entirely in accord with the proposal that pairing a context
with nausea endows that context with the ability to evoke a CR of nausea.

Other signs of nausea

Although they produce results consistent with the suggestion that contextual cues can come to evoke nausea as a CR, the test procedures just
described are rather indirect, and doubts may remain. Suppose, for
example, that the only thing the rat learns during training is that something
unpleasant happened in the context. It would not be surprising then if it
refused to consume a novel substance when returned to the threatening
context (the result obtained with the consumption test). The outcome
would thus be a consequence of conditioned fear rather than conditioned
nausea. (It may be noted that Parker, e.g., 2003, has advanced just such an
analysis for certain cases of flavour aversion learning.) The results of the
blocking test are rather more difficult to explain away in these terms; none
the less, it would be comforting if we could provide a more direct assay of
the state of nausea that could be applied to this training situation.

Although they cannot vomit, rats show a characteristic set of orofacial
responses, such as tongue protrusion and open-mouthed gaping, when
presented with an unpleasant tasting substance, responses similar to those
that accompany vomiting in rodent species that are capable of this feat (see
Figure 2.1). A neutral (or even a preferred flavour, such as that of saccharin)
proves capable of evoking these same reactions after having been paired
with a nausea-inducing injection of LiCl. Limebeer, Hall, and Parker (2006)
made use of this taste-reactivity test to assess the conditioned properties of
contextual cues. As usual, training consisted of pairing a distinctive context
with an injection of LiCl. On the subsequent test, the rats were placed in the
context and a solution of saccharin was infused into the mouth by means of
a cannula. In spite of the fact that the saccharin had not itself been
associated with LiCl, the rats showed the standard rejection reactions –
simply being in a context that had been associated with LiCl was enough to
evoke responses taken to be characteristic of nausea. Indeed, the rats tended
to show these responses to some extent simply on being placed in the
context, prior to the presentation of the saccharin – a behaviour pattern
quite absent in control subjects that had not received the initial context–
LiCl pairings. These results confirm the proposal that experience of nausea

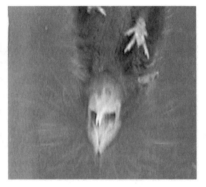

Rat Gape   Shrew Retch

Figure 2.1 Right: A shrew (a species capable of vomiting) just before the expulsion phase of the reflex; left: a rat's reaction to an unpleasant taste. Although incapable of vomiting, the rat shows the characteristic open-mouthed gape of the initial phase (the response scored in the experiment discussed here). (Photograph courtesy of L. Parker.)

in a particular context can endow that context with the ability to evoke nausea as a conditioned response and validate the use of this experimental arrangement as an animal model for the investigation of ANV.

Interventions based on the laws of association: animal studies

We have described a set of conditioning procedures that are obvious candidates with which to work in our aim of developing a strategy that might reduce the occurrence of clinical aversion and avoidance. In these procedures, as in the clinic, the subject experiences an unpleasant event in the presence of certain contextual cues. But, the co-occurrence of two events does not necessarily mean that an association will be formed between them. Studies of standard conditioning procedures have revealed a number of factors that prevent association formation or restrict the strength of any association that may be formed. Can knowledge of these factors help us to devise procedures that can be used in the clinic to alleviate some of the unwanted side-effects of treatment? A first step in answering this question is to investigate the effectiveness of these factors in experimental studies of context conditioning in animals, and work of this sort forms the focus of this section of the chapter. In a later section we turn to direct studies of the clinical situation in people.

Scapegoating by the addition of a salient cue

It is well established, from experiments using a wide range of conditioning procedures, that if a compound CS composed of two stimuli is paired with a US, then the more salient stimulus will be learned about most readily, and that this will detract from learning about the other stimulus – the less salient cue is said to suffer **overshadowing**. For the cases of clinical context aversions that we are considering, the potential of overshadowing is clear. Adding a salient cue at the time of the critical treatment should serve to restrict or overshadow unwanted learning about the clinical context; instead, the patient would learn about the added cue, which would serve as a *scapegoat*. Perhaps the most obvious problem with this procedure is in the choice of an appropriate scapegoat cue. After all, if this cue is to acquire aversive properties it needs to be a stimulus that is unlikely to be encountered by the patient on future occasions. It must therefore be a rather unusual or novel cue. Bernstein, Webster, and Bernstein (1982) applied this principle successfully in the treatment of food aversions acquired by patients receiving chemotherapy. In their study, they showed that paediatric cancer patients given an unusual flavour at the time of treatment were less likely to exhibit aversions to the tastes of standard foods usually consumed during the course of treatment.

Potentiation and selective association

The overshadowing procedure clearly has potential as a technique for reducing the context-aversion conditioning responsible for ANV. However, it is necessary to proceed with caution. Overshadowing is not the guaranteed outcome of adding an extra cue; indeed, in some cases enhanced learning about the other cue has been obtained (an effect known as **potentiation**; see LoLordo & Droungas, 1989). The studies outlined below suggest that potentiation is particularly likely to be found for nausea-based learning with an exteroceptive target cue such as a context.

As we noted, Garcia and his colleagues have put forward the notion that certain cues are relatively poor at functioning as CSs when paired with certain reinforcers. In the case of illness-based conditioning, it is suggested that only gustatory stimuli (such as tastes and odours) are readily able to enter into an association with illness; exteroceptive cues, such as those provided by a particular place or context, are said to be less able to support learning that is based upon an interoceptive consequence such as gastric distress (e.g., Garcia & Koelling, 1966). What is more, it has been proposed that there are certain circumstances in which contextual cues *can* acquire aversive properties when paired with illness. In particular, there is evidence to suggest that contextual conditioning might be more readily observed when the animal is allowed to consume a fluid of some sort at the time of the context–US pairing (e.g., Boakes, Westbrook, & Barnes, 1992; Mitchell & Heyes, 1996). This potentiation effect is of practical importance for the idea of using scapegoating as a technique for controlling contextual aversions, as it implies that, far from producing the desired effect of reducing such learning, the addition of a second cue could enhance the problem. It is of the first importance, therefore, to determine if context-nausea conditioning is indeed potentiated by the presence of a salient added cue. Experimental study, using the animal model described above, has allowed us to examine this possibility.

Demonstrating overshadowing in context-nausea conditioning

Evidence that has been taken to support the view that the presence of a novel taste stimulus can potentiate context-nausea learning has come from experiments using the consumption test. It will be recalled that one method of assessing the strength of a context aversion (following context–LiCl pairings) is to measure the willingness of the animal to consume a flavoured solution in the presence of the contextual cues. Subjects given previous context-illness conditioning trials show a greater tendency to shun the test flavour than control subjects for whom no such pairings had been given. It has been demonstrated that rats given access to a novel flavour at the time of conditioning will show an enhanced tendency to shun a novel test flavour when reexposed to the context (e.g., Best, Brown, & Sowell 1984; Boakes et al., 1992), and it is this result that has been taken to indicate the occurrence of a potentiation effect. But another interpretation is possible. Symonds and Hall (1999) have pointed out that findings of this sort could be explained in terms of simple generalization. A flavour that is presented at the time of context conditioning will itself acquire aversive properties by entering into an association with illness. On test, any enhanced tendency to shun the test flavour could then be a consequence, not of potentiation of learning about the context, but of generalization of an aversion from the scapegoat flavour to the test flavour (see also Symonds & Hall, 1997; Symonds et al., 1998).

In order to assess the true effects of a scapegoat flavour presented at the time of conditioning it is necessary to use a test procedure that avoids this possible confound. Symonds and Hall (1999) made use of the blocking procedure, described previously. Following the conditioning phase in which the target context was paired with LiCl, subjects were given compound conditioning in which the context was presented in compound with a novel taste, followed by an injection of LiCl. The strength of the previously established context–illness association was then measured by assessing the extent to which acquisition of an aversion to the novel taste was blocked. The important feature of this procedure is that strong contextual learning would be evidenced by a willingness to consume the test flavour (that is, potentiation of learning about the context would be expected to enhance the extent to which the context would block the acquisition of an aversion to the test flavour). If potentiation were found in these circumstances, it could not then be explained in terms of generalization of an aversion from the taste added during conditioning to that used on test.

Using this test, Symonds and Hall (1999) found no sign of potentiation; rather they found evidence for an overshadowing effect. In their experiment the addition of a novel flavour (the sour taste of an acid) at the time of context conditioning was found to reduce the ability of the context to block conditioning to the test flavour, indicating that conditioning to the context had been restricted by the novel flavour. They concluded that the potentiation effect (at least in the case of context-nausea conditioning) was an artifact produced by the use of the consumption test and that such conditioning is subject to the overshadowing process predicted by standard associative theory. The scapegoat procedure remains a potentially useful intervention that could be developed for use in the clinical setting.

Pre-exposure to the target context

Exposure to the cue to be used as the CS prior to the start of conditioning will retard the acquisition of a CR to that cue. This *latent inhibition* effect has been well-documented for a range of conditioning preparations (Lubow, 1989), and although it has usually been reported using discrete stimuli such as tones, lights, and flavours (as opposed to a complex set of cues such as a context), its potential as an intervention for alleviating contextual aversions is clear. Preexposure to aspects of the clinical context (to the dentist's chair or drill, or to the hospital setting in which chemotherapy is to take place) could be a useful therapy for reducing context aversion.

Interestingly, one factor of importance in determining the likelihood that ANV will develop is the age of the patient; children appear to be more susceptible than adults (Burish & Carey, 1986). This observation prompts the speculation that younger patients suffer more than older ones simply because the latter are likely to have had more experience of the hospital environment, possibly in the absence of any ill-effects – for these, the contextual cues will have undergone latent inhibition. Similarly, for the case of dental phobia, Davey (1989) has identified prior experience of the dental setting as being an important factor in determining the degree to which dental phobias develop. Patients who experience a painful dental treatment but do not acquire an aversion to the clinic are often those who have a history of repeated dental visits that did not involve the experience of pain or discomfort. Again, this is consistent with the possibility that a process of latent inhibition can operate during exposure to the dental clinic.

But, as was the case with overshadowing, the proposal to make use of the latent inhibition procedure carries with it some potential problems. First, although latent inhibition is a robust effect that has been repeatedly obtained when a simple stimulus is used as the CS, things may be different for complex cues such as those that constitute a context. In particular, it has been found that prior exposure to a context that is to be used as a CS can, under some circumstances, *facilitate* rather than retard subsequent conditioning. The second problem is that, even if it could be established that contextual cues are able to undergo latent inhibition, the use of preexposure as a therapeutic procedure could be rather time-consuming and costly. For instance, devising a regime for reducing dental anxiety or ANV based upon latent inhibition would potentially involve allowing the patient a number of visits to the dental clinic or hospital prior to treatment, something unlikely to find favour with those charged with the efficient use of an expensive facility. Ideally, then, there is a need to establish both the reality of contextual latent inhibition, and also to find a way of enhancing its effectiveness, preferably by increasing the impact of fewer pre-exposure trials, for example, giving stickers or lollies to children undergoing routine dental checkups. Laboratory experiments employing animal models have yielded information relevant to both these needs.

Unitization and latent inhibition

Kiernan and Westbrook (1993), using rats as their subjects, investigated the effects of pre-exposure to the context on the acquisition of conditioned fear of the context (assessed by the freezing response, described above). They found that after a series of exposures (each of about 20 min), acquisition of conditioned freezing was retarded; that is they found a latent inhibition effect. But with briefer pre-exposure (2-min trials), fear conditioning was facilitated. One explanation for this biphasic effect is that during the initial phase of preexposure to a complex context the various aspects of the environment become linked together (by a process known as *unitization*; see McLaren, Kaye, & Mackintosh, 1989). A unitized context is better able to evoke a CR than one perceived as a set of separate features. But with extended pre-exposure to the context, this unitized stimulus will itself undergo latent inhibition, with the result that facilitation of conditioning gives way to retardation. Regardless of the mechanism that supports this effect, from a practical perspective it is worth bearing in mind that exposure to the context may facilitate, rather than retard, the acquisition of fear to the context.

Similar preexposure effects have been obtained with context-nausea conditioning. In a series of unpublished studies conducted in our laboratory we have found that brief pre-exposure to the context, prior to the context–LiCl pairing, either has no effect, or marginally enhances the magnitude of the conditioned aversion. Only when the duration of pre-exposure is increased (to at least six 30-min sessions) is the latent inhibition effect observed (Hall, Symonds, & Rodriguez, 2009).

Results of this sort give some support to the proposal that latent inhibition could be a potentially useful procedure for reducing context conditioning in the clinic. But they make clear the necessity of giving a substantial amount of pre-exposure if the unwelcome effects of unitization are to be avoided. This observation makes it all the more essential to find a way of facilitating the latent inhibition process, so that the effect can be obtained after fewer preexposure trials.

Enhancing the magnitude of latent inhibition: Predictions from learning theory

According to the account of latent inhibition developed by Hall (1991) the effect depends on a learning process in which the subject learns that the pre-exposed cue is associated with no event. Rodriguez and Hall (2008; see also Hall & Rodriguez, 2010) explored the implications of applying the general theory of classical conditioning, proposed by Pearce and Hall (1980), to this form of learning. They pointed out that, according to this theory, the presence of an added salient cue during pre-exposure to the context should speed the acquisition of the stimulus–no event association, and accordingly the development of latent inhibition should be enhanced.

Hall et al. (2009) tested this prediction for latent inhibition in context-nausea learning. In one of their experiments rats received six sessions of pre-exposure to the context prior to the conditioning trials in which the context was paired with LiCl. A subsequent consumption test showed a small latent inhibition effect; that is the context aversion was somewhat less marked than that shown by rats given conditioning without pre-exposure. Their new result came from rats that were allowed access to a novel flavour (such as the sour taste of acid or the sweet taste of saccharin) during pre-exposure. These animals showed significantly more latent inhibition; that is, they showed less evidence of having formed an aversion to the context. In a subsequent experiment Hall et al. showed that adding a salient cue was capable of generating latent inhibition in animals given only four pre-exposure trials; an amount of pre-exposure that, in the absence of the added cue, would be incapable of producing the effect.

These results imply that if latent inhibition is to be employed in the clinic, it may be best to give pre-exposure in conjunction with presentation of a salient, but irrelevant, stimulus. Of course, the generality of the results reported by Hall et al. (2009) may need to be confirmed over a range of stimuli and conditioning procedures, but the basic principles appear to be in place; latent inhibition can be observed with contextual cues, and we have reason to believe that the size of the effect can be enhanced under certain circumstances. The next step is to explore the extent to which these principles, derived from animal studies, apply to our own species.

Applying conditioning principles to the human clinical population

However convinced we may be about the generality of the basic laws of associative learning, it needs to be demonstrated empirically that over-shadowing and latent inhibition are effective for people in the clinical context. It is one thing to demonstrate these effects by administering **footshocks** in a Skinner box or by injecting rats with LiCl, but the results for patients undergoing stressful treatments in the clinical setting may be quite different. If there is any merit in our attempts to describe clinical context aversions in terms of a conditioning process, then the real proof will lie in showing that these conditions can be alleviated by therapies based upon the learning principles that we have identified. What we will describe in this section are a number of preliminary attempts to examine the potential of such therapies for human subjects, both for healthy volunteers (studied in the laboratory) and for patients in the clinical environment.

Overshadowing

Overshadowing occurs when a second stimulus is presented in compound with the target CS during conditioning and the added cue restricts the level of conditioning that develops to the target CS. We have shown that such an effect can be obtained when the CS is a context, the added cue is a novel flavour, and the US a state of nausea. This observation encourages us to think that overshadowing may have potential as an intervention for the alleviation of ANV.

An early report by Greene and Seime (1987) gives grounds for optimism. They described the effect of giving a single oncology patient a dose of lemon flavour before chemotherapy; the outcome was that the patient complained far less of anticipatory symptoms over the course of her treatment when compared with her reaction to the treatment cycle experienced prior to receiving the lemon flavour. This observation is open to a number of explanations, but similar results have come from a more systematic study reported by Stockhorst, Wiener et al. (1998). In this, patients suffering from cancer were presented with a fluid to drink prior to each chemotherapy session of their treatment cycle. For half of the patients (the control group), this fluid was plain water, but for the others (the experimental group) the drink consisted of a novel flavour. These flavours were chosen to be rather unusual in their taste properties, such that the patients were unlikely ever to encounter them again (or, indeed, to have encountered them before). The authors found that the experimental group reported rather less anticipatory symptoms than the control group.

A further outcome of the study by Stockhorst, Wiener et al. (1998) is also worthy of note. They found that the overshadowing treatment served not only to reduce the incidence of anticipatory symptoms, but also reduced the extent to which the patients complained of *post-treatment* nausea and vomiting (i.e., the procedure appeared to attenuate the direct effects of the chemotherapy agent). In terms of the conditioning model, this seems to indicate that the overshadowing treatment is capable of reducing the observed magnitude of the UR. Why should this occur? One possibility, offered by Stockhorst et al., is based on the fact that posttreatment nausea is measured in the presence of the clinical cues that constitute the clinic (the CS for conditioned nausea). If the clinic evokes conditioned nausea, this could summate with the unconditioned nausea produced by the chemotherapy. The overshadowing treatment will then reduce the size of the post-treatment effect by attenuating its conditioned component. Direct evidence for the reality of such a summation effect has been provided by a study by Symonds and Hall (2002), using the animal model described above. (Interestingly, in this case it was the clinical study that led to the animal experiment, rather than the other way round.) These observations imply that the overshadowing technique (or indeed any other intervention capable of reducing conditioning) may be potentially more powerful than we originally supposed, as it may reduce not only anticipatory symptoms, but also those that are suffered immediately after treatment. In a sense this result appears to bear a similarity to a placebo response, which may itself have its basis in conditioning (see Klosterhalfen & Enck, this volume).

Further work will be needed to establish the generality of the overshadowing effect in the clinical context, and to refine the procedures, but these initial results are encouraging. Moreover, there is no reason to suppose that the effectiveness of this intervention will be restricted to the chemotherapy clinic. In principle, it should have the potential to be effective in other clinical settings and its application to dental phobia, for example, seems worthy of investigation.

Latent inhibition

Our second proposed intervention technique rests on the finding that nonreinforced stimulus exposure will retard future conditioning to that stimulus. We have demonstrated a clear effect for context-nausea conditioning with rats; perhaps, giving pre-exposure to the clinic will be capable of reducing the extent to which chemotherapy patients develop ANV. But it is a big jump from the animal conditioning laboratory to the clinic, and preliminary validation with human subjects would be worthwhile.

This issue has been addressed in a study by Klosterhalfen et al. (2005). The subjects were healthy individuals who volunteered to undergo the nausea-inducing experience of being rotated in a specially constructed rotation chair, of the sort used in aviation medicine for investigating motion sickness. (The chair is shown in Figure 2.2; as may be evident it constitutes, in itself, a context that participants find quite salient.) In appropriately selected subjects (those prone to motion sickness) rotation will induce a state of nausea. Moreover, after one or two rotations they will show conditioned nausea akin to the ANV effect; the subjects will report a feeling of nausea when simply returned to the experimental apparatus. To discover whether latent inhibition can be produced with this procedure, Klosterhalfen et al. simply placed the subjects in the chair either one or a few times prior to the first rotation trial. They found (at least for female subjects; perhaps because they are more prone to reporting symptoms of nausea than are males), that those given three pre-exposure trials to the context showed a significant decrease in the degree of anticipatory nausea reported in the experimental context on a test session given after the

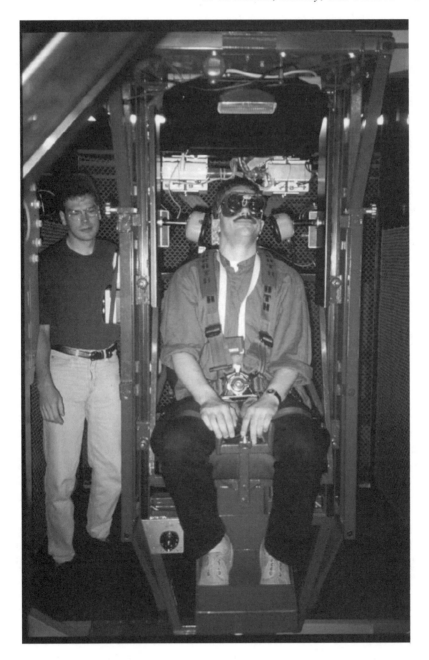

Figure 2.2 Rotation chair used to induce nausea. In the experiment described here, volunteers experienced five 1-min rotations, separated by 1-min rest periods, at a speed of $120°$ s^{-1}. During rotation they were required to move their head slowly up and down every 6 s, with the eyes closed. (Photograph courtesy of P. Enck.)

rotation trial. These results are encouraging; but it remains the case that it would probably be unacceptable to advocate an intervention that required a patient to attend a clinic three times, for no apparent reason, before the course of treatment is initiated. We must hope, then, that the procedure found to be effective in enhancing latent inhibition in rats (that of adding an extra salient stimulus during preexposure) will also work for people. Investigation of this possibility is currently under way.

As was the case with overshadowing, we do not suppose that latent inhibition will be of use only in the oncology clinic. We have already presented reasons for thinking that prior exposure to the dental clinic may be an important factor in determining a patient's reaction to a painful dental experience. And given the evidence showing that contextual latent inhibition can be demonstrated in both animals and humans, it will be no surprise that context exposure has been proposed as a possible therapy for dental fear. Van den Hout and Merckelback (1991) have suggested that a series of nonaversive exposures to the clinical setup (perhaps consisting of a number of sham treatments) might serve to protect patients (especially children) against the development of dental anxiety. Similarly, Weinstein (1990) has also proposed that invasive dental techniques should be postponed until as late as possible in life, a strategy that would allow the latent inhibition process to operate for as long as possible.

Conclusions

The study of classical conditioning and the laws that govern this form of learning is of interest in its own right, and the laboratory study of such learning in animals has generated theories of ever-increasing complexity and sophistication. But the basic principle remains simple. Pairing two events can establish an association between them, and when one of these events is of motivational significance (the US), the other (the CS) will acquire the power to evoke new responses appropriate to the motivational state engendered by the first. This process will operate in the real world as much as in the laboratory. The outcome will often be beneficial – an organism that develops a tendency to approach a previously neutral stimulus that has been associated with food, or to avoid one that has been associated with an aversive event, will be at an advantage.

We have focussed here, however, on cases in which this form of learning bestows no advantage – chemotherapy is unpleasant enough in itself, without the added distress produced by ANV. In many medical procedures the pairing of an aversive event with a given set of cues is inevitable (in spite of our best efforts, many medical treatments involve pain or discomfort, and the clinic is the only place in which they can be carried out). But the good news is that experimental work has shown that pairings do not necessarily result in association formation. It is well established that pre-exposure to the CS (latent inhibition) or the presence of a competing cue (overshadowing) can restrict the extent to which pairings result in an effective CS–US association. In this chapter we have demonstrated that these processes operate in a conditioning procedure of clinical relevance (context conditioning in the rat) and have described the initial stages of attempts to apply them to human volunteer subjects and to patients. The next step will be to move to direct clinical trials of interventions based on learning theory principles in the clinic itself.

References

Aapro, M. S., Molassiotis, A., & Oliver, I. (2005). Anticipatory nausea and vomiting. *Supportive Care in Cancer, 13*, 117–121.

American Psychiatric Association (1994). *Diagnostic and statistical manual of mental disorders* (4th ed.). Washington, DC: Author.

Andrykowski, M. A., & Redd, W. H. (1987). Longtitudinal analysis of the development of anticipatory nausea. *Journal of Consulting and Clinical Psychology, 55*, 36–41.

Barlow, D. H. (1988). *Anxiety and its disorders.* New York, NY: Guilford Press.

Bernstein, I. L., Webster, W. L., & Bernstein, I. D. (1982). Food aversions in children receiving chemotherapy for cancer. *Cancer, 50*, 2961–2963.

Best, M. R., Brown, E. R., & Sowell, M. K. (1984). Taste-mediated potentiation of noningestional stimuli in rats. *Learning and Motivation, 15*, 244–258.

Boakes, R. A., Tarrier, N., Barnes, W. B., & Tattersall, M. H. N. (1993). Prevalence of anticipatory nausea and other side-effects in cancer patients receiving chemotherapy. *European Journal of Cancer, 29A*, 866–870.

Boakes, R. A., Westbrook, R. F., & Barnes, B. W. (1992). Potentiation by a taste of toxicosis-based context conditioning: Effects of varying the test fluid. *Quarterly Journal of Experimental Psychology, 45B*, 303–325.

Burish, T. G., & Carey, M. P. (1986). Conditioned aversive responses in cancer chemotherapy patients: Theoretical and development analysis. *Journal of Consulting and Clinical Psychology, 54*, 593–600.

Davey, G. C. L. (1989). Dental phobias and anxieties: Evidence for conditioning processes in the acquisition and modulation of a learned fear. *Behaviour Research and Therapy, 27*, 51–58.

De Jongh, A., Muris, P., Ter Horst, G., & Duyx, M. P. (1995). Acquisition and maintenance of dental anxiety: The role of conditioning experiences and cognitive factors. *Behaviour Research and Therapy, 33*, 205–210.

Domjan, M. (1977). Selective suppression of drinking during a limited period following aversive drug treatment in rats. *Journal of Experimental Psychology: Animal Behavior Processes, 3*, 66–76.

Fanselow, M. S. (1990). Factors governing one trial contextual fear conditioning. *Animal Learning & Behavior, 18*, 264–270.

Garcia, J., & Koelling, P. A. (1966). Relation of cue to consequence in avoidance learning. *Psychonomic Science, 4*, 123–124.

Garcia, J., Brett, L. P., & Rusiniak, K. W. (1989). Limits of Darwinian conditioning. In S. B. Klein & R. R Mowrer (Eds.), *Contemporary learning theories: Instrumental conditioning theory and the impact of biological constraints on learning* (pp. 181–203). Hillsdale, NJ: Lawrence Erlbaum Associates, Inc.

Greene, P. G., & Seime, R. J. (1987). Stimulus control of anticipatory nausea in cancer chemotherapy. *Journal of Behaviour Therapy and Experimental Psychiatry*, *18*, 61–64.

Hall, G. (1991). *Perceptual and associative learning*. Oxford: Clarendon Press.

Hall, G., & Rodriguez, G. (2010). Associative and nonassociative processes in latent inhibition: An elaboration of the Pearce–Hall model. In R. E. Lubow & I. Weiner (Eds.), *Latent inhibition: Data, theories, and applications to schizophrenia* (pp. 114–136). Cambridge, UK: Cambridge University Press.

Hall, G., Symonds, M., & Rodriguez, M. (2009). Enhanced latent inhibition in context aversion conditioning. *Learning and Motivation*, *40*, 62–73.

Kamin, L. J. (1969). Predictability, attention, surprise, and conditioning. In B. M. Campbell & R. M. Church (Eds.), *Punishment and aversive behavior* (pp. 279–296). New York, NY: Appleton-Century-Crofts.

Kiernan, M. J., & Westbrook, R. F. (1993). Effects of exposure to a to-be-shocked environment upon the rat's freezing response. *Quarterly Journal of Experimental Psychology*, *46B*, 271–288.

Klosterhalfen, S., Kellermann, S., Stockhorst, U., Wolf, J., Kirschbaum, C., & Hall, G. (2005). Latent inhibition of rotation-chair induced nausea in healthy male and female volunteers. *Psychosomatic Medicine*, *67*, 335–340.

Limebeer, C. L., Hall, G., & Parker, L. A. (2006). Exposure to a lithium-paired context elicits gaping in rats: A model of anticipatory nausea. *Physiology & Behavior*, *88*, 398–403.

LoLordo, V. M., & Droungas, A. (1989). Selective associations and adaptive specializations: Taste aversions and phobias. In S. B Klein & R. R. Mowrer (Eds.), *Contemporary learning theories: Instrumental conditioning theory and the impact of biological constraints on learning* (pp. 145–179). Hillsdale, NJ: Lawrence Erlbaum Associates, Inc.

Lubow, R. E. (1989). *Latent inhibition and conditioned attention theory*. New York, NY: Cambridge University Press.

McLaren, I. P. L., Kaye, H., & Mackintosh, N. J. (1989). An associative theory of the representation of stimuli: Applications to perceptual learning and latent inhibition. In R. G. M. Morris (Ed.), *Parallel distributed processing: Implications for psychology and neurobiology* (pp. 102–140). Oxford, UK: Clarendon Press.

Marks, I. M. (1987). *Fears, phobias, and rituals*. New York, NY: Oxford University Press.

Mitchell, C., & Heyes, C. (1996). Simultaneous overshadowing and potentiation of taste and contextual cues by a second taste in toxicosis conditioning. *Learning and Motivation*, *27*, 38–72.

Morrow, G. R., & Rosenthal, S. N. (1996). Models, mechanisms, and management of anticipatory nausea and emesis. *Oncology*, *53 (Suppl. 1)*, 4–7.

Morrow, G. R., Roscoe, J. A., Kirshner, J. J., Hynes, H. E., & Rosenbluth, R. J. (1998). Anticipatory nausea and vomiting in the era of 5-HT3 antiemetics. *Supportive Care in Cancer*, *6*, 244–247.

Parker, L. A. (2003). Taste avoidance and taste aversion: Evidence for two different processes. *Learning & Behavior*, *31*, 165–172.

Pavlov, I. P. (1960). *Conditioned reflexes*. New York, NY: Dover. (Original work published 1927.)

Pearce, J. M., & Hall, G. (1980). A model for Pavlovian learning: Variations in the effectiveness of conditioned but not of unconditioned stimuli. *Psychological Review, 87*, 532–552.

Rodriguez, G., & Hall, G. (2008). Potentiation of latent inhibition. *Journal of Experimental Psychology: Animal Behavior Processes, 34*, 352–360.

Rodriguez, M., Lopez, M., Symonds, M., & Hall, G. (2000). Lithium-induced context aversion in rats as a model of anticipatory nausea in humans. *Physiology & Behavior, 71*, 571–579.

Stockhorst, U., Klosterhalfen, S., & Steingruber, H. J. (1998). Conditioned nausea and further side-effects in cancer chemotherapy: A review. *Journal of Psychophysiology, 12*, 14–33.

Stockhorst, U., Wiener, J. A., Klosterhalfen, S., Klosterhalfen, W., Aul, C., & Steingruber, H. J. (1998). Effects of overshadowing on conditioned nausea in cancer patients: An experimental study. *Physiology & Behavior, 64*, 743–753.

Symonds, M., & Hall, G. (1997). Contextual conditioning with lithium-induced nausea as the US: Evidence from a blocking procedure. *Learning and Motivation, 28*, 200–215.

Symonds, M., & Hall, G. (1999). Overshadowing not potentiation of illness-based contextual conditioning by a novel taste. *Animal Learning & Behavior, 27*, 379–390.

Symonds, M., & Hall, G. (2002). Post-injection suppression of drinking is modified by the presence of contextual cues: Implications for both anticipatory and post-treatment nausea in humans. *Animal Learning & Behavior, 30*, 355–362.

Symonds, M., Hall, G., Lopez, M., Loy, I., Ramos, A., & Rodriguez, M. (1998). Is fluid consumption necessary for the formation of context-illness associations? An evaluation using consumption and blocking tests. *Learning and Motivation, 29*, 168–183.

Townend, E., Dimigen, G., & Fung, D. (2000). A clinical study of dental anxiety. *Behaviour Research and Therapy, 38*, 31–46.

Van den Hout, M., & Merckelbach, H. (1991). Classical conditioning: Still going strong. *Behavioural Psychotherapy, 19*, 59–79.

Watson, J. B., & Rayner, R. (1920). Conditioned emotional reactions. *Journal of Experimental Psychology, 3*, 1–14.

Weinstein, P. (1990). Breaking the worldwide cycle of pain, fear and avoidance: Uncovering risk factors and promoting prevention for children. *Annals of Behavioral Medicine, 12*, 141–147.

3 Associative learning and phobias

Andy P. Field and Helena M. Purkis

Associative learning offers one of the earliest explanations of how phobic reactions to stimuli might be acquired. Conditioning as a model for phobia first arose from a famous demonstration by Watson and Rayner (1920) involving a white rat, a hammer, an iron bar, and a small child. The authors wanted to demonstrate that aversive and avoidant responses could be acquired to a previously neutral stimulus. In their study, a 9-month-old child, Albert B (or little Albert), was tested to see whether he was fearful of various stimuli (including a white rat and the noise made by banging a claw hammer on an iron bar). Watson and Rayner established that Albert was not initially fearful of the rat, but was scared by the noise. Albert was then placed in a room with the rat. Every time he touched the rat, or the rat approached him, an experimenter hit the iron bar with the hammer. After several trials in which the rat was paired with the loud noise, Albert started to display signs of anxiety when the rat was presented alone (i.e., without the noise). The authors did not propose a theory of phobia acquisition on the basis of their findings. However, the implication from this study was that experiencing a neutral stimulus in temporal proximity to some fear-inducing or traumatic event could create an excessive, persistent fear (i.e., a phobia) to that stimulus.

From a conditioning perspective, the rat is a conditional stimulus (CS), the loud noise is an unconditional stimulus (US), and the loud noise evokes an automatic response (anxiety), called the unconditional response (UR). After the repeated pairing of the CS and US, and the formation of an association between the CS and US in memory, the CS comes to evoke a conditional response, CR. In this case, the conditional response is similar to the unconditional response, i.e., anxiety.

From a clinical perspective, at the time the study was conducted, conditioning was understood to have two important characteristics: it was governed by the law of equipotentiality, and it displayed **extinction**. According to the law of equipotentiality, any predictor (CS) is able to enter into an association with any outcome (US), and all predictors have the same potential to be associated with any outcome. The implication of this law for theories of phobia acquisition is that a phobia can potentially be developed to any stimulus, provided that stimulus is, at some point, experienced alongside a trauma. Extinction refers to the effect whereby the strength of a conditioned response (CR) to a stimulus will decline over successive trials when the predictor (CS) is presented alone (without the US). The implication of extinction for theories of phobia is that exposure to the CS (the feared stimulus) in the absence of the fear-evoking stimulus (the US) allows the phobic/anxious response (CR) to extinguish. This simple idea formed the basis for behaviour therapy (see Wolpe, 1961), which remains successful in the treatment of specific phobias (Öst, 1996, 2008; Öst, Svensson, Hellstrom, & Lindwall, 2001; Silverman, Pina, & Viswesvaran, 2008).

Associative learning and other pathways to fear

The basic idea that associative learning underpins phobia acquisition has had to weather many theoretical storms. One seminal review (Rachman, 1977) astutely noted that anxious responses develop not just from direct traumatic experience, but also through indirect pathways such as learning by observing others' reactions (vicarious learning) or learning through receiving threat-relevant information. Although direct conditioning, **vicarious conditioning** and learning via instruction are, *prima facie*, different pathways, Field (2006) has argued that they have the same underlying mechanism: An association between a CS and US drives them all. For example, in vicarious learning a person experiences a stimulus (a CS) and someone else's reaction to it. This reaction might be distressing enough to act as a US (Mineka & Cook, 1993). A second possibility is that an observed fear response is a CS that has acquired a fear-evoking quality through some prior co-occurrence with a traumatic event (US). The observational learning episode itself is, therefore, the co-occurrence of a new CS2 with the CS1 of the fear response (i.e. **second-order conditioning**). A stimulus (CS2), therefore, acquires a second-order fear response through co-occurrence with a fear response that has previously been associated with a traumatic outcome. Unfortunately, there is no available evidence to distinguish these two interpretations of what occurs in observational learning (see Mineka & Cook, 1993). However, as Field points out, all that really matters is that vicarious learning is a form of associative learning at the procedural level and the associative structure of a vicarious learning episode can be conceptualized in much the same way as a direct conditioning episode.

According to Field (2006), verbal threat information can also be conceptualized from an associative learning standpoint in which information is regarded as a US. This idea is somewhat similar to the way in which associative learning models explain other situations in which USs are not biologically significant (e.g., **causal learning**). In terms of fear acquisition, it is plausible that throughout childhood, a child experiences many causal learning/conditioning trials in which a stimulus (such as an animal) consistently predicts negative information ("don't touch that", "be careful of the animal", "that animal bites"). This scenario is associative learning at both a procedural level (learning results from pairing a stimulus with an outcome) and a behavioural level (beliefs or behaviours are acquired by pairing a stimulus with meaningful information about it). Field goes on to suggest that threat information produces (or strengthens) an association between a CS and a threat representation (and, of course, information can change this representation too). It is worth noting that according to some theorists the need for an "association" to be assumed in such associative models is debatable (De Houwer, 2009; Mitchell, De Houwer, & Lovibond, 2009).

The clinical implications of vicarious and informational episodes representing types of associative learning is that these forms of learning should exhibit the other functional characteristics of so-called direct conditioning that we describe in this chapter. As such, we make the assumption that when we discuss functional characteristics of "conditioning" or "associative learning" they could apply to direct traumatic experiences, vicarious experiences, and the provision of threat information. As such, associative learning, as a theoretical framework, potentially has enormous power to explain how fears develop. As this chapter will hopefully show, much of the criticism of associative learning models stems from a misunderstanding of the scope and underlying principles of associative learning theory.

General evidence for associative models of fears and phobia

Ethical considerations (more strictly enforced now than in little Albert's time) prevent experimental study of the role of associative learning in the development of anxiety in childhood. However, evidence from laboratory-based research in adults and from naturalistic studies supports the premise that associative learning is the primary mechanism through which fears develop. Pavlovian fear conditioning is a standard laboratory paradigm in both human and animal research. When a neutral CS is paired with a sufficiently aversive US, a fear response will be acquired to the CS (Pavlov, 1927). A considerable amount of work has been devoted to mapping the neural circuitry involved in fear responding (LeDoux, 2000, 2003; Phelps, 2006; Phelps & LeDoux, 2005), establishing that the amygdala is central to the automatic processing of emotional, and particularly fear-related information (LeDoux, 2003; Morris, Öhman, & Dolan, 1998; Phelps, 2006; Phelps & LeDoux, 2005). Recent research reports that when a stimulus signals an aversive event, such as a shock, the stimulus, regardless of its valence, prompts a physiological profile consistent with defensive activation (Bradley, Moulder, & Lang, 2005). It has also been demonstrated that fear conditioning changes the valence of a CS from positive to negative. Pictures of animals initially rated as positive (dogs, fish, birds) were presented in an associative learning paradigm, in which one type of animal was paired with an aversive shock US, and another type of animal was presented in absence of shock. Animals from the category that had been paired with shock were found to be implicitly more negative, as indexed by affective priming, and were rated as more negative than animals from the category not paired with shock (Purkis & Lipp, 2009). These few articles barely scratch the surface of the 747 published papers with "Fear Conditioning" in their title in the period 1959–2010[1]; associative learning as a mechanism for fear acquisition has been well and truly established.

Several naturalistic studies support the idea that a single traumatic event can lead to clinical levels of anxiety of objects related to the trauma. After the sinking of a cruise ship, 25 teenage female survivors were found to have excessive fears relating to ships, water travel, swimming, and water, and moreover their fear generalized to other modes of transport (Yule, Udwin, & Murdoch, 1990). Similarly, child survivors ($N = 29$) of a severe lightening strike had a greater number and more intense fear of thunderstorms, lightening, and tornadoes than controls (Dollinger, O'Donnell, & Staley, 1984).

There is also retrospective evidence that anxious children (or their parents) will attribute fears to traumatic experiences. In a review of seven studies that had looked at self-reported attributions of fear, associative learning was endorsed by up to 91 percent of children (King, Gullone, & Ollendick, 1998). Nearly all of the endorsements favoured the three pathways to fear: direct conditioning, vicarious learning, or verbal threat information. The weighted mean percentage of children or parents endorsing these three pathways was 94 percent. Fear of water, however, is a notable exception: In the aforementioned review, 78 percent of parents endorsed a "fear at first contact" explanation and no one attributed this fear to conditioning; and in another study (Menzies & Clarke, 1993) only 1 of 50 parents explained their child's water phobia with conditioning (13 others suggested vicarious learning).

If we consider verbal threat information and vicarious learning as pathways driven by associative learning then there is considerable experimental evidence that fear cognitions, avoidance, and physiological responses can be learnt through associative learning (see Askew & Field, 2008; Muris & Field, 2010, for reviews). Briefly, when children are given threat information about a novel animal (in our research, these are usually Australian marsupials) it changes their fear beliefs for over 6 months (Field, Argyris, & Knowles, 2001; Field, Lawson, & Banerjee, 2008), creates processing biases about future encounters with the animal (Field & Lawson, 2008; Muris et al., 2009), and during an approach task increases their heart rate (Field & Schorah, 2007) and makes them avoid the animal in a behavioural task (Field & Lawson, 2003). Similarly, when children view their mothers (Gerull & Rapee, 2002) or pictures of strangers expressing fear to novel stimuli this increases their threat cognitions and avoidance of these animals (Askew & Field, 2007); infants also tend to show avoidance of strangers after seeing their socially anxious mothers' reactions to the stranger (Murray, Cooper, Creswell, Schofield, & Sack, 2007).

Phenomena in associative learning

Having established that associative learning is a viable and well-supported pathway to fear, we now turn our attention to the functional characteristics of associative learning that have a direct implication for how fears and phobias are developed (and, hence, prevented or treated). Research has established a great deal about the processes involved in an associative learning procedure and the factors that moderate conditioned responses. Nonetheless, there are many widespread myths (see Rescorla, 1988) about associative learning which continue to hinder the development of associative learning theory as a framework for studying the development of phobias. This section explores some important aspects of associative learning (and ignores quite a few more) that are, perhaps, not as widely known within the clinical domain as they should be.

Associative learning can occur after only one trial

Many clinical psychologists view associative learning as something that occurs over several trials. This belief is certainly true in laboratory settings using reasonably innocuous stimuli. In fact, in eyeblink conditioning studies that employ tones as CSs and puffs of air (that induce eyeblink) as USs, associative learning may take hundreds of trials. The idea that associative learning requires repeated trials is particularly problematic for associative learning models of fear acquisition because it is unlikely that an organism would have repeated exposure to a particular stimulus and the same traumatic outcome (a person would have to be extremely unlucky to experience a traumatic outcome every time they were up high, were in an enclosed space, or saw a spider or snake). However, in the right conditions, conditioned responses can be acquired very rapidly. Rescorla (1980) demonstrated conditioned responding in only eight trials and the use of 8–10 conditioning trials per CS is now standard in laboratory based associative learning paradigms. Even eight stimulus–trauma trials is a reasonable amount of "bad luck" in the real world. However, there is good evidence for one-trial learning, especially when the outcome is very aversive. Campbell, Sanderson, and Laverty (1964) paired a neutral tone with an injection of scoline, a curare derivate that induces transient respiratory paralysis. In this case, one trial was sufficient to establish a conditioned fear response to the tone that did not extinguish, and in fact became stronger across 100 extinction trials. Garcia, McGowan, and Green (1972) demonstrated one-trial learning using illness and shock as an aversive US (see also Izquierdo, Barros, Medina, & Izquierdo, 2000; Izquierdo, Barros, Ardenghi, et al., 2000); and Öhman, Eriksson, and Olofsson (1975) obtained one-trial learning to both fear-relevant (snakes) and fear-irrelevant (houses) stimuli when an intense shock was used as a US. These studies demonstrate that a fear response can be conditioned to a stimulus in one trial if it is paired with a sufficiently intense US.

The nature of the CS

At the beginning of the chapter, we discussed the principle of equipotentiality. This was a tenet of early learning theory (Pavlov, 1927) that associative relationships were equally likely to be formed between conditional and unconditional stimuli, regardless of the specifics of the stimuli or responses involved. However, a famous piece of research by Garcia and Koelling derailed this theory (Garcia, Ervin, & Koelling, 1966; Garcia & Koelling, 1966). The drinking behaviour of rats was measured after presentations of various combinations of cues and outcomes associated with their drinking water: lights and sounds with shocks and radiation. The conclusion was that rats were more likely to associate tastes with illness than with shock, and light and noise with shock than with illness. Seligman (1971) used this research to support the assertion that the theory of equipotentiality was flawed and that associations such as taste and nausea that have an obvious survival benefit could represent associations that are biologically "prepared" to be learned.

Seligman (1971) argued that phobias differed from conditioned fear reactions because they were selective, occurred often to a limited range of stimuli, were irrational, and were resistant to extinction. He therefore proposed that phobias might be special instances of fear conditioning that occurred when fear was conditioned to stimuli that were prepared to enter into a fear association. In the absence of better criteria, Seligman defined these "fear-relevant stimuli" as those that are commonly associated with phobia, such as snakes, spiders, or heights.

Early conditioning studies confirmed that pictures of fear-relevant stimuli were more effectively associated with fear than were pictures of nonfear-relevant stimuli. Greater resistance to extinction in electrodermal responding was demonstrated following conditioning with pictures of fear-relevant stimuli, snakes, compared with pictures of nonfear-relevant stimuli, houses and faces, when a fear evoking electric shock was used as the US (Öhman, Erixon, & Lofberg, 1975). In fact all the predictions derived from Seligman's (1971) account of prepared learning have been tested extensively (see Öhman & Mineka, 2001, for a review). There is good evidence that fear can be conditioned more robustly to fear-relevant than to nonfear-relevant stimuli. Whether this reflects an evolutionary preparedness or social learning factors is debated, because there is good evidence that culturally fear-relevant stimuli, such as pointed guns, are as effective as CS as are evolutionarily fear-relevant stimuli (Davey, 1995; Hugdahl & Johnsen, 1989). That certain stimuli have a greater capacity to be feared could go some way towards explaining why some fears seem to require so little associative learning, such as fear of water. What seems certain is that all stimulus associations are not created equal; the nature of the CS has an impact on fear learning.

Associative learning is mediated by CS–US associations

Conditioning is often referred to as associative learning,[2] reflecting the acquisition of CS–US associations, in both learning generally (e.g., Davey, 1989a; Mackintosh, 1983) and the acquisition of phobias (e.g., Davey, 1989b, 1997; Field, 2006; Field & Davey, 2001). Contemporary perspectives posit that associative learning reflects a mental linking of the relevant events and stimuli encountered during a learning episode (Hall, 2002; Pearce & Bouton, 2001). Broadly speaking, there are two competing theories regarding the specific associations that are formed during associative learning: (1) stimulus–response (S–R), an association is formed between the CS and the UR (i.e., between the to-be-feared stimulus and the organism's reaction to the trauma); or (2) stimulus–stimulus (S–S), an association is formed between the CS and the US (i.e., between the to-be-feared stimulus and the trauma itself). The majority of research favours the latter explanation: that animals and humans learn associations between the CS and US during associative learning, and that this association mediates the CR.

There are two converging streams of evidence that CRs are mediated by CS–US associations. First, in studies in which the UR is prevented, CRs still occur. For instance, when the drug curare, which blocks all skeletal responses, is used during associative learning, conditioned skeletal responses to the CS are still present when the drug has worn off (Solomon & Turner, 1962). Second, revaluation of the US has an effect on the CR: Rescorla (1974) presented rats with a weak shock as a US to produce a CR. Following associative learning, the rats were exposed to a stronger shock than was used during associative learning, but without any presentations of the CS. Subsequent presentations of the CS produced stronger conditioned responses than were observed during the initial associative learning. Rescorla concluded that exposure to the stronger shocks had led to US-revaluation; the US was revalued as more aversive than it had been during associative learning. This finding demonstrates that conditioned responses are mediated by CS–US associations, and that CRs can be influenced by experiences outside of the original learning trials.

However, the processes involved in associative learning are far more complex than this simple CS–US association model suggests. Learning is not simply the association of two stimuli but is influenced by past learning and contextual variables, during which associations are formed between representations of multiple events (including relationships generated by other associations). Associative learning, far from being a simple association between two events, is a complex process that provides an organism with a highly detailed representation of its environment.

Associative learning reflects past experience

Organisms are a product of their experiences: they do not enter con-ditioning episodes as empty vessels, instead they bring with them prior experiences and prior relationships between CSs and USs. There are many associative learning phenomena that reflect the influence of prior associ-ations on the formation of new associations. When cues that are predictive of a US have different learning histories, cue competition is observed. One type of cue competition is blocking (Kamin, 1968). In a typical blocking experiment, in trials in the first phase, a CS (CS1, such as a light) predicts the US. In trials in the second phase, a compound CS (CS1 and CS2, a light and a tone) predicts the US. Compared with a group who are exposed only to the second phase, the blocking group will show reduced conditioned responding to CS2. For the blocking group, CS1 already reliably predicts the US and this "blocks" learning about CS2 in the second stage. The group that was not pre-exposed to CS1–US contingencies, however, shows equal associative learning to CS1 and CS2.

Another form of cue competition occurs when the CS is presented in compound with a stimulus that already has an inhibitory relationship with the US. Inhibitory conditioning is acquired when a CS comes to predict the absence of a US. Imagine that in trials in the first phase, CS1 is presented with the US (e.g., light – shock), and in the second phase, CS1 is presented with CS2 in the absence of the US (e.g., light + tone – no shock). Given that CS1 reliably predicted the US, CS2 will form an inhibitory relationship with the US (i.e., the tone predicts the absence of shock). Now imagine that CS2, the inhibitory stimulus, is paired with a new stimulus, CS3, in the presence of the shock US (e.g., tone + buzzer – shock). Given that CS2 already has an inhibitory relationship with the US, the new stimulus, CS3, should acquire a magnified conditioned response to the US (buzzer really predicts shock), compared with a group who were presented with CS3 in isolation with the US. This phenomenon is known as super-learning or super-conditioning (Aitken, Larkin, & Dickinson, 2000; Rescorla, 1971). Super-conditioning implies that learning history will affect the magnitude of an acquired fear response: If at the time at which a CS becomes associated with trauma an inhibitory stimulus is present, it would be reasonable to expect a much greater acquired fear response. There are many other forms of cue competition that can be achieved through altering the extent to which CSs are predictive of USs.

Two related phenomena demonstrate that learning also occurs when, behaviourally speaking, no learning appears to have taken place. The first phenomenon is latent inhibition, which results from CS pre-exposure; presentations of the CS in absence of the US prior to conditioning trials. Associative learning takes significantly longer after CS pre-exposure than when there is no pre-exposure of the CS (Lubow, 1973; Lubow & Moore, 1959). Latent inhibition implies that it is more difficult to condition a response to a familiar stimulus than to a novel stimulus. Studies with fear of dogs (Doogan & Thomas, 1992) and of dental fear (Ten Berge, Veerkamp, & Hoogstraten, 2002) suggest that acquisition of fear was less likely after a history of nontraumatic experiences.

A subtly different phenomenon is learned irrelevance (or learned helplessness), which occurs when uncorrelated presentations of CSs and USs are pre-exposed prior to associative learning (unlike latent inhibition, pre-exposure includes CSs and USs, but the CS does not reliably predict the US). This kind of pre-exposure retards the subsequent conditioning of correlated CS–US presentations (Mackintosh, 1973). Both latent inhibition and learned irrelevance demonstrate that the overall power of a CS to predict a US is crucial (in both cases the overall correlation between the CS and US is reduced). These, in combination with cue competition suggest that it is possible to learn about the absence of relationships and respond accordingly (Mackintosh, 1973, for example, believed that during pre-exposure to uncorrelated CS–US presentations, what is learned is that the CS is irrelevant).

Thus, associative learning episodes are affected by knowledge acquired from prior experience of the relationships between CSs and USs. In clinical terms, this means that the power of a particular conditioning episode will depend, to some extent, on prior experience. To place these functional characteristics within a clinical context let us take a hypothetical example of a boy who, when stroking a cat, is scratched. Prior (nontraumatic) exposure to cats (for example, having one as a pet) should protect the boy from acquiring a fear of cats after being scratched (*latent inhibition*). If the boy has been scratched many times before but has not known what scratched him or has associated scratches with different unrelated stimuli (rose bushes, falling over on concrete, etc.), then this should weaken the association between cats and trauma after he is scratched by one (*learned irrelevance*). If he already associates similar painful scratches with another animal (for example, perhaps he has been scratched by dogs in the past) then this prior association should block the association between the cat and trauma (*blocking*). Finally, if the boy was in a context in which cues predicted safety at the time when the cat scratches him, then he should acquire a greater fear CR to the cat than if he had been among cues that predicted threat (*super-learning*).

The acquisition of fear and phobia in a complex environment is therefore complicated by many factors. However, this complexity provides an explanation for why people who experience the same trauma differ in their acquisition of fears. People have different learning histories, with regard to trauma and with regard to the stimuli that a trauma may be paired with. One obvious implication of the fact that learning history has a strong influence on fear acquisition is that fear may be acquired through associative learning processes more easily at younger ages (Field, 2006) because learning histories become more varied and complex with age. To use the example above, all other things being equal, a boy of 8 years old has had more time to have experienced cats, more time to have experienced them more often, and more time to have acquired a positive, longer, and more protective learning history, than has a girl of 1 year old.

Associative learning does not depend upon contiguity

Contiguity is neither necessary nor sufficient for associative learning to occur (Rescorla, 1968), which in clinical terms means that the to-be-feared stimulus need not occur at the same time as the traumatic event. As we have seen above, associative learning relies on the base rate of the US, and thus the predictive power of the CS, which is not the same thing as contiguity. Clinically speaking, the base rate experience of the trauma will influence the acquisition, or not, of a phobia. Contiguity on the other hand, is not only insufficient, but also unnecessary. This point can also be drawn from situations in which an inhibitory association is conditioned. In a situation in which the US is experienced in absence of a CS, the expectation, based on stimulus contiguity, would be that nothing is learned. But clearly, if this was the case, it would be impossible to demonstrate phenomena that reflect conditioned inhibition. The truth is that even in the absence of CS–US contiguity, information about stimuli and their associations can be learned. This finding explains why not all phobia sufferers remember a traumatic event, because the trauma might not have occurred contiguously with the stimulus that they now fear.

The CR and UR are not necessarily the same

It is now accepted that a CS can elicit a variety of responses that are related to the US, but do not necessarily match the response elicited by the US. For example, when rats are exposed to an aversive outcome such as a shock, they respond with behaviours such as increased heart rate, squeaking, and jumping. But when a CS is paired with a shock, the CS tends to elicit anticipatory responses (that are opposite to the behaviours elicited by the US) such as a decrease in heart rate and "freezing" (Black, 1971). Moreover, the response that is conditioned via the US can depend on the nature of the CS. Pinel and Treit (1979) showed that if a tone CS predicts a shock US, then rats will freeze when presented with the tone. However, if a localized prod is used as a CS (with the same shock US), presentations of the prod will elicit behaviours aimed at burying the prod. Thus CRs to the same US differ depending on the nature of the CS that predicts it. These findings again highlight that the associative learning of a phobia is not as simple as experiencing the to-be-feared stimulus during a traumatic event and subsequently feeling anxiety. The response a person experiences during an associative learning episode, rather than anxiety itself, may be related to anxiety and will depend on the nature of the CS and the US. With this in mind, retrospective studies (in adults and children) of fear acquisition are likely to underestimate associative learning experiences simply because they present participants with an inaccurate and oversimplified explanation of the experience involved.

The CS does not always produce a CR following associative learning

When conditioned responding is contingent upon the presence or absence of a predictive cue in addition to the CS, this is called feature modulation or occasion setting. Rescorla (1991) demonstrated that if a CS was reinforced only when accompanied by another stimulus (called a "feature") the CR would occur only if that feature was present. Feature modulation differs from cue competition, in that the feature can precede the presentation of the CS and the stimuli do not need to overlap. In a feature-positive design the presence of the feature indicates that the CS will be followed by the US, and in a feature-negative design the presence of the feature indicates that the CS will not be followed by the US. The phenomenon of feature modulation reinforces that associative learning is dependent on context.

From a clinical perspective, feature modulation may shed light on the differences in subjective experiences of stimuli following associative learning. Conditioning may often occur in the presence of a modulating stimulus. In subsequent encounters with the CS, the presence or absence of the modulating stimulus would then influence whether a CR occurs. From an associative learning perspective, although an association has been formed between CS and US, it will have no behavioural impact if the modulating stimulus is not present. Conversely, if there is no modulating stimulus during conditioning, or if the modulating stimulus always co-occurs with the CS, then subsequent encounters with the CS have a high likelihood of producing a response. For example, a student who makes an embarrassing mistake while playing soccer on a football pitch might not develop a generalized social anxiety, because the mistake–embarrassment association may be moderated by the salient context of, for example, the game of football in which learning took place, and not the more general social context. The implication for treatment programmes is that they must discover which moderators exist, and exposure to the CS should be performed within the context of these moderators (Bouton, Mineka, & Barlow, 2001).

Overshadowing refers to the finding that when a compound CS (i.e., two or more stimuli presented at the same time) signals a US, only the more salient of the two CSs, when presented alone, will evoke a CR. This is because, during learning, responses to the less salient stimuli are overshadowed. (Imagine, for example, that you eat a meal that subsequently makes you ill. Overshadowing implies that you would be likely to attribute the illness to the most distinctive or salient component or flavour present in the meal.) There is a tendency to assume that conditioning takes place between one stimulus (viewed as a whole) and another stimulus (also viewed as a whole). However, a given stimulus is actually a combination of many features (in the way that a meal is made up of many distinct flavours). Conditioning is not simply the association of one stimulus with another, but the association of multiple stimulus features with other stimulus features (see the section on conditioning being driven by CS–US associations). Fear and anxiety can be evoked by certain specific features of the CS; the strength of conditioned responding during subsequent exposure to the CS will be modulated by the degree to which those features are present in that particular example of the stimulus.

Conditioning can occur without an actual CS and US

We previously referred to the notion that conditioning is a mental linking of relevant events and stimuli during a learning episode (Hall, 2002). Behaviour is elicited on the basis of a mental representation of an associ-ation between stimuli. Given this, it is perhaps not so strange that con-ditioning can occur with mental representations of the CS and US. Previous research has demonstrated that CRs can be acquired (using flavour CSs) without the presence of the actual CS or US at the time of learning, but rather with mental representations of these stimuli. Learning from rep-resentations of stimuli has been shown in two ways. When a mental representation of a CS is paired with a US, the actual CS acquires a CR; and, if a mental representation of a CS (CS1) is paired with a second stimulus (CS2) that was previously paired with a US, CS1 acquires a CR. In the latter case, CS2 is presumed to evoke a mental representation of the US. In both these cases, a mental representation of the CS is paired with a mental representation of the US, and therefore learning has occurred in the absence of the actual CS and US (Dwyer, 1999, 2001, 2003; Dwyer, Mackintosh, & Boakes, 1998).

It has also been demonstrated that a predictor can act as an outcome for other potential predictors; this is called second-order conditioning (Rescorla, 1980). In this case, CS1 is paired with an outcome, and then CS2 is paired with CS1. CS2 comes to evoke the same response as CS1, suggesting that the CS2 has formed a direct association to the original US (although this was only ever paired with CS1). The implication is that when CS1 and CS2 are paired, CS1 evokes a representation of the US that becomes associated with CS2. There is some evidence in humans that devaluing the US after second-order conditioning eliminates the conditional response to CS2 (Davey & McKenna, 1983). Moreover, a US represen-tation can be used in place of an actual US to produce associative learning. These lines of evidence support that mental representations of CS and US are sufficient for associative learning to occur.

Field (2006) suggests that this research has important implications for associative learning accounts of fear acquisition. It may be possible to acquire a conditioned fear response to a stimulus without that stimulus ever being present at the time of the trauma, merely by thinking about the stimulus at the time of the trauma. Moreover, it may be possible to acquire a conditioned fear response merely by thinking about a particular stimulus and a traumatic event simultaneously. Such possibilities go some way to provide an explanation as to why phobia sufferers often do not remember explicit associative learning episodes. Fear acquisition seemingly occurs through more complex scenarios than simply experiencing a stimulus in the presence of trauma. A person may have no memory of the object of his or her fear co-occurring with a traumatic event, because the object may never have been paired directly with the trauma. Nonetheless, the acquired fear still stems from associative learning processes.

The US need not be biologically significant

USs stimuli are often defined as biologically significant events, as traditionally, an UR involves a physiological response. However, humans can readily associate stimuli with other stimuli that do not evoke URs. Studies of causal learning support that humans can learn predictive relations between neutral stimuli and neutral outcomes (see De Houwer & Beckers, 2002; Dickinson, 2001; Shanks, Holyoak, & Medin, 1996, for reviews). Causal learning paradigms include such tasks as predicting whether pictures of butterflies will mutate when exposed to radiation (Collins & Shanks, 2002; Lober & Shanks, 2000) and whether certain foods predict an allergic reaction (e.g., Aitken et al., 2000; Le Pelley & McLaren, 2003). In these paradigms, the US does not evoke an UR in the traditional sense. Nevertheless, humans readily learn the contingencies (e.g., they can accurately predict allergic reactions after several trials on which they receive feedback about whether their predictions are correct). Causal learning is a recognized form of associative learning (the cause acts as the CS and the outcome acts as the US), data from causal learning studies fit predictions from associative learning models (De Houwer & Beckers, 2002; Dickinson, 2001; Le Pelley & McLaren, 2003; Lober & Shanks, 2000), learning is mediated by the statistical contingency between the CS and US (Perales & Shanks, 2003), and is subject to blocking, super-learning, learned inhibition, and negative contingency learning (see Dickinson, 2001, for a review).

Models of associative learning can be successfully applied to situations in which the US is innocuous, and there is no obvious CR (or UR for that matter), and such associations seem to be governed by the same laws as traditional associative learning. This is important because it demonstrates the generality of associative learning. Throughout the lifespan, many associations will be formed between potentially fear-related stimuli and any number of seemingly innocuous USs. These stimuli may or may not generate anxiety at the time of learning, and may or may not come to elicit anxiety in the future.

Extinction does not break the CS–US association

As discussed in the section on one-trial learning, associations between CS and US can be formed very quickly. Though evidence for one-trial learning generally requires the presentation of an intense US, there is incidental evidence that associations are formed just as quickly with a less intense US. The difference lies in whether, and for how long, a response is displayed to the CS after the US ceases to be presented.

In conditioning trials with random presentations of CS and US, responses are initially evoked by the CS, but these diminish following further training with this contingency. Nonetheless, Rescorla (2000) demonstrated that CS–US associations were formed during such training. This research confirmed that CS–US associations were formed very early and rapidly. However, as training continued the CS lost its power to evoke a CR, even though the CS–US associations remained intact. This finding is particularly interesting because it implies that CS–US associations can (1) form in very few trials and (2) that subsequent random presentations of the CS and US do not eliminate the association. As Field (2006) points out, the absence of a behavioural manifestation of a stimulus–trauma association (i.e., fear or anxiety) does not imply that the stimulus–trauma association has not been formed. It may remain latent and emerge to have a behavioural effect at some later stage.

This leads on to work in extinction of fear responding, which, of course, has enormous implications for the treatment of phobias. In an extinction para-digm, the CS is presented alone (without presentations of the US), and this exposure results in a gradual decline in the CR until it is no longer evoked. Given that CS–US associations survive random presentations, it is probably no surprise that they also survive extinction (even if the CR is extinguished). Associative learning models of fear have been criticized because they predict extinction of fear responses, yet this extinction does not seem to occur with phobias. One such argument is that following a traumatic event, subsequent exposure to the now feared stimulus most likely occurs in absence of trauma, thus the fear response should extinguish. (To use our earlier example, if a boy is scratched by a cat then in all probability subsequent cats that he encounters will not scratch him, so his anxiety CR should decline.) A supporting argument is that when treated through exposure therapy (that, in its simplest form, is a series of extinction trials) anxiety sometimes returns. There are several counter arguments, including avoidance: The boy who is scratched by a cat and becomes anxious may subsequently avoid cats and so would never experience cats in the absence of trauma. Second, a mental representation of a US can maintain responding, thus if an encounter with the fear-evoking stimulus evokes a mental representation of the traumatic event, this could maintain the fear response (Field, 2006).

However, the argument that anxiety can return after extinction largely arises out of a misconception about associative learning that extinction is forever. Recent research with extinction is completely consistent with the view that CS–US associations not only survive subsequent random CS–US presentations, but also survive extinction procedures (Bouton, 1994). Although conditioned responding to a CS declines across presentations of the CS, in the absence of the US, several phenomena suggest that the underlying CS–US association survives. All three phenomena involve the reemergence of conditioned responding after the extinguishing of the CR has been observed during extinction.

In renewal, there is a context change between conditioning and extinction. Conditioning (e.g., a tone CS with a shock US) is conducted in one location, and extinction trials (the tone alone) are conducted in a different location, and CRs to the tone extinguish. However, when the extinguished CS (tone) is presented in the original location (the context in which it was conditioned), CRs reoccur; i.e., the response is renewed.

In spontaneous recovery, weak CRs return merely after the passage of time. This effect is similar to renewal, if time is viewed as a context (Bouton & Swartzentruber, 1991), in that extinction trials occur in a different temporal context to conditioning. Though the CS cannot be re-experienced in the original temporal context, it is experienced in a different context to both conditioning and extinction. The clinical implication of these phenomena is that conditioned fear responses may remain after a traumatic event, if subsequent, nontraumatic, encounters are in a different context or at a different time. As such, it is important for clinicians to identify the parameters of fear as closely as possible, and to try to extinguish fear responses within those contexts. This is consistent with the common practice in behaviour therapy to apply extinction in multiple contexts.

A related phenomenon is reinstatement, in which CRs to the CS reappear if the US is presented again on its own, following extinction. As with renewal, reinstatement is context dependent: The CS must be experienced in the same context as the reinstating stimulus (the US) for CRs to be reinstated. The clinical implication is that after fear responses are extinguished, a subsequent experience of the original trauma could reinstate the CR (provided the feared stimulus is later experienced in the same context).

From a clinical perspective, it seems clear that the prediction that fear responses should extinguish over subsequent exposures is not as simple as it seems. The extent to which fear extinction is successful will depend upon factors such as context, and therefore the success of exposure therapy may depend in part on matching the context of exposure to the context in which the initial trauma occurred. This issue is considered in more detail in the chapter by Bouton, Winterbauer, and Vurbic.

Traumatic incidents might not be traumatic at the time

In discussing that conditioning reflects CS–US associations, we briefly mentioned revaluation of the US. In Rescorla (1974), rats were conditioned with a weak shock, and then presented with a strong shock in absence of the CS. Subsequent presentations of the CS elicited stronger CRs than were originally obtained during conditioning, because the US had been revalued as more threatening. US revaluation is just as potent in humans: habituation of the US following conditioning results in a more favourable assessment of the US, and in reduced CRs on subsequent presentations of the CS (Davey & McKenna, 1983). On the other hand, when the US is revalued as more negative, stronger CRs are observed on subsequent presentations of the CS. Davey, de Jong, and Tallis (1993) report three case studies of people who had USs revalued (for example, a girl whose parents inflated the aversiveness of an encounter with a spider by telling her of lots of potentially bad things that could have happened).

The clinical implication of revaluation is that if a person has formed a stimulus–trauma association (that survives extinction and subsequent random exposure to the stimulus and/or trauma), then all it would take to re-evoke a conditioned response is for the US to be revalued. US revaluation rules out the need to find specific traumatic associative learning events in a patient's history, as the US may have become traumatic subsequent to the learning episode. Moreover, US revaluation explains why some individuals experience a stimulus in the presence of a traumatic event yet do not develop phobic symptoms; the traumatic event may have subsequently been devalued.

Associative learning and "cognitive" features of phobias

Associative learning and the acquisition of attentional biases

Stimuli that are associated with fear are subject to attentional bias; they attract attention preferentially from other stimuli in the environment (see Hadwin & Field, 2010, for a review). An attentional bias is shown for fear-relevant stimuli whether the threat is of phylogentic origin, such as snakes, spiders, or angry faces (Lipp, 2006; Lipp, Price, & Tellegen, 2009; Öhman, Flykt, & Esteves, 2001; Rinck, Reinecke, Ellwart, Heuer, & Becker, 2005), or of ontogenetic origin, such as weapons and syringes (Blanchette, 2006; Brosch & Sharma, 2005). Though fear-relevant stimuli are preferentially attended by unselected participants, preferential attention towards these stimuli is further enhanced if the participant has a high level of fear or anxiety towards the stimulus (Waters, Lipp, & Spence, 2004). Anxiety is therefore correlated with attentional allocation; stimuli that are related to fear or threat are preferentially attended (Mogg & Bradley, 1998). Furthermore, if these biases are trained in nonanxious adults their anxiety increases (e.g., Mathews & Mackintosh, 2000; Wilson, MacLeod, Mathews, & Rutherford, 2006; Yiend, Mackintosh, & Mathews, 2005) and if these biases are untrained in clinically anxious individuals they become less anxious (e.g., Amir, Beard, Burns, & Bomyea, 2009; Schmidt, Richey, Buckner, &

Timpano, 2009; see MacLeod & Bridle, 2009). Attentional bias to threat has, on this basis, been proposed to play a causal role in human anxiety (Mathews & MacLeod, 2002).

Recent research suggests that attentional biases can be trained to neutral stimuli through fear conditioning. Koster, Crombez, Van Damme, Verschuere, and De Houwer (2004) embedded a conditioning paradigm within an attention task. Participants completed an exogenous cueing task where one stimulus was always followed by an aversive noise. Responses on the task confirmed that the threatening cue captured and held attention. Similarly, Purkis and Lipp (2009) observed that pictures of birds, fish, and dogs captured attention in a dot probe task following a fear conditioning paradigm with these stimuli.

It is not clear what contribution associative learning makes to the process of attentional biases. Field and Lester (2010b) speculate that attentional biases are learnt via operant learning principles in which a response (attention to a threat stimulus) is reinforced. They adopt Dickinson and colleague's distinction between goal-directed and habitual instrumental learning (Dickinson, Balleine, Watt, Gonzalez, & Boakes, 1995). Dickinson argues that goal-directed instrumental learning requires two separate learning systems: an habitual learning system that is used for stimulus–response learning only and does not encode details of the outcome, and a separate system that learns goal-directed action and so does encode information about the outcome. Given that the habitual learning system functions more prominently than the goal-directed system in infants (Klossek, Russell, & Dickinson, 2008) and that attentional biases do not require any understanding of the implicational meaning of a response, Field and Lester argue that attentional biases to threat might be acquired through the habitual system.

Although an instrumental learning account of attentional bias modification paradigms seems plausible, Field and Lester suggest that in the real world children are probably not reinforced for directing attention to threat (because there is not a "correct" response to reinforce). Instead, in the face of a threat stimulus they pick up on other people's attention (through social referencing) or the consequences (an external agent removes them from the situation). As such, it might be reasonable to assume that a stimulus–outcome association is learned through Pavlovian associative learning. Such an association would, therefore, be subject to the various constraints that we have described within this chapter.

Associative learning and the acquisition of interpretation biases

Anxiety also affects the way in which ambiguous information is processed. Recent research suggests that anxious individuals exhibit strong interpretation biases (see Hadwin & Field, 2010, for a review). When presented with ambiguous information, low anxious individuals are more likely to provide a positive interpretation whereas highly anxious individuals are more likely to provide a negative interpretation. After hearing sentences such as "The doctor examined little Emma's growth", or "The farmer gave Dave the sack", anxious participants were more likely to endorse related recognition items that referred to cancer (as compared to height), and job (as compared to bag) than were nonanxious controls (Eysenck, Mogg, May, Richards, & Mathews, 1991). Similarly, when presented with ambiguous information that could be interpreted positively, neutrally, or negatively (for instance, "I was surprised to be called to see my boss today"), highly anxious individuals regularly endorsed a threatening or negative interpretation (Davey, Hampton, Farrell, & Davidson, 1992; MacLeod & Cohen, 1993; Mathews, Richards, & Eysenck, 1989). It may the case that interpretation biases maintain a state of anxiety, or it may be that an anxious state of mind makes it easier to construe threat-related interpretations of events. It has been shown that spider fearful individuals, for instance, could generate more reasons as to why spiders were harmful and fewer reasons why they were safe compared to nonfearful individuals (Cavanagh & Davey, 2003).

As for attentional biases, there is no coherent theory of how associative learning explains the learning of interpretation biases. Field and Lester (2010b) suggest that in contrast to attentional biases, interpretation biases require an understanding of the implicational meaning of responses. As such they should not only take advantage of the more complex learning system that drives goal-directed operant learning, but should also be more influenced by cognitive development (see Field & Lester, 2010a). However, although interpretation biases *could* be learnt over successive trials through an association being formed between an ambiguous cue and a threat response (interpretation) – the stimulus–response learning system – in reality, Field and Lester believe that children probably learn a simple stimulus–outcome association (i.e., "when faced with ambiguity the outcome will be bad"). As we have seen, representations can themselves be powerful USs, so the underlying association can be formed regardless of whether the child actually experiences a bad outcome or is merely told that the outcome will be bad (Dickinson, 2001; Field, 2006). Field and Lester also note that "outcomes" need not be real: imagined outcomes will be sufficient to create associative connections. As such, the feedback a child receives in the face of ambiguity might not be traumatic or negative in itself, but it could trigger imagery or cognitions that are traumatic to the child; as we have seen, these mental representations can act as a powerful negative outcome.

Summary

This chapter has been an attempt to summarize some contemporary phenomena in associative learning and how these relate to the acquisition and treatment of phobias. In the last 15 years, theoretical models acknowledge many of the points that we have made about conditioning and for different perspectives to ours we recommend looking at these models (Davey, 1997; Mineka & Zinbarg, 2006; Öhman & Mineka, 2001). We began by looking at the basic associative model of conditioning, and the evidence that different pathways to fear can be thought of in terms of associative learning. We then reviewed some of the more important phenomena of associative learning and discussed their clinical implications for the acquisition and treatment of fears. We concluded the review with a brief look at two extremely important cognitive phenomena in anxiety (attentional and interpretation biases) and speculated on how associative learning can inform models of how these biases develop.

Notes

1 Source: PubMed (http://www.ncbi.nlm.nih.gov/pubmed).
2 The observant among you will have noticed that we have already used the terms interchangeably in this chapter.

References

Aitken, M. R. F., Larkin, M. J. W., & Dickinson, A. (2000). Super-learning of causal judgements. *Quarterly Journal of Experimental Psychology Section B: Comparative and Physiological Psychology*, *53*(1), 59–81.

Amir, N., Beard, C., Burns, M., & Bomyea, J. (2009). Attention modification program in individuals with generalized anxiety disorder. *Journal of Abnormal Psychology*, *118*(1), 28–33. doi: 10.1037/a0012589.

Askew, C., & Field, A. P. (2007). Vicarious learning and the development of fears in childhood. *Behaviour Research and Therapy*, *45*, 2616–2627.

Askew, C., & Field, A. P. (2008). The vicarious learning pathway to fear 40 years on. *Clinical Psychology Review*, *28*, 1249–1265.

Black, A. H. (1971). Autonomic aversive conditioning in infrahuman subjects. In F. R. Brush (Ed.), *Aversive conditioning and learning* (pp. 3–104). New York, NY: Academic Press.

Blanchette, I. (2006). Snakes, spiders, guns, and syringes: How specific are evolutionary constraints on the detection of threatening stimuli? *Quarterly Journal of Experimental Psychology*, *59*(8), 1484–1504. doi: 10.1080/02724980543000204.

Bouton, M. E. (1994). Context, ambiguity, and classical-conditioning. *Current Directions in Psychological Science*, *3*(2), 49–53.

Bouton, M. E., Mineka, S., & Barlow, D. H. (2001). A modern learning theory perspective on the etiology of panic disorder. *Psychological Review*, *108*(1), 4–32.

Bouton, M. E., & Swartzentruber, D. (1991). Sources of relapse after extinction in Pavlovian and instrumental learning. *Clinical Psychology Review*, *11*(2), 123–140.

Bradley, M. M., Moulder, B., & Lang, P. J. (2005). When good things go bad: The reflex physiology of defense. *Psychological Science*, *16*(6), 468–473.

Brosch, T., & Sharma, D. (2005). The role of fear-relevant stimuli in visual search: A comparison of phylogenetic and ontogenetic stimuli. *Emotion*, *5*(3), 360–364. doi: 10.1037/1528-3542.5.3.360.

Campbell, D., Sanderson, R. E., & Laverty, S. G. (1964). Characteristics of a conditioned-response in human-subjects during extinction trials following a single traumatic conditioning trial. *Journal of Abnormal and Social Psychology, 68*(6), 627–639.

Cavanagh, K., & Davey, G. (2003). Access to information about harm and safety in spider fearful and nonfearful individuals: When they were good they were very very good but when they were bad they were horrid. *Journal of Behavior Therapy and Experimental Psychiatry, 34*(3–4), 269–281. doi: 10.1016/j.jbtep.2003.10.003.

Collins, D. J., & Shanks, D. R. (2002). Momentary and integrative response strategies in causal judgment. *Memory & Cognition, 30*(7), 1138–1147.

Davey, G. C. L. (1989a). *Ecological learning theory*. London: Routledge.

Davey, G. C. L. (1989b). UCS revaluation and conditioning models of acquired fears. *Behaviour Research and Therapy, 27*(5), 521–528.

Davey, G. C. L. (1995). Preparedness and phobias: Specific evolved associations or a generalized expectancy bias. *Behavioral and Brain Sciences, 18*(2), 289–297.

Davey, G. C. L. (1997). A conditioning model of phobias. In G. C. L. Davey (Ed.), *Phobias: A handbook of theory, research and treatment* (pp. 301–322). Chichester, UK: John Wiley.

Davey, G. C. L., de Jong, P. J., & Tallis, F. (1993). UCS inflation in the etiology of a variety of anxiety disorders: Some case-histories. *Behaviour Research and Therapy, 31*(5), 495–498.

Davey, G. C. L., Hampton, J., Farrell, J., & Davidson, S. (1992). Some characteristics of worrying: Evidence for worrying and anxiety as separate constructs. *Personality and Individual Differences, 13*(2), 133–147.

Davey, G. C. L., & McKenna, I. (1983). The effects of postconditioning revaluation of CS1 and UCS following Pavlovian second-order electrodermal conditioning in humans. *Quarterly Journal of Experimental Psychology, 35B*, 125–133.

De Houwer, J. (2009). The propositional approach to associative learning as an alternative for association formation models. *Learning & Behavior, 37*(1), 1–20. doi: 10.3758/lb.37.1.1.

De Houwer, J., & Beckers, T. (2002). A review of recent developments in research and theories on human contingency learning. *Quarterly Journal of Experimental Psychology, 55B*, 289–310.

Dickinson, A. (2001). Causal learning: An associative analysis. *Quarterly Journal of Experimental Psychology Section B: Comparative and Physiological Psychology, 54*(1), 3–25.

Dickinson, A., Balleine, B., Watt, A., Gonzalez, F., & Boakes, R. A. (1995). Motivational control after extended instrumental training. *Animal Learning & Behavior, 23*(2), 197–206.

Dollinger, S. J., O'Donnell, J. P., & Staley, A. A. (1984). Lightning-strike disaster: Effects on children's fears and worries. *Journal of Consulting and Clinical Psychology, 52*(6), 1028–1038.

Doogan, S., & Thomas, G. V. (1992). Origins of fear of dogs in adults and children: The role of conditioning processes and prior familiarity with dogs. *Behaviour Research and Therapy, 30*(4), 387–394.

Dwyer, D. M. (1999). Retrospective revaluation or mediated conditioning? The effect of different reinforcers. *Quarterly Journal of Experimental Psychology Section B: Comparative and Physiological Psychology, 52*(4), 289–306.

Dwyer, D. M. (2001). Mediated conditioning and retrospective revaluation with

LiCl then flavour pairings. *Quarterly Journal of Experimental Psychology Section B: Comparative and Physiological Psychology, 54*(2), 145–165.

Dwyer, D. M. (2003). Learning about cues in their absence: Evidence from flavour preferences and aversions. *Quarterly Journal of Experimental Psychology Section B: Comparative and Physiological Psychology, 56*(1), 56–67.

Dwyer, D. M., Mackintosh, N. J., & Boakes, R. A. (1998). Simultaneous activation of the representations of absent cues results in the formation of an excitatory association between them. *Journal of Experimental Psychology: Animal Behavior Processes, 24*(2), 163–171.

Eysenck, M. W., Mogg, K., May, J., Richards, A., & Mathews, A. (1991). Bias in interpretation of ambiguous sentences related to threat in anxiety. *Journal of Abnormal Psychology, 100*(2), 144–150.

Field, A. P. (2006). Is conditioning a useful framework for understanding the development and treatment of phobias? *Clinical Psychology Review, 26*(7), 857–875.

Field, A. P., Argyris, N. G., & Knowles, K. A. (2001). Who's afraid of the big bad wolf: A prospective paradigm to test Rachman's indirect pathways in children. *Behaviour Research and Therapy, 39*(11), 1259–1276.

Field, A. P., & Davey, G. C. L. (2001). Conditioning models of childhood anxiety. In W. K. Silverman & P. A. Treffers (Eds.), *Anxiety disorders in children and adolescents: Research, assessment and intervention* (pp. 187–211). Cambridge, UK: Cambridge University Press.

Field, A. P., & Lawson, J. (2003). Fear information and the development of fears during childhood: Effects on implicit fear responses and behavioural avoidance. *Behaviour Research and Therapy, 41*(11), 1277–1293.

Field, A. P., & Lawson, J. (2008). The verbal information pathway to fear and subsequent causal learning in children. *Cognition & Emotion, 22*(3), 459–479.

Field, A. P., Lawson, J., & Banerjee, R. (2008). The verbal information pathway to fear in children: The longitudinal effects on fear cognitions and the immediate effects on avoidance behavior. *Journal of Abnormal Psychology, 117*(1), 214–224.

Field, A. P., & Lester, K. J. (2010a). Is there room for 'development' in models of information processing biases to threat in children and adolescents? *Clinical Child and Family Psychology Review, 13*, 315–332.

Field, A. P., & Lester, K. J. (2010b). Learning of information processing biases in anxious children and adolescents. In J. A. Hadwin & A. P. Field (Eds.), *Information processing biases and anxiety: A developmental perspective* (pp. 253–278). Chichester, UK: Wiley-Blackwell.

Field, A. P., & Schorah, H. (2007). The negative information pathway to fear and heart rate changes in children. *Journal of Child Psychology and Psychiatry, 48*(11), 1088–1093.

Garcia, J., Ervin, F. R., & Koelling, R. A. (1966). Learning with prolonged delay of reinforcement. *Psychonomic Science, 5*(3), 121–122.

Garcia, J., & Koelling, R. A. (1966). Relation of cue to consequence in avoidance learning. *Psychonomic Science, 4*, 123.

Garcia, J., McGowan, B. K., & Green, K. F. (1972). Biological constraints on conditioning. In A. H. Black & W. F. Prokasy (Eds.), *Classical conditioning II: Current research and theory* (pp. 3–27). New York, NY: Appleton-Century-Crofts.

Gerull, F. C., & Rapee, R. M. (2002). Mother knows best: Effects of maternal modelling on the acquisition of fear and avoidance behaviour in toddlers. *Behaviour Research and Therapy, 40,* 279–287.

Hadwin, J. A., & Field, A. P. (2010). *Information processing biases and anxiety: A developmental perspective.* Chichester, UK: Wiley-Blackwell.

Hall, G. (2002). Associative structures in Pavlovian and instrumental conditioning. In C. R. Gallistel (Ed.), *Stevens' handbook of experimental psychology* (Vol. 3, 3rd ed., pp. 1–45). New York, NY: John Wiley & Sons.

Hugdahl, K., & Johnsen, B. H. (1989). Preparedness and electrodermal fear-conditioning: Ontogenetic vs phylogenetic explanations. *Behaviour Research and Therapy, 27*(3), 269–278.

Izquierdo, L. A., Barros, D. M., Ardenghi, P. G., Pereira, P., Rodrigues, C., Choi, H., et al. (2000). Different hippocampal molecular requirements for short- and long-term retrieval of one-trial avoidance learning. *Behavioural Brain Research, 111*(1–2), 93–98.

Izquierdo, L. A., Barros, D. H., Medina, J. H., & Izquierdo, I. (2000). Novelty enhances retrieval of one-trial avoidance learning in rats 1 or 31 days after training unless the hippocampus is inactivated by different receptor antagonists and enzyme inhibitors. *Behavioural Brain Research, 117*(1–2), 215–220.

Kamin, L. J. (1968). 'Attention-like' processes in classical conditioning. In M. R. Jones (Ed.), *Miami symposium on the prediction of behavior: Aversive stimulation* (pp. 9–32). Coral Gables, FL: University of Miami Press.

King, N. J., Gullone, E., & Ollendick, T. (1998). Etiology of childhood phobias: Current status of Rachman's three pathways theory. *Behaviour Research and Therapy, 36*(3), 297–309.

Klossek, U. M. H., Russell, J., & Dickinson, A. (2008). The control of instrumental action following outcome devaluation in young children aged between 1 and 4 years. *Journal of Experimental Psychology: General, 137*(1), 39–51. doi: 10.1037/0096-3445.137.1.39.

Koster, E. H. W., Crombez, G., Van Damme, S., Verschuere, B., & De Houwer, J. (2004). Does imminent threat capture and hold attention? *Emotion, 4*(3), 312–317. doi: 10.1037/1528-3542.4.3.312.

Le Pelley, M. E., & McLaren, I. P. L. (2003). Learned associability and associative change in human causal learning. *Quarterly Journal of Experimental Psychology Section B: Comparative and Physiological Psychology, 56*(1), 68–79.

LeDoux, J. E. (2000). Emotion circuits in the brain. *Annual Review of Neuroscience, 23,* 155–184.

LeDoux, J. E. (2003). The emotional brain, fear, and the amygdala. *Cellular and Molecular Neurobiology, 23*(4–5), 727–738.

Lipp, O. V. (2006). Of snakes and flowers: Does preferential detection of pictures of fear-relevant animals in visual search reflect on fear-relevance? *Emotion, 6*(2), 296–308.

Lipp, O. V., Price, S. M., & Tellegen, C. L. (2009). Emotional faces in neutral crowds: Detecting displays of anger, happiness, and sadness on schematic and photographic images of faces. *Motivation and Emotion, 33*(3), 249–260. doi: 10.1007/s11031-009-9136-2.

Lober, K., & Shanks, D. R. (2000). Is causal induction based on causal power? Critique of Cheng (1997). *Psychological Review, 107*(1), 195–212.

Lubow, R. E. (1973). Latent inhibition. *Psychological Bulletin, 79*(6), 398–407.

Lubow, R. E., & Moore, A. U. (1959). Latent inhibition: The effect of nonreinforced pre-exposure to the conditional stimulus. *Journal of Comparative and Physiological Psychology, 52*(4), 415–419.

Mackintosh, N. J. (1973). Stimulus selection: Learning to ignore stimuli that predict no change in reinforcement. In R. A. Hinde & L. S. Hinde (Eds.), *Constraints of learning* (pp. 75–96). London, UK: Academic Press.

Mackintosh, N. J. (1983). *Conditioning and associative learning.* Oxford, UK: Oxford University Press.

MacLeod, C., & Cohen, I. L. (1993). Anxiety and the interpretation of ambiguity: A text comprehension study. *Journal of Abnormal Psychology, 102*(2), 238–247.

Mathews, A., & Mackintosh, B. (2000). Induced emotional interpretation bias and anxiety. *Journal of Abnormal Psychology, 109*(4), 602–615.

Mathews, A., & MacLeod, C. (2002). Induced processing biases have causal effects on anxiety. *Cognition & Emotion, 16*(3), 331–354.

Mathews, A., Richards, A., & Eysenck, M. (1989). Interpretation of homophones related to threat in anxiety-states. *Journal of Abnormal Psychology, 98*(1), 31–34.

Menzies, R. G., & Clarke, J. C. (1993). The etiology of childhood water phobia. *Behaviour Research and Therapy, 31*(5), 499–501.

Mineka, S., & Cook, M. (1993). Mechanisms involved in the observational conditioning of fear. *Journal of Experimental Psychology: General, 122*(1), 23–38.

Mineka, S., & Zinbarg, R. (2006). A contemporary learning theory perspective on the etiology of anxiety disorders: It's not what you thought it was. *American Psychologist, 61*(1), 10–26.

Mitchell, C. J., De Houwer, J., & Lovibond, P. F. (2009). The propositional nature of human associative learning. *Behavioral and Brain Sciences, 32*(2), 183–198. doi: 10.1017/s0140525x09000855.

Mogg, K., & Bradley, B. P. (1998). A cognitive-motivational analysis of anxiety. *Behaviour Research and Therapy, 36*(9), 809–848.

Morris, J. S., Öhman, A., & Dolan, R. J. (1998). Conscious and unconscious emotional learning in the human amygdala. *Nature, 393*(6684), 467–470.

Muris, P., & Field, A. P. (2010). The role of verbal threat information in the development of childhood fear. "Beware the Jabberwock!" *Clinical Child and Family Psychology Review, 13*, 129–150.

Muris, P., Rassin, E., Mayer, B., Smeets, G., Huijding, J., Remmerswaal, D., et al. (2009). Effects of verbal information on fear-related reasoning biases in children. *Behaviour Research and Therapy, 47*(3), 206–214. doi: 10.1016/J.Brat.2008.12.002.

Murray, L., Cooper, P., Creswell, C., Schofield, E., & Sack, C. (2007). The effects of maternal social phobia on mother–infant interactions and infant social responsiveness. *Journal of Child Psychology and Psychiatry, 48*(1), 45–52.

Öhman, A., Eriksson, A., & Olofsson, C. (1975). One-trial learning and superior resistance to extinction of autonomic responses conditioned to potentially phobic stimuli. *Journal of Comparative and Physiological Psychology, 88*(2), 619–627.

Öhman, A., Erixon, G., & Lofberg, I. (1975). Phobias and preparedness: Phobic versus neutral pictures as conditioned stimuli for human autonomic responses. *Journal of Abnormal Psychology, 84*(1), 41–45.

Öhman, A., Flykt, A., & Esteves, F. (2001). Emotion drives attention: Detecting the snake in the grass. *Journal of Experimental Psychology: General, 130*(3), 466–478.

Öhman, A., & Mineka, S. (2001). Fears, phobias, and preparedness: Toward an evolved module of fear and fear learning. *Psychological Review, 108*(3), 483–522.

Öst, L.-G. (1996). One-session group treatment of spider phobia. *Behaviour Research and Therapy*, *34*(9), 707–715.

Öst, L.-G. (2008). Efficacy of the third wave of behavioral therapies: A systematic review and meta-analysis. *Behaviour Research and Therapy*, *46*(3), 296–321. doi: 10.1016/j.brat.2007.12.005.

Öst, L.-G., Svensson, L., Hellstrom, K., & Lindwall, R. (2001). One-session treatment of specific phobias in youths: A randomized clinical trial. *Journal of Consulting and Clinical Psychology*, *69*(5), 814–824.

Pavlov, I. P. (1927). *Conditioned reflexes*. Oxford, UK: Oxford University Press.

Pearce, J. M., & Bouton, M. E. (2001). Theories of associative learning in animals. *Annual Review of Psychology*, *52*, 111–139.

Perales, J. C., & Shanks, D. R. (2003). Normative and descriptive accounts of the influence of power and contingency on causal judgement. *Quarterly Journal of Experimental Psychology Section A: Human Experimental Psychology*, *56*, 977–1007.

Phelps, E. A. (2006). Emotion and cognition: Insights from studies of the human amygdala. *Annual Review of Psychology*, *57*, 27–53. doi: 10.1146/annurev.psych. 56.091103.070234.

Phelps, E. A., & LeDoux, J. E. (2005). Contributions of the amygdala to emotion processing: From animal models to human behavior. *Neuron*, *48*(2), 175–187. doi: 10.1016/j.neuron.2005.09.025.

Pinel, J. P. J., & Treit, D. (1979). Conditioned defensive burying in rats: Availability of burying materials. *Animal Learning & Behavior*, *7*(3), 392–396.

Purkis, H. M., & Lipp, O. V. (2009). Are snakes and spiders special? Acquisition of negative valence and modified attentional processing by non-fear-relevant animal stimuli. *Cognition & Emotion*, *23*(3), 430–452. doi: 10.1080/02699930801993973.

Rachman, S. (1977). Conditioning theory of fear-acquisition: Critical-examination. *Behaviour Research and Therapy*, *15*(5), 375–387.

Rescorla, R. A. (1968). Probability of shock in presence and absence of CS in fear conditioning. *Journal of Comparative and Physiological Psychology*, *66*(1), 1–5.

Rescorla, R. A. (1971). Variations in the effectiveness of reinforcement following prior inhibitory conditioning. *Learning and Motivation*, *2*, 113–123.

Rescorla, R. A. (1974). Effect of inflation of unconditioned stimulus value following conditioning. *Journal of Comparative and Physiological Psychology*, *86*(1), 101–106.

Rescorla, R. A. (1980). *Pavlovian second-order conditioning: Studies in associative learning*. Hillsdale, NJ: Lawrence Erlbaum Associates, Inc.

Rescorla, R. A. (1988). Pavlovian conditioning: It's not what you think it is. *American Psychologist*, *43*(3), 151–160.

Rescorla, R. A. (1991). Combinations of modulators trained with the same and different target stimuli. *Animal Learning & Behavior*, *19*(4), 355–360.

Rescorla, R. A. (2000). Associative changes with a random CS–US relationship. *Quarterly Journal of Experimental Psychology Section B: Comparative and Physiological Psychology*, *53*(4), 325–340.

Rinck, M., Reinecke, A., Ellwart, T., Heuer, K., & Becker, E. S. (2005). Speeded detection and increased distraction in fear of spiders: Evidence from eye movements. *Journal of Abnormal Psychology*, *114*(2), 235–248. doi: 10.1037/0021-843x.114.2.235.

Schmidt, N. B., Richey, J. A., Buckner, J. D., & Timpano, K. R. (2009). Attention training for generalized social anxiety disorder. *Journal of Abnormal Psychology*, *118*(1), 5–14. doi: 10.1037/a0013643.

See, J., MacLeod, C., & Bridle, R. (2009). The reduction of anxiety vulnerability through the modification of attentional bias: A real-world study using a home-based cognitive bias modification procedure. *Journal of Abnormal Psychology*, *118*(1), 65–75. doi: 10.1037/a0014377.

Seligman, M. E. P. (1971). Phobias and preparedness. *Behavior Therapy*, *2*(3), 307–320.

Shanks, D. R., Holyoak, K. J., & Medin, D. L. (Eds.). (1996). *The psychology of learning and motivation: Causal learning*, Vol. 34. San Diego: Academic Press.

Silverman, W. K., Pina, A. A., & Viswesvaran, C. (2008). Evidence-based psycho-social treatments for phobic and anxiety disorders in children and adolescents. *Journal of Clinical Child and Adolescent Psychology*, *37*(1), 105–130. doi: 10.1080/15374410701817907.

Solomon, R. L., & Turner, L. H. (1962). Discriminative classical-conditioning in dogs paralyzed by curare can later control discriminative avoidance responses in the normal state. *Psychological Review*, *69*(3), 202–219.

Ten Berge, M., Veerkamp, J. S. J., & Hoogstraten, J. (2002). The etiology of childhood dental fear: The role of dental and conditioning experiences. *Journal of Anxiety Disorders*, *16*(3), 321–329.

Waters, A. M., Lipp, O. V., & Spence, S. H. (2004). Attentional bias toward fear-related stimuli: An investigation with nonselected children and adults and children with anxiety disorders. *Journal of Experimental Child Psychology*, *89*(4), 320–337. doi: 10.1016/j.jecp.2004.06.003.

Watson, J. B., & Rayner, R. (1920). Conditioned emotional reactions. *Journal of Experimental Psychology*, *3*, 1–14.

Wilson, E. J., MacLeod, C., Mathews, A., & Rutherford, E. M. (2006). The causal role of interpretive bias in anxiety reactivity. *Journal of Abnormal Psychology*, *115*(1), 103–111.

Wolpe, J. (1961). The systematic desensitization treatment of neurosis. *Journal of Nervous Mental Disease*, *132*, 189–203.

Yiend, J., Mackintosh, B., & Mathews, A. (2005). Enduring consequences of experimentally induced biases in interpretation. *Behaviour Research and Therapy*, *43*(6), 779–797.

Yule, W., Udwin, O., & Murdoch, K. (1990). The Jupiter sinking: Effects on children's fears, depression and anxiety. *Journal of Child Psychology and Psychiatry and Allied Disciplines*, *31*(7), 1051–1061.

4 Vulnerabilities underlying human drug dependence:

Goal valuation versus habit learning

Lee Hogarth and Henry W. Chase

Individual differences in susceptibility to dependence

There are two steps towards becoming a drug addict, according to Bardo, Donohew, and Harrington (1996). The individual must first try the drug recreationally and then he or she must continue to use the drug to the point where mounting harms justify the clinical diagnosis of dependence. Whether or not an individual tries a drug in the first instance appears to be a function of a number of demographic and psychosocial factors such as drug availability in the neighbourhood; accepting attitudes among parents, siblings, and peers; expectancies concerning the likely pleasurable effect of the drug; as well as disobedient and undercontrolled temperament (Hawkins, Catalano, & Miller, 1992; Kirisci, Vanyukov, & Tarter, 2005; Leventhal & Schmitz, 2006; Wagner & Anthony, 2002). However, these variables are not of concern in this chapter. Rather, we are interested in identifying how exposure to the drug interacts with the individual's psychological constitution, to drive the uptake and maintenance of drug use initially, and the perseveration of drug use longitudinally.

Epidemiological data have confirmed that drug dependence is a matter of individual vulnerability rather than a simple function of drug exposure. Anthony, Warner, and Kessler (1994), for example, interviewed 8098 residents of the United States to determine the percentage of respondents who reported having ever consumed drugs, and the percentage with a history of drug dependence, defined by endorsement of clinical criteria. For tobacco smoking shown in the top row of Table 4.1, 75.6 percent of the sample had tried smoking, yet only 24.1 percent reported a history of nicotine dependence. These data suggest that should an individual try smoking, approximately 31.9 percent become nicotine dependent, while the remaining 68.1 percent of individuals who tried smoking apparently did not become dependent and/or quit altogether (see also Donny & Dierker, 2007; Hughes, Helzer, & Lindberg, 2006; Hyland, Rezaishiraz, Bauer, Giovino, & Cummings, 2005). The same story can be told of the other drug classes, for example, alcohol, where approximately 15.4 percent of people who have tried alcohol become dependent (see also Gill, 2002; Grant et al., 2004).

Table 4.1 Percentage of sample (*n* = 8098) from the National Comorbidity Survey data gathered in 1990–1992 (persons aged 15–54 years old) who reported ever using drugs (left column) and ever developing drug dependence (middle column). The right column shows the percentage of people who reported trying the drug who also reported clinical dependence

	Percentage who ever-used	Percentage with a history of dependence	Percent of ever-users who became dependent
Tobacco	75.6	24.1	31.9
Alcohol	91.5	14.1	15.4
Other drugs	51.0	7.5	14.7
Cannabis	46.3	4.2	9.1
Cocaine	16.2	2.7	16.7
Stimulant	15.3	1.7	11.2
Anxiolytics	12.7	1.2	9.2
Analgesics	9.7	0.7	7.5
Psychedelics	10.6	0.5	4.9
Heroin	1.5	0.4	23.1
Inhalants	6.8	0.3	3.7

Source: Anthony et al. (1994), Table 2.

Overall, therefore, one might propose a rule of thumb, wherein should one try a drug of any class there is a 13.4 percent chance of becoming dependent (the mean of the right column). However, it is important to note that this value estimates the *minimum* risk of becoming dependent, because serious addicts are less likely to have responded to the survey, so the true risk remains unknown. Nevertheless, the key point for the present discussion is that dependence is a matter of individual vulnerability rather than an inevitable consequence of experimental drug use.

Paradoxical claims regarding constitutional vulnerabilities

Contemporary addiction theory makes paradoxical claims about the constitutional vulnerabilities underlying drug dependence. A substantive body of evidence, described below, supports the claim that drug dependence is mediated by a hypersensitivity of the reward system to activation by drugs of abuse, which gives rise to greater intentions, expectations, craving, and desire for drugs. These theories envisage the addict as a rational agent who chooses or decides to engage in drug use behaviour because he or she anticipates the resulting experience of the drug to be highly rewarding. By contrast, another set of empirical data supports the view that drug dependence is mediated by a progressive loss of intentional control over drug use, accompanied by a transition to automatic or habitual control by environmental drug associated stimuli. These theories envisage the addict as an automaton, inasmuch as his or her behaviour is elicited directly by cues in the environment, without the addict choosing to undertake this behaviour intentionally, or in contradiction to his or her intentions to quit. These two positions are paradoxical inasmuch as the addicts' behaviour apparently cannot be intentionally chosen and automatically elicited at the same time. The question therefore, is which constitutional vulnerability is critical for the formation of dependence: reward hypersensitivity or accelerated habit learning (or some combination of both)?

Reward hypersensitivity

The core premise of reward hypersensitivity theory is that individuals vary in the sensitivity of their brain reward systems to activation by drugs of abuse, and the differential experience of drug reward gives rise to different magnitudes of drug-related behaviour across individuals (e.g. Hiroi & Scott, 2009; Yacubian & Buchel, 2009). Evidence for this proposal comes from the finding that the extent to which drugs such as amphetamine (Drevets et al., 2001) or smoking (Barrett, Boileau, Okker, Pihl, & Dagher, 2004) release dopamine in the striatum – the brain substrate of reward (Wise & Rompre, 1989) – predicts subjective reports of rewarding effect of the drug. In analyzing such data, Volkow, Fowler, Wang, Baler, and Telang (2009) have argued that the relationship between the dopamine response to drug administration and the subjective appraisal of the rewarding effect shows an inverted-U shaped curve (see also Le Foll et al., 2009). Specifically, a small dopamine response yields little experience of reward, a substantial dopamine response is aversive, whereas an intermediate dopamine response is maximally rewarding, and underlies vulnerability to dependence. Whatever the precise nature of the underlying brain response, it is clear that subjective experience of drug reward has been associated with greater preference and uptake of drug use (de Wit, Uhlenhuth, & Johanson, 1986; Fergusson, Horwood, Lynskey, & Madden, 2003; Scherrer et al., 2009; Stoops et al., 2007).

Reward hypersensitivity theory has also been supported by human instrumental tasks that have shown that dependence is associated with higher rates of responding for drugs (for a review see Hursh & Silberberg, 2008). For example, Moeller et al. (2009) allowed cocaine addicts to choose to view cocaine-related pictures or control pictures and the preference for selecting the cocaine pictures was associated with cocaine use in the previous 30 days. Similarly, in a study by Perkins et al. (2002), smokers could self-administer nicotine or placebo nasal spray and the preference for the nicotine spray predicted latency to relapse following cessation (see also Bisaga, Padilla, Garawi, Sullivan, & Haney, 2007; Bühler et al., 2010). Furthermore, the drug demand questionnaire has been developed to assess willingness to pay for drugs, and is regarded as analogous to these instrumental tasks (Bickel, Marsch, & Carroll, 2000; Jacobs & Bickel, 1999). Critically, higher levels of drug demand are associated with level of drug dependence assessed by questionnaire (Greenwald, 2008; Murphy & MacKillop, 2006; MacKillop et al., 2008, 2010) and the propensity to relapse following cessation (MacKillop & Murphy, 2007; Murphy, Correia, Colby, & Vuchinich, 2005; Murphy et al., 2006), confirming that dependence is associated with hypersensitivity to drug reward.

Goal-directed action

Although the research above indicates that dependent individuals experience drugs as more rewarding and engage in drug seeking more frequently, a question remains as to the precise learning processes that enable the experience of reward to strengthen the behaviour. Goal-directed theory (de Wit & Dickinson, 2009) argues that the experience of drug reward establishes a veridical mental representation of the drug, which encodes both the perceptual identity of the drug (shape, smell, location, etc.) and its reward or incentive value (that includes both pleasure, rush, euphoria, etc. as well relief from discomfort and dysphoria, etc.). Vulnerable individuals, as a consequence of experiencing greater drug reward, therefore, acquire a drug representation that has a higher incentive value. Moreover, drug seeking, according to goal-directed theory, is intentional in the sense of being mediated by knowledge of the contingency between the response (R) and receipt of the drug outcome (O), and by the represented reward value of the O, which provides evaluative feedback to determine the propensity to perform the R (see Figure 4.1). In other words, dependent individuals engage in drug seeking more frequently because they expect to experience greater drug reward as a consequence of performing this response (R–O).

Evidence for this goal-directed account of dependence comes from the finding that expectations about the beneficial effects of the drug, either

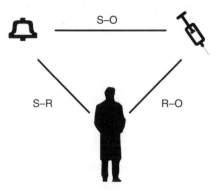

Figure 4.1 Potential associative learning processes involved in human drug use behaviour. Drug users learn three types of association: (1) The predictive Pavlovian contingency between drug stimuli (S) and the drug outcome (O); (2) the causal instrumental contingency between drug-seeking response (R) and the drug outcome (O); and (3) a direct association between the drug stimulus (S) and the drug seeking response (R). These binary associations can be linked in a number of ways to drive addictive behaviour.

pleasure/reward, alleviation of discomfort or cognitive enhancement, are associated with more frequent drug use behaviour (Hides, Kavanagh, Dawe, & Young, 2009; Morawska & Oei, 2005; Palfai, 2002; Urban, 2010) and with the propensity to relapse (Herd, Borland, & Hyland, 2009; W. R. Miller, Westerberg, Harris, & Tonigan, 1996). On the grounds of such evidence, it has been suggested that positive drug expectations are the final common path through which the multifarious risk factors for dependence augment drug use behaviour (Leventhal & Schmitz, 2006), and how risk of dependence is transmitted from parents to their children (Campbell & Oei, 2010). Finally, the proposal that positive drug expectancies play a causal role in mediating drug use behaviour has inspired a variety of cognitive-behavioural interventions which have sought to influence these expectancies in the hope of producing a sustained reduction in drug use behaviour (Jones, Corbin, & Fromme, 2001).

The measurement of subjective craving, like drug expectancy, also supports the claim that an explicit representation of the drug is important in mediating drug use behaviour. Although craving is sensitive to a variety of manipulations (Skinner & Aubin, 2010; Tiffany, Warthen, & Goedeker, 2007), it is clear that craving encodes the current incentive value of the drug; being augmented by abstinence and decreased by satiety (Jarvik et al., 2000; Tiffany & Drobes, 1991; Willner, Hardman, & Eaton, 1995). Furthermore, craving can be modulated by the strength of the contingency between the instrumental drug-seeking response and probability of receiving the drug (Carter & Tiffany, 2001), that is, by perceived drug availability (Droungas, Ehrman, Childress, & O'Brien, 1995; Juliano & Brandon, 1998). Finally, craving has been associated with propensity to relapse following cessation (Allen, Bade, Hatsukami, & Center, 2008; Killen & Fortmann, 1997). Thus, craving fits the criteria of the drug representation proposed by goal-directed theory, by encoding the R–O contingency and the current reward value of the O, and predicting the propensity to perform the R.

Outcome revaluation

Although these foregoing studies are suggestive, none has provided direct evidence for the causal status of drug expectancies in mediating drug use behaviour. Such evidence has come principally from animal studies that have employed the outcome revaluation procedure (Dickinson, 1989). In one such design by Olmstead, Lafond, Everitt, and Dickinson (2001), for example, rats were initially trained on a seeking–taking chain in which they first had to press a seeking lever to gain access to a taking lever that in turn delivered intravenous cocaine. By the goal-directed account, rats' performance of the seeking response was controlled by an expectation of drug reward to be gained through access to the taking lever. To test this, Olmstead et al. (2001) extinguished the taking lever by ceasing its production of cocaine delivery, in the absence of the seeking lever. The fact that this manipulation led to an immediate reduction in rats' performance of the seeking response indicated that the drug-seeking response was goal-directed, being controlled by an expectation of its consequences, that is, by an expectation of access to the now nonrewarded taking lever. Importantly, this test was conducted in extinction (where the seeking response did not produce access to the taking lever), such that the reduction in performance of the seeking response must have been mediated by an expectation of its consequences, rather than direct experience of those consequences modulating the propensity to perform the response through stimulus–response/reinforcement learning (Hull, 1943).

Hutcheson, Everitt, Robbins, and Dickinson (2001) employed a similar design with heroin, but instead of extinguishing the taking lever to reduce its value, rats experienced heroin in withdrawal so that they could learn that the drug had a greater incentive value in that state. The finding that when again placed in withdrawal rats immediately increased their performance of the seeking lever in extinction indicated that this response was controlled by an expectation of the incentive value of the drug to be gained as a consequence of that response. Thus, expectations concerning the positive value of drug effects was demonstrably causal in determining the propensity to engage in drug-seeking behaviour.

To examine the causal status of drug expectancy in mediating human drug-seeking behaviour, we developed a human drug revaluation procedure based upon these animal methods (Hogarth & Chase, 2011). Human revaluation procedures have been used previously to study the neural substrates (de Wit, Corlett, Aitken, Dickinson, & Fletcher, 2009; Tricomi, Balleine, & O'Doherty, 2009; Valentin, Dickinson, & O'Doherty, 2007), developmental maturation (Kenward, Folke, Holmberg, Johansson, & Gredeback, 2009; Klossek, Russell, & Dickinson, 2008), and effects of conflict (de Wit, Niry, Wariyar, Aitken, & Dickinson, 2007) and stress (Schwabe & Wolf, 2009, 2010) on goal-directed control of behaviour. However, as far as we were aware, this study was the first to use the revaluation procedure to assess the goal-directedness of human drug seeking.

Student smokers were first trained on a concurrent choice task based on a procedure by Herrnstein (1961; see also Baum, 1974; H. L. Miller, 1976), where they could press one key to earn one quarter of a cigarette or a second key to earn one quarter of a chocolate bar that were added to their totals over trials. Importantly, each key had only a 50 percent chance of being effective in any trial, and the uncertainty about which key would be effective ensured that participants shifted frequently between the two choices. Relatively young smokers were recruited, half of whom were daily smokers and half nondaily smokers, to ensure broad variance in dependence level within the sample. The key finding was that the preference for the tobacco key was significantly correlated with a multitude of dependence criteria including cigarettes smoked per day, smoking days per week, age of smoking onset, *Diagnostic and Statistical Manual* (DSM) nicotine dependence score (Donny

& Dierker, 2007; Grant et al., 2003), cigarette dependence score (Etter, Le Houezec, & Perneger, 2003), minutes to morning cigarette, and the questionnaire of smoking urges (QSU) factors 1 and 2 (Cappelleri et al., 2007; Cox, Tiffany, & Christen, 2001). These results indicate that the reward value of the tobacco outcome "You win ¼ of a cigarette" increased linearly across dependence, consistent with the drug hypervaluation theory and prior studies noted above. This association between dependence status and preference for the drug choice can be explained by a number of theories.

To test whether choice of the tobacco key was specifically mediated by an expectation of the incentive value of the tobacco outcome (the goal-directed account), this outcome was devalued by allowing smokers to smoke ad libitum to satiety (Hogarth & Chase, 2011, Experiment 1). Subsequently, in the test phase, participants were again given the opportunity to perform the choice task, but this time in extinction, where the two responses no longer produced their respective rewards. This design was critical to ensure that choice between the two keys could not be influenced by direct experience of the outcomes in the sated state. Rather, any reduction in tobacco choice in the extinction test would indicate that this response was goal-directed; being mediated by knowledge of the response–outcome (R–O) contingencies established in training, combined with knowledge of the current low value of the tobacco outcome.

The results showed that all participants selectively reduced their choice of the tobacco key following the satiety manipulation indicating that the tobacco-seeking response was indeed goal-directed, that is, was determined by an expectation of the incentive value of the tobacco outcome earned by the response. The implication, therefore, was that dependent individuals' preference for the tobacco key in concurrent training arose from their hypervaluation of the tobacco outcome as the goal of intentional drug seeking. Thus, hypervaluation of the drug as an instrumental goal appears to confer an important vulnerability to the uptake of drug use. Finally, dependence was not associated with differences in the magnitude of the devaluation effect, suggesting that, in contrast to drug hypervaluation, the capacity for goal-directed control over drug seeking did not vary as a function of dependence (see Naqvi & Bechara, 2009; Heyman, 2009 for further discussion of the role of goal-directed learning in addiction).

Commensuration

The studies reviewed above collectively show that drug preference, demand, and craving are not only associated with the uptake of drug use, but also with the maintenance and relapse to drug use, suggesting that hypervaluation of the drug as an instrumental goal may confer vulnerability to dependence across the lifetime of drug use. Indeed, drug hypervaluation could explain the perseveration of drug use despite mounting costs, which is the hallmark of clinical dependence (Deroche-Gamonet, Belin, & Piazza,

2004; Pelloux, Everitt, & Dickinson, 2007; Vanderschuren & Everitt, 2004). The behavioural economic concept of elasticity regards the acceptance of costs to obtain a commodity as the key quantitative marker of the essential value of that commodity (Hursh & Silberberg, 2008). This claim is supported by the finding that dependence is associated with shallower discount functions of drug demand as financial or work costs are increased, that is, dependent individuals are prepared to accept greater costs to obtain the drug (Bickel et al., 2000; Heyman, 1996, 2000; Hursh & Silberberg, 2008; MacKillop & Murphy, 2007; MacKillop et al., 2008). The complimentary economic concept of commensuration, derived from prospect theory (Kahneman & Tversky, 1979), adds the point that the propensity to engage in drug seeking reflects an integration of expectations about the reward and punishment associated with the outcome (Dayan & Daw, 2008; Padoa-Schioppa, 2007; Rangel, Camerer, & Montague, 2008; Stalnaker, Takahashi, Roesch, & Schoenbaum, 2009; Talmi, Dayan, Kiebel, Frith, & Dolan, 2009; Ursu, Clark, Stenger, & Carter, 2008; Vlaev, Seymour, Dolan, & Chater, 2009). Thus, hypervaluation of the drug as a goal could drive perseveration of drug use under mounting costs simply because the expected value of the drug is higher, requiring a more substantial negative expectancy to reduce the overall utility of drug seeking to zero. Thus, theoretically, the acquisition of hypervalued goal-directed drug seeking could represent a singular vulnerability that confers risk for both the uptake and clinical perseveration of drug use.

Accelerated habit learning

In contrast to goal-directed theory, habit theory argues that drug seeking is elicited automatically by drug associated stimuli, without engaging an expectation of the consequences of this behaviour. This habit account has compelling face validity because addicts' drug use behaviour is viewed as being automatically compelled by environmental drug cues rather than intentionally chosen, and as such, encapsulates the loss of willed control over drug use that is a hallmark of dependence.

Again, the revaluation procedure has provided the principal method for demonstrating the habitual status of drug use behaviour. For example, in a study by Dickinson, Wood, and Smith (2002), rats acquired two instrumental responses, one for alcohol and one for food pellets, before one of these outcomes was devalued by pairing it with lithium chloride induced sickness. When the rats were again given the opportunity to respond for each outcome in extinction, it was found that whereas performance of the food-seeking response was reduced by the devaluation treatment, performance of the alcohol-seeking response was not. These findings suggest that whereas food seeking was goal-directed, being controlled by an expectation of the current incentive value of the food outcome, by contrast, alcohol seeking was habitual, being elicited directly by stimuli in the instrumental context without engaging an expectation of the current reward value of alcohol (for corroboratory evidence see Glasner, Overmier, & Balleine, 2005; Miles, Everitt, & Dickinson, 2003).

Chronic drug pre-exposure has also been shown to render rats more prone to habit learning. Nelson and Killcross (2006) pre-exposed rats to amphetamine for 7 days, before a 7-day injection-free period. Rats then acquired an instrumental response for sucrose before this outcome was devalued by lithium chloride induced sickness. Finally, rats were again given the opportunity to perform the sucrose-seeking response in extinction, such that any reduction in responding must be mediated by knowledge of the R–O contingency and the current incentive value of the sucrose outcome. The key finding was that whereas placebo pre-exposed rats reduced their sucrose seeking, indicating that their sucrose seeking was goal-directed, amphetamine pre-exposed rats did not, indicating that their sucrose seeking was habitual, being elicited by cues in the instrumental context with engaging knowledge of the current incentive value of sucrose (for corroboratory evidence see Jedynak, Uslaner, Esteban, & Robinson, 2007; Nordquist et al., 2007; Schoenbaum & Setlow, 2005). The implication is that vulnerability to dependence may be mediated by individual differences in the predilection for habit learning.

Cue-reactivity

Human drug cue reactivity studies, at first sight, appear to be well suited to test the prediction of habit theory that dependence will be associated with more substantial conditioned responding to drug paired cues (Di Chiara et al., 1999; Jentsch & Taylor, 1999). Indeed, such studies have established that drug users show greater reactivity to drug cues compared with control cues, relative to nondrug users (for reviews see Carter & Tiffany, 1999; Rohsenow, Childress, Monti, Niaura, & Abrams, 1991). However, studies that have explored the relationship between cue reactivity and dependence level or relapse have yielded inconsistent results (for reviews see Drummond, 2000; Perkins, 2009), although others have sought to defend against this critique (Ferguson & Shiffman, 2009; Shiffman, 2009; Tiffany & Wray, 2009). Such data have led Drummond (2000) to argue that even if a convincing association were demonstrated between cue reactivity and dependence, it would remain uncertain whether greater reactivity was a consequence of dependent individuals having undergone greater drug conditioning trials in their natural environment prior to the experiment, or due to a pre-existing predilection for stimulus control that was responsible for their dependence. On top of this, Robbins and Ehrman (1992) have pointed out that where drug-related pictures and words (etc.) are used, one cannot be sure if the response is conditioned or mediated by unconditioned differences in the familiarity, arousal, or valence of the drug cues. These two interpretational limitations can be negated by conducting conditioning in the laboratory, because where exposure to conditioning trials is matched, greater reactivity in the dependent group could be attributed more readily to a trait-based predilection for stimulus control.

On this rationale, we established a laboratory drug conditioning procedure to test whether conditioned responding varied as a function of dependence level. Figure 4.2 shows the pooled data from five replications of a dis-crimination procedure in which smokers learned that a tobacco-seeking response (key press) earned one quarter of a cigarette only in the presence of stimulus A but not stimulus B (Hogarth, Dickinson, & Duka, 2009; Hogarth, Dickinson, Hutton, Elbers, & Duka, 2006; Hogarth, Dickinson, Janowski, Nikitina, & Duka, 2008; Hogarth, Dickinson, Wright, Kouvaraki, & Duka, 2007). The key finding of this procedure was that the tobacco paired stimulus (A) elicited conditioned behaviour only in aware participants for whom this stimulus elicited an expectation of the tobacco outcome, but not for participants who failed to acquire explicit knowledge of the S–O contin-gencies arranged in the procedure. This dependency of conditioned respond-ing upon explicit predictive knowledge has been confirmed in human conditioning studies (Lovibond & Shanks, 2002; Mitchell, De Houwer, & Lovibond, 2009), and drug conditioning studies (see Hogarth & Duka, 2006 for a review). Thus, in humans, knowledge of the S–O contingencies appears necessary for conditioning responding to the S.

The question at stake is whether stimulus control over these behaviours varied as a function of participants' dependence level. To address this question, 66 aware participants shown in Figure 4.2 were dichotomized with respect to nicotine dependence by splitting them into 3 percentiles around the number of cigarettes smoked per day. Contrasts were then made between the group that smoked the most (regular-smokers, $n = 22$) with the group that smoked the least (social-smokers, $n = 23$). As can be seen in Figure 4.3, the acquisition of control by the tobacco paired stimulus over drug-expectancy, drug seeking, attentional bias, and evaluative ratings of stimuli were matched between the high and low smokers groups (con-firmed statistically). Moreover, the same null group effects were obtained when participants were dichotomized by their level of nicotine dependence assessed by the Fagerstrom Tolerance Questionnaire (Fagerstrom & Schneider, 1989). Thus, in this design, where exposure to conditioning trials was matched, we found no evidence for differential stimulus control across levels of dependence. These data, therefore, provide no evidence for a pre-existing constitutional predilection for drug conditioning underlying drug dependence.

The nature of stimulus control

Despite the null difference in stimulus control across levels of dependence in our relatively young smoker sample, there is no doubt that Pavlovian conditioning plays an important role in mediating drug seeking (see the

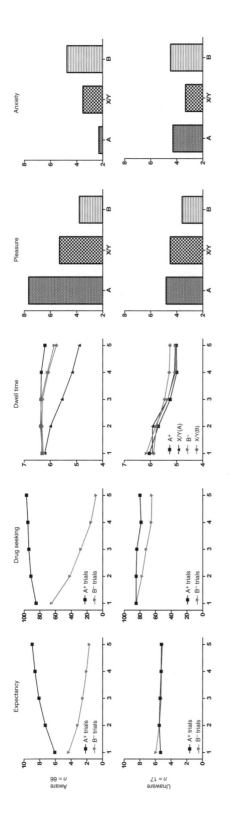

Figure 4.2 Pooled data from five replications of a schedule in which smokers learned that a tobacco-seeking key press response earned one quarter of a cigarette in trials containing stimuli AX or AY, but not trials containing stimuli BX or BY. Participants who reported higher expectancies of drug reward in trials containing stimulus A than B were defined as aware. Only in aware participants did stimulus A control performance of the tobacco-seeking response, command dwell time attentional bias, and elicit differential evaluative ratings of pleasure and anxiety. Unaware participants, by contrast, for whom the stimulus A did not elicit an expectation of the tobacco outcome showed no such conditioned responding, despite having equal exposure to the S–O contingency as the aware group. These data indicate that acquisition of explicit knowledge about the S–O contingency during conditioning was necessary for the S to elicit conditioned behaviour.

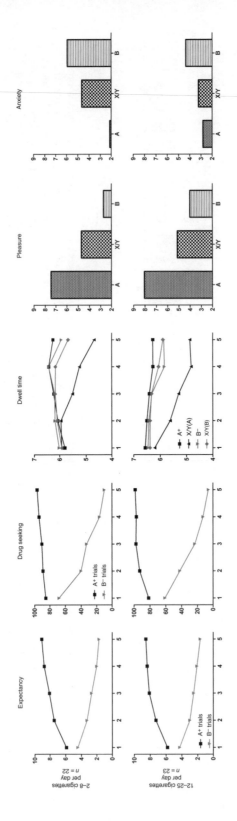

Figure 4.3 Equivalent acquisition of stimulus control over drug conditioned behaviour in regular- and social-smokers, who differed in the number of cigarettes smoked per day.

chapter by Bouton, Winterbauer, & Vurbic, this volume), and it remains possible that individual differences in stimulus control may function as an important vulnerability at a later stage of the drug use career. For these reasons, it is important to consider the precise associative mechanisms that could underlie human drug conditioning. There are two of the main "habitual" associative architectures that we will consider here. The first is S–R/reinforcement learning (Hull, 1943). According to this model, drug consumption reinforces the association between the environmental stimulus (S) that predicted the drug and the motoric response sequence (R) that gave access to the drug. As a consequence of the formation of this S–R association, when the drug S is next encountered it elicits the drug seeking R directly, without engaging a representation of the outcome. By this account, the drug user is an automaton inasmuch as their behaviour is elicited directly by environmental drug cues without making contact with an expectation of the O (see Figure 4.1).

The second habit structure is so-called S–O–R learning (Balleine & O'Doherty, 2010; de Wit & Dickinson, 2009; Ostlund & Balleine, 2008). On this view, S that predict the drug outcome (O) come to elicit a representation or expectation of that O. In turn, this expectation of the drug O elicits Rs that produce that O. By this account, the drug user is a cognitive agent inasmuch as an expectation of the drug, elicited by the S, controls drug seeking. Crucially, however, this representation is thought to only encode the perceptual features of the drug O and not its incentive value. Thus, the representation of the drug O acts as a discriminative stimulus that elicits drug seeking, but such control is nevertheless habitual, because no contact was made with knowledge of the R–O contingency or the current incentive value of the O.

This S–O–R theory differs from S–R theory in making three predictions. The first is that drug stimuli should elicit an expectation of the drug, which we have confirmed in Figure 4.2. The second prediction is that drug stimuli should be able to transfer control to instrumental responses trained separately with the same outcome. Third, such transfer of control should be autonomous to changes in the current reward value of the drug. We now turn to these latter two predictions of S–O–R theory.

Transfer of stimulus control

Transfer of control procedures have been used to demonstrate the causal status of the outcome representation in driving instrumental performance (see Balleine & Ostlund, 2007 for a review). For example, Colwill and Rescorla (1988) trained two stimuli with different rewarding outcomes, and separately trained two instrumental responses with the same outcomes. The finding in the test phase (conducted in extinction) that each stimulus selectively enhanced performance of the response that earned the same outcome demonstrated that such control must have been mediated by the stimulus retrieving the outcome representation that was common to the response. In contrast, S–R/reinforcement theory cannot explain this transfer effect because the Ss and the Rs were never contiguously reinforced in this procedure.

Although transfer of control procedures have been developed for humans (Bray, Rangel, Shimojo, Balleine, & O'Doherty, 2008; Gámez & Rosas, 2007; Paredes-Olay, Abad, Gámez, & Rosas, 2002; Talmi, Seymour, Dayan, & Dolan, 2008), previous applications of this design to elucidate cue effects in addiction have only partially implemented the full methodology (Ludwig, Wikler, & Stark, 1974; Mucha, Pauli, & Angrilli, 1998; Perkins, Epstein, Grobe, & Fonte, 1994). Consequently, we devised a transfer paradigm for human smokers (Hogarth et al., 2007) based upon the animal procedure of Colwill and Rescorla (1988). Smokers first learned that two stimuli predicted one quarter of a cigarette and 5 pence, respectively, before two responses were trained with these same outcomes. The finding that in the transfer test (conducted in extinction) each stimulus selectively enhanced performance of the response that had earned the same outcome demonstrated that the outcome expectancy retrieved by the stimuli was causal in mediating action selection. As before, S–R/reinforcement could not explain this transfer effect because the Ss and the Rs were never contiguously reinforced. These data are therefore consistent with the view that drug cues mediate drug seeking through S–O–R rather than S–R learning. Importantly, no evidence was found that the magnitude of this transfer effect varied as a function of dependence (although the sample size and recruitment protocol were not explicitly designed to assess this hypothesis) supporting Figure 4.3 in suggesting that stimulus control is equivalent across dependence level.

Autonomy of transfer

Further studies using the transfer procedure have established that the transfer effect is autonomous of changes in the incentive value of the outcome, suggesting the outcome representation retrieved by the S does not encode the current value of the O (Corbit, Janak, & Balleine, 2007; Holland, 2004; Rescorla, 1994). The problem with then applying S–O–R theory as a general account of Pavlovian control, however, is the finding that in other paradigms, Pavlovian conditioned responses (Colwill & Motzkin, 1994; Dickinson & Balleine, 2002) and transfer of control (Colwill & Rescorla, 1990a, 1990b; Corbit et al., 2007; Dickinson & Dawson, 1987; Rescorla, 1991) have been shown to be sensitive to manipulations of outcome value. Work is ongoing to comprehensively explain these diverse findings (Balleine & Ostlund, 2007; Dickinson & Balleine, 2002).

Studies of drug cue effects on human drug-related behaviour have supported the autonomous S–O–R account (for reviews see Drummond, 2000; Tiffany et al., 2007). For example, Tiffany, Cox, and Elash (2000) and Waters et al. (2004) found that the administration of nicotine replacement medication versus placebo reduced the overall level of smokers' tobacco craving, indicating that the incentive value of smoking had been reduced, but the capacity of smoking cues to enhance craving was unaffected by this manipulation. Similarly, Drobes and Tiffany (1997) and Maude-Griffin and Tiffany (1996) found that decreasing the incentive value of smoking by specific satiety reduced craving but did not influence the capacity of smoking cues to enhance craving. Such data have led Tiffany et al. (2007) to conclude that whereas baseline craving reflects an explicit evaluation of the reward value of the drug, cue-elicited craving reflects an automatic Pavlovian priming effect. We would identify these two processes as goal-directed R–O and the autonomous S–O–R learning, respectively.

To test S–O–R theory of addiction more formally, we undertook two transfer studies. In the first study, smokers were trained on a discrimination procedure in which one stimulus was paired with the winning of one quarter of a cigarette, before this stimulus was tested for capacity to transfer of control over the probability of puffing in an ad libitum smoking session (Hogarth, Dickinson, & Duka, 2010). The results showed that across the smoking session, puff probability and craving declined, reflecting a decrease in the incentive value of smoking with satiety, but the capacity of the stimulus to enhance puff probability and craving remained unchanged across the session. These data indicate that the capacity of the drug-paired S to motivate drug-taking behaviour did not make contact with the current incentive value of the drug, and for this reason, such stimulus control can be deemed automatic or habitual. Importantly, as before, exploratory analysis found no evidence that such control varied as a function of dependence (although the study was not formally designed for this purpose) consistent with Figure 4.3.

In the second study (Hogarth & Chase, 2011, experiment 2), smokers were recruited on the basis of whether they were daily or nondaily smokers (to ensure broad variance in dependence level), and were run on a devaluation procedure similar to that described earlier. Participants first completed a concurrent choice task to earn cigarette and chocolate points before one of these outcomes was devalued through exposure to health warning about the consumption of these outcomes (i.e. "Smoking causes fatal lung cancer" or "Eating too many calories is the main cause of obesity"). In the test that followed, participants again had the opportunity to press the two keys but this time in extinction. Thus, any modification of choice must be mediated by knowledge of the R–O contingencies and the current value ascribed to the Os. The results showed again that initial preference for the drug response was associated with dependence level, there was an outcome-specific devaluation effect, that is, a selective reduction in choice of the devalued outcome in the extinction test, and dependence was not associated with any variation in the magnitude of this devaluation effect. The data therefore confirmed our previous conclusions that uptake of drug use is associated with hypervaluation of the drug as a goal of intentional drug seeking, and not with differences in predilection for habitual stimulus control over drug seeking.

The critical finding, however, was that in the transfer test where a cigarette or chocolate picture was presented (at random) to determine their impact on choice between the two responses (in extinction), it was found that each stimulus increased the choice of the response associated with the same outcome by approximately 20 percent (compared to baseline). As this test was conducted in extinction and these stimuli had not previously been trained with the responses, this outcome-specific transfer effect must have mediated by each stimulus retrieving a representation of the outcome earned by the response (replicating Hogarth et al., 2007). Critically, in accordance with the autonomous S–O–R theory, the transfer effect was not modulated by the devaluation treatment, suggesting that the O representation retrieved by the S did not encode the current incentive value of the O, but rather, retrieved only the perceptual features of the O which elicited the associated response automatically. Importantly, despite having directly demonstrated automatic stimulus control over drug seeking, individual differences in dependence were not associated with this effect. These data therefore provided strong evidence that individual differences in the uptake of drug use in relatively young drug users is conferred by the hyper-valuation of the drug as a goal of intentional drug seeking, rather than by the formation of autonomous stimulus control over drug seeking.

Impulsivity and habit formation

Recent evidence has converged on the view that individuals' differences in impulsivity (measured by failures of inhibitory control in animals and by the endorsement of statements concerning the thoughtlessness of action in humans) appears be associated with variations in dependence, particularly in later stage drug users when drug-related harms are more apparent (Belin, Mar, Dalley, Robbins, & Everitt, 2008; Biederman et al., 1997; Diergaarde et al., 2008; Doran, Spring, McChargue, Pergadia, & Richmond, 2004; Economidou, Pelloux, Robbins, Dalley, & Everitt, 2009; Flory & Manuck, 2009; Franques, Auriacombe, & Tignol, 2000; Moeller et al., 2001). Consistent with this claim, in our studies of young adult smokers, we have consistently found that impulsivity is largely orthogonal to dependence status, allowing us to dissociate these two individual difference variables. The implication is that although variations in dependence may not be associated with accelerated habit formation, impulsivity appears to be.

We recently undertook two studies to examine habit formation in high impulsive smokers. In the first study (Hogarth, Chase, & Baess, in press), smokers were recruited and dichotomized into a low and high impulsive group based upon their score on the Barratt's Impulsiveness Scale (BIS-11; Flory & Manuck, 2009; Patton, Stanford, & Barratt, 1995; Stanford et al.,

2009). They were then trained on a concurrent choice task for chocolate and water points before one of these outcomes was devalued through specific satiety (i.e., consumption of water or chocolate to satiety). Finally, in the test phase, choice between the two outcomes was tested in extinction. The key result was that despite the two groups reporting equal decline in hedonic appraisal of the devalued outcome, high impulsivity was associated with a smaller outcome-specific devaluation effect, that is, a smaller reduction in choice of the devalued outcome in the extinction test. This finding accords with the view that high impulsive individuals have weaker goal-directed control over their instrumental performance, and instead, tend to be prompted to respond directly by contextual cues without knowledge of the consequences.

A second study corroborated this claim (Hogarth, 2011). Smokers were assessed for impulsivity in the BIS-11 and craving to smoke in the questionnaire of smoking urges (Cox et al., 2001) before completing an ad libitum smoking session in which the number of puffs consumed was recorded. The key finding was that whereas subjective craving predicted consumption in low impulsive group, craving was decoupled from consumption in the high impulsive group. That is, the correlation between craving and drug consumption was moderated by impulsivity. These data accord with the view that whereas low impulsive smokers puffing behaviour was goal-directed, being mediated by an explicit representation of the incentive value of smoking, by contrast, high impulsive smokers drug taking was apparently habitual, in being decoupled from the representation of incentive value and instead controlled automatically by cues embedded in the environment and/or the smoking sequence (Nemeth-Coslett & Griffiths, 1984a, 1984b; Rose, 2006; see also Kirkeby & Robinson, 2005).

Conclusion

The evidence gathered for this chapter supports the claim that vulnerability to dependence is conferred by two dissociable associative learning processes recruited by drugs of abuse. Individual differences in the uptake of drug use appears to be conferred by hypervaluation of the drug as a goal in intentional drug seeking, that is, by the recruitment of goal-directed learning. By contrast, impulsivity appears to be associated with a propensity to acquire habitual control of instrumental behaviour, which may emerge as an important vulnerability for the clinical perseveration of drug use in the face of mounting costs, when the cognitive or intentional regulation of drug use behaviour would otherwise drive quitting (Economidou et al., 2009; Everitt et al., 2008; Goldstein et al., 2009; Heyman, 2009; Volkow et al., 2010). Data reviewed elsewhere converge on this view, suggesting that these two vulnerabilities may be dissociated at the genetic (Consortium, 2010; Hiroi & Scott, 2009) and neuroanatomical (Balleine & O'Doherty, 2010) levels. The clinical implication is that dual strategies for treatment and prevention are required to stream clients depending upon whether the goal-directed or habit learning process functions as a predominant cause of that client's drug use behaviour.

Acknowledgement

This work was supported by a Medical Research Council grant number G0701456 held by Lee Hogarth.

References

Allen, S. S., Bade, T., Hatsukami, D., & Center, B. (2008). Craving, withdrawal, and smoking urges on days immediately prior to smoking relapse. *Nicotine & Tobacco Research, 10*, 35–45.

Anthony, J. C., Warner, L. A., & Kessler, R. C. (1994). Comparative epidemiology of dependence on tobacco, alcohol, controlled substances, and inhalants: Basic findings from the National Comorbidity Survey. *Experimental and Clinical Psychopharmacology, 2*, 244–268.

Balleine, B. W., & O'Doherty, J. P. (2010). Human and rodent homologies in action control: Corticostriatal determinants of goal-directed and habitual action. *Neuropsychopharmacology, 35*, 48–69.

Balleine, B. W., & Ostlund, S. B. (2007). Still at the choice point. In B. W. Balleine, K. Doya, & J. O'Doherty (Eds.), *Annals of the New York Academy of Sciences: Vol. 1104. Reward and decision making in corticobasal ganglia networks* (pp. 147–171). New York, NY: New York Academy of Sciences.

Bardo, M. T., Donohew, R. L., & Harrington, N. G. (1996). Psychobiology of novelty seeking and drug seeking behavior. *Behavioural Brain Research, 77*, 23–43.

Barrett, S. P., Boileau, I., Okker, J., Pihl, R. O., & Dagher, A. (2004). The hedonic response to cigarette smoking is proportional to dopamine release in the human striatum as measured by positron emission tomography and [C-11]raclopride. *Synapse, 54*, 65–71.

Baum, W. M. (1974). 2 types of deviation from matching law: Bias and under-matching. *Journal of the Experimental Analysis of Behavior, 22*, 231–242.

Belin, D., Mar, A. C., Dalley, J. W., Robbins, T. W., & Everitt, B. J. (2008). High impulsivity predicts the switch to compulsive cocaine-taking. *Science, 320*, 1352–1355.

Bickel, W. K., Marsch, L. A., & Carroll, M. E. (2000). Deconstructing relative reinforcing efficacy and situating the measures of pharmacological reinforcement with behavioral economics: A theoretical proposal. *Psychopharmacology, 153*, 44–56.

Biederman, J., Wilens, T., Mick, E., Faraone, S. V., Weber, W., Curtis, S., et al. (1997). Is ADHD a risk factor for psychoactive substance use disorders? Findings from a four-year prospective follow-up study. *Journal of the American Academy of Child and Adolescent Psychiatry, 36*, 21–29.

Bisaga, A., Padilla, M., Garawi, F., Sullivan, M. A., & Haney, M. (2007). Effects of alternative reinforcer and craving on the choice to smoke cigarettes in the laboratory. *Human Psychopharmacology: Clinical and Experimental, 22*, 41–47.

Bray, S., Rangel, A., Shimojo, S., Balleine, B., & O'Doherty, J. P. (2008). The neural mechanisms underlying the influence of Pavlovian cues on human decision making. *Journal of Neuroscience, 28*, 5861–5866.

Bühler, M., Vollstädt-Klein, S., Kobiella, A., Budde, H., Reed, L. J., Braus, D. F., et al. (2010). Nicotine dependence is characterized by disordered reward processing in a network driving motivation. *Biological Psychiatry, 67*, 745–752.

Campbell, J. M., & Oei, T. P. (2010). A cognitive model for the intergenerational transference of alcohol use behavior. *Addictive Behaviors, 35*, 73–83.

Cappelleri, J. C., Bushmakin, A. G., Baker, C. L., Merikle, E., Olufade, A. O., & Gilbert, D. G. (2007). Multivariate framework of the brief questionnaire of smoking urges. *Drug and Alcohol Dependence, 90*, 234–242.

Carter, B. L., & Tiffany, S. T. (1999). Meta-analysis of cue-reactivity in addiction research. *Addiction, 94*, 327–340.

Carter, B. L., & Tiffany, S. T. (2001). The cue-availability paradigm: The effects of cigarette availability on cue reactivity in smokers. *Experimental and Clinical Psychopharmacology, 9*, 183–190.

Colwill, R. M., & Motzkin, D. K. (1994). Encoding of the unconditioned stimulus in Pavlovian conditioning. *Animal Learning & Behavior, 22*, 384–394.

Colwill, R. M., & Rescorla, R. A. (1988). Associations between the discriminative stimulus and the reinforcer in instrumental learning. *Journal of Experimental Psychology: Animal Behavior Processes, 14*, 155–164.

Colwill, R. M., & Rescorla, R. A. (1990a). Effects of reinforcer devaluation on discriminative control of instrumental behavior. *Journal of Experimental Psychology: Animal Behavior Processes, 16*, 40–47.

Colwill, R. M., & Rescorla, R. A. (1990b). Evidence for the hierarchical structure of instrumental learning. *Animal Learning & Behavior, 18*, 71–82.

Consortium TTaG (2010). Genome-wide meta-analyses identify multiple loci associated with smoking behavior. *Nature Genetics, 42*, 441–447.

Corbit, L. H., Janak, P. H., & Balleine, B. W. (2007). General and outcome-specific forms of Pavlovian–instrumental transfer: The effect of shifts in motivational state and inactivation of the ventral tegmental area. *European Journal of Neuroscience, 26*, 3141–3149.

Cox, L. S., Tiffany, S. T., & Christen, A. G. (2001). Evaluation of the brief questionnaire of smoking urges (QSU-brief) in the laboratory and clinical settings. *Nicotine and Tobacco Research, 3*, 7–16.

Dayan, P., & Daw, N. D. (2008). Decision theory, reinforcement learning, and the brain. *Cognitive Affective & Behavioral Neuroscience, 8*, 429–453.

de Wit, H., Uhlenhuth, E. H., & Johanson, C. E. (1986). Individual differences in the reinforcing and subjective effects of amphetamine and diazepam. *Drug and Alcohol Dependence, 16*, 341–360.

de Wit, S., Corlett, P. R., Aitken, M. R., Dickinson, A., & Fletcher, P. C. (2009). Differential engagement of the ventromedial prefrontal cortex by goal-directed and habitual behavior toward food pictures in humans. *Journal of Neuroscience, 29*, 11330–11338.

de Wit, S., & Dickinson, A. (2009). Associative theories of goal-directed behaviour: A case for animal–human translational models. *Psychological Research, 73*, 463–476.

de Wit, S., Niry, D., Wariyar, R., Aitken, M. R. F., & Dickinson, A. (2007). Stimulus–outcome interactions during instrumental discrimination learning by rats and humans. *Journal of Experimental Psychology: Animal Behavior Processes, 33*, 1–11.

Deroche-Gamonet, V., Belin, D., & Piazza, P. V. (2004). Evidence for addiction-like behavior in the rat. *Science, 305*, 1014–1017.

Di Chiara, G., Tanda, G., Bassareo, V., Pontieri, F., Acquas, E., Fenu, S., et al. (1998). Drug addiction as a disorder of associative learning: Role of nucleus accumbens shell/extended amygdala dopamine. In J. F. McGinty (Ed.), *Annals of the New York Academy of Sciences: Vol. 877. Advancing from the ventral striatum to the extended amygdala: Implications for neuropsychiatry and drug abuse* (pp. 461–485). New York, NY: New York Academy of Sciences.

Dickinson, A. (1989). Expectancy theory in animal conditioning. In S. B. Klein & R. R. Mowrer (Eds.), *Pavlovian conditioning and the status of traditional learning theory* (pp. 279–308). Hillsdale, NJ: Lawrence Erlbaum Associates, Inc.

Dickinson, A., & Balleine, B. W. (2002). The role of learning in the operation of motivational systems. In C. R. Gallistel (Ed.), *Stevens' handbook of experimental psychology: Vol. 3. Learning, motivation and emotion* (3rd ed., pp. 497–533). New York, NY: Wiley.

Dickinson, A., & Dawson, G. R. (1987). Pavlovian processes in the motivational control of instrumental performance. *Quarterly Journal of Experimental Psychology Section B: Comparative and Physiological Psychology, 39*, 201–213.

Dickinson, A., Wood, N., & Smith, J. W. (2002). Alcohol seeking by rats: Action or habit? *Quarterly Journal of Experimental Psychology Section B: Comparative and Physiological Psychology, 55*, 331–348.

Diergaarde, L., Pattij, T., Poortvliet, I., Hogenboom, F., de Vries, W., Schoffelmeer, A. N. M., et al. (2008). Impulsive choice and impulsive action predict vulnerability to distinct stages of nicotine seeking in rats. *Biological Psychiatry, 63*, 301–308.

Donny, E. C., & Dierker, L. C. (2007). The absence of DSM-IV nicotine dependence in moderate-to-heavy daily smokers. *Drug and Alcohol Dependence, 89*, 93–96.

Doran, N., Spring, B., McChargue, D., Pergadia, M., & Richmond, M. (2004). Impulsivity and smoking relapse. *Nicotine & Tobacco Research, 6*, 641–647.

Drevets, W. C., Gautier, C., Price, J. C., Kupfer, D. J., Kinahan, P. E., Grace, A. A., et al. (2001). Amphetamine-induced dopamine release in human ventral striatum correlates with euphoria. *Biological Psychiatry, 49*, 81–96.

Drobes, D. J., & Tiffany, S. T. (1997). Induction of smoking urge through imaginal and in vivo procedures: Physiological and self-report manifestations. *Journal of Abnormal Psychology, 106*, 15–25.

Droungas, A., Ehrman, R., Childress, A., & O'Brien, C. (1995). Effects of smoking cues and cigarette availability on craving and smoking behavior. *Addictive Behaviors, 20*, 657–673.

Drummond, D. C. (2000). What does cue-reactivity have to offer clinical research? *Addiction, 95*, S129–S144.

Economidou, D., Pelloux, Y., Robbins, T. W., Dalley, J. W., & Everitt, B. J. (2009). High impulsivity predicts relapse to cocaine-seeking after punishment-induced abstinence. *Biological Psychiatry, 65*, 851–856.

Etter, J. F., Le Houezec, J., & Perneger, T. V. (2003). A self-administered questionnaire to measure dependence on cigarettes: The Cigarette Dependence Scale. *Neuropsychopharmacology, 28*, 359–370.

Everitt, B. J., Belin, D., Economidou, D., Pelloux, Y., Dalley, J. W., & Robbins, T. W. (2008). Neural mechanisms underlying the vulnerability to develop compulsive drug-seeking habits and addiction. *Philosophical Transactions of the Royal Society B, 363*, 3125–3135.

Fagerstrom, K., & Schneider, N. G. (1989). Measuring nicotine dependence: A review of the Fagerstrom Tolerance Questionnaire. *Journal of Behavioral Medicine, 12*, 159–182.

Ferguson, S. G., & Shiffman, S. (2009). Cue-induced cravings for cigarettes. *Current Cardiovascular Risk Reports, 3*(6), 385–390.

Fergusson, D. M., Horwood, L. J., Lynskey, M. T., & Madden, P. A. F. (2003). Early reactions to cannabis predict later dependence. *Archives of General Psychiatry, 60*, 1033–1039.

Flory, J. D., & Manuck, S. B. (2009). Impulsiveness and cigarette smoking. *Psychosomatic Medicine, 71*, 431–437.

Franques, P., Auriacombe, M., & Tignol, J. (2000). Addiction and personality. *Encephale–Revue de Psychiatrie Clinique Biologique et Therapeutique, 26*, 68–78.

Gámez, M., & Rosas, J. M. (2007). Associations in human instrumental conditioning. *Learning and Motivation, 38*, 242–261.

Gill, J. S. (2002). Reported levels of alcohol consumption and binge drinking within the UK undergraduate student population over the last 25 years. *Alcohol and Alcoholism, 37*, 109–120.

Glasner, S. V., Overmier, J. B., & Balleine, B. W. (2005). The role of Pavlovian cues in alcohol seeking in dependent and nondependent rats. *Journal of Studies on Alcohol, 66*, 53–61.

Goldstein, R. Z., Craig, A. D., Bechara, A., Garavan, H., Childress, A. R., Paulus, M. P., et al. (2009). The neurocircuitry of impaired insight in drug addiction. *Trends in Cognitive Sciences, 13*, 372–380.

Grant, B. F., Dawson, D. A., Stinson, F. S., Chou, S. P., Dufour, M. C., & Pickering, R. P. (2004). The 12-month prevalence and trends in DSM-IV alcohol abuse and dependence: United States, 1991–1992 and 2001–2002. *Drug and Alcohol Dependence, 74*, 223–234.

Grant, B. F., Dawson, D. A., Stinson, F. S., Chou, P. S., Kay, W., & Pickering, R. (2003). The Alcohol Use Disorder and Associated Disabilities Interview Schedule-IV (AUDADIS-IV): Reliability of alcohol consumption, tobacco use, family history of depression and psychiatric diagnostic modules in a general population sample. *Drug and Alcohol Dependence, 71*, 7–16.

Greenwald, M. K. (2008). Behavioral economic analysis of drug preference using multiple choice procedure data. *Drug and Alcohol Dependence, 93*, 103–110.

Hawkins, J. D., Catalano, R. F., & Miller, J. Y. (1992). Risk and protective factors for alcohol and other drug problems in adolescence and early adulthood: Implications for substance-abuse prevention. *Psychological Bulletin, 112*, 64–105.

Herd, N., Borland, R., & Hyland, A. (2009). Predictors of smoking relapse by duration of abstinence: Findings from the International Tobacco Control (ITC) Four Country Survey. *Addiction, 104*, 2088–2099.

Herrnstein, R. J. (1961). Relative and absolute strength of response as a function of frequency of reinforcement. *Journal of the Experimental Analysis of Behavior, 4*, 267–272.

Heyman, G. M. (1996). Resolving the contradictions of addiction. *Behavioral and Brain Sciences, 19*, 561–574.

Heyman, G. M. (2000). An economic approach to animal models of alcoholism. *Alcohol Research & Health, 24,* 132–139.

Heyman, G. M. (2009). *Addiction: A disorder of choice.* Cambridge, MA: Harvard University Press.

Hides, L., Kavanagh, D. J., Dawe, S., & Young, R. M. (2009). The influence of cannabis use expectancies on cannabis use and psychotic symptoms in psychosis. *Drug and Alcohol Review, 28,* 250–256.

Hiroi, N., & Scott, D. (2009). Constitutional mechanisms of vulnerability and resilience to nicotine dependence. *Molecular Psychiatry, 14,* 653–667.

Hogarth, L. (2011). The role of impulsivity in the aetiology of drug dependence: Reward sensitivity versus automaticity. *Psychopharmacology, 215,* 567–580.

Hogarth, L., & Chase, H. W. (2011). Parallel goal-directed and habitual control of human drug-seeking: Implications for dependence vulnerability. *Journal of Experimental Psychology: Animal Behavior Processes, 37,* 261–276.

Hogarth, L., Chase, H. W., & Baess, K. (in press). Impaired goal-directed control in human impulsivity. *Quarterly Journal of Experimental Psychology.*

Hogarth, L., Dickinson, A., & Duka, T. (2009). Detection versus sustained attention to drug cues have dissociable roles in mediating drug seeking behaviour. *Experimental and Clinical Psychopharmacology, 17,* 21–30.

Hogarth, L., Dickinson, A., & Duka, T. (2010). The associative basis of cue elicited drug taking in humans. *Psychopharmacology, 208,* 337–351.

Hogarth, L., Dickinson, A., Hutton, S. B., Elbers, N., & Duka, T. (2006). Drug expectancy is necessary for stimulus control of human attention, instrumental drug-seeking behaviour and subjective pleasure. *Psychopharmacology, 185,* 495–504.

Hogarth, L., Dickinson, A., Janowski, M., Nikitina, A., & Duka, T. (2008). The role of attentional bias in mediating human drug seeking behaviour. *Psychopharmacology, 201,* 29–41.

Hogarth, L., Dickinson, A., Wright, A., Kouvaraki, M., & Duka, T. (2007). The role of drug expectancy in the control of human drug seeking. *Journal of Experimental Psychology: Animal Behavior Processes, 33,* 484–496.

Hogarth, L., & Duka, T. (2006). Human nicotine conditioning requires explicit contingency knowledge: Is addictive behaviour cognitively mediated? *Psychopharmacology, 184,* 553–566.

Holland, P. C. (2004). Relations between Pavlovian-instrumental transfer and reinforcer devaluation. *Journal of Experimental Psychology: Animal Behavior Processes, 30,* 258–258.

Hughes, J. R., Helzer, J. E., & Lindberg, S. A. (2006). Prevalence of DSM/ICD-defined nicotine dependence. *Drug and Alcohol Dependence, 85,* 91–102.

Hull, C. L. (1943). *Principles of behavior.* New York, NY: Appleton-Century-Crofts.

Hursh, S. R., & Silberberg, A. (2008). Economic demand and essential value. *Psychological Review, 115,* 186–198.

Hutcheson, D. M., Everitt, B. J., Robbins, T. W., & Dickinson, A. (2001). The role of withdrawal in heroin addiction: Enhances reward or promotes avoidance? *Nature Neuroscience, 4,* 943–947.

Hyland, A., Rezaishiraz, H., Bauer, J., Giovino, G. A., & Cummings, K. M. (2005). Characteristics of low-level smokers. *Nicotine & Tobacco Research, 7,* 461–468.

Jacobs, E. A., & Bickel, W. K. (1999). Modeling drug consumption in the clinic using simulation procedures: Demand for heroin and cigarettes in opioid-dependent outpatients. *Experimental and Clinical Psychopharmacology*, 7, 412–426.

Jarvik, M. E., Madsen, D. C., Olmstead, R. E., Iwamoto-Schaap, P. N., Elins, J. L., & Benowitz, N. L. (2000). Nicotine blood levels and subjective craving for cigarettes. *Pharmacology Biochemistry & Behavior*, 66, 553–558.

Jedynak, J. P., Uslaner, J. M., Esteban, J. A., & Robinson, T. E. (2007). Methamphetamine-induced structural plasticity in the dorsal striatum. *European Journal of Neuroscience*, 25, 847–853.

Jentsch, J. D., & Taylor, J. R. (1999). Impulsivity resulting from frontostriatal dysfunction in drug abuse: Implications for the control of behavior by reward-related stimuli. *Psychopharmacology*, 146, 373–390.

Jones, B. T., Corbin, W., & Fromme, K. (2001). A review of expectancy theory and alcohol consumption. *Addiction*, 96, 57–72.

Juliano, L. M., & Brandon, T. H. (1998). Reactivity to instructed smoking availability and environmental cues: Evidence with urge and reaction time. *Experimental and Clinical Psychopharmacology*, 6, 45–53.

Kahneman, D., & Tversky, A. (1979). Prospect theory: An analysis of decision under risk. *Econometrica*, 47, 263–291.

Kenward, B., Folke, S., Holmberg, J., Johansson, A., & Gredeback, G. (2009). Goal directedness and decision making in infants. *Developmental Psychology*, 45, 809–819.

Killen, J. D., & Fortmann, S. P. (1997). Craving is associated with smoking relapse: Findings from three prospective studies. *Experimental and Clinical Psychopharmacology*, 5, 137–142.

Kirisci, L., Vanyukov, M., & Tarter, R. (2005). Detection of youth at high risk for substance use disorders: A longitudinal study. *Psychology of Addictive Behaviors*, 19, 243–252.

Kirkeby, B. S., & Robinson, M. D. (2005). Impulsive behavior and stimulus–response variability in choice reaction time. *Journal of Research in Personality*, 39, 263–277.

Klossek, U. M. H., Russell, J., & Dickinson, A. (2008). The control of instrumental action following outcome devaluation in young children aged between 1 and 4 years. *Journal of Experimental Psychology: General*, 137, 39–51.

Le Foll, B., Chefer, S. I., Kimes, A. S., Shumway, D., Stein, E. A., Mukhin, A. G., et al. (2009). Baseline expression of alpha 4 beta 2*nicotinic acetylcholine receptors predicts motivation to self-administer nicotine. *Biological Psychiatry*, 65, 714–716.

Leventhal, A. M., & Schmitz, J. M. (2006). The role of drug use outcome expectancies in substance abuse risk: An interactional–transformational model. *Addictive Behaviors*, 31, 2038–2062.

Lovibond, P. F., & Shanks, D. R. (2002). The role of awareness in Pavlovian conditioning: Empirical evidence and theoretical implications. *Journal of Experimental Psychology: Animal Behavior Processes*, 28, 3–26.

Ludwig, A. M., Wikler, A., & Stark, L. H. (1974). First drink: Psychobiological aspects of craving. *Archives of General Psychiatry*, 30, 539–547.

MacKillop, J., Miranda, Jr, R., Monti, P. M., Ray, L. A., Murphy, J. G., Rohsenow, D. J., et al. (2010). Alcohol demand, delayed reward discounting, and craving in relation to drinking and alcohol use disorders. *Journal of Abnormal Psychology*, 119, 106–114.

MacKillop, J., & Murphy, J. G. (2007). A behavioral economic measure of demand for alcohol predicts brief intervention outcomes. *Drug and Alcohol Dependence*, *89*, 227–233.

MacKillop, J., Murphy, J. G., Ray, L. A., Eisenberg, D. T. A., Lisman, S. A., Lum, J. K., et al. (2008). Further validation of a cigarette purchase task for assessing the relative reinforcing efficacy of nicotine in college smokers. *Experimental and Clinical Psychopharmacology*, *16*, 57–65.

Maude-Griffin, P. M., & Tiffany, S. T. (1996). Production of smoking urges through imagery: The impact of affect and smoking abstinence. *Experimental and Clinical Psychopharmacology*, *4*, 198–208.

Miles, F. J., Everitt, B. J., & Dickinson, A. (2003). Oral cocaine seeking by rats: Action or habit? *Behavioral Neuroscience*, *117*, 927–938.

Miller, H. L. (1976). Matching-based hedonic scaling in the pigeon. *Journal of the Experimental Analysis of Behavior*, *26*, 335–347.

Miller, W. R., Westerberg, V. S., Harris, R. J., & Tonigan, J. S. (1996). What predicts relapse? Prospective testing of antecedent models. *Addiction*, *91*, S155–S172.

Mitchell, C. J., De Houwer, J., & Lovibond, P. F. (2009). The propositional nature of human associative learning. *Behavioral and Brain Sciences*, *32*, 183–198.

Moeller, F. G., Dougherty, D. M., Barratt, E. S., Schmitz, J. M., Swann, A. C., & Grabowski, J. (2001). The impact of impulsivity on cocaine use and retention in treatment. *Journal of Substance Abuse Treatment*, *21*, 193–198.

Moeller, S. J., Maloney, T., Parvaz, M. A., Dunning, J. P., Alia-Klein, N., Woicik, P. A., et al. (2009). Enhanced choice for viewing cocaine pictures in cocaine addiction. *Biological Psychiatry*, *66*, 169–176.

Morawska, A., & Oei, T. P. S. (2005). Binge drinking in university students: A test of the cognitive model. *Addictive Behaviors*, *30*, 203–218.

Mucha, R. F., Pauli, P., & Angrilli, A. (1998). Conditioned responses elicited by experimentally produced cues for smoking. *Canadian Journal of Physiology and Pharmacology*, *76*, 259–268.

Murphy, J. G., Barnett, N. P., Colby, S. M., Correia, C. J., Mackillop, J., & Vuchinich, R. E. (2006). Relative reinforcing value of alcohol predicts response to a brief intervention. *Alcoholism: Clinical and Experimental Research*, *30*, 250A–250A.

Murphy, J. G., Correia, C. J., Colby, S. M., & Vuchinich, R. E. (2005). Using behavioral theories of choice to predict drinking outcomes following a brief intervention. *Experimental and Clinical Psychopharmacology*, *13*, 93–101.

Murphy, J. G., & MacKillop, J. (2006). Relative reinforcing efficacy of alcohol among college student drinkers. *Experimental and Clinical Psychopharmacology*, *14*, 219–227.

Naqvi, N. H., & Bechara, A. (2009). The hidden island of addiction: The insula. *Trends in Neurosciences*, *32*, 56–67.

Nelson, A., & Killcross, S. (2006). Amphetamine exposure enhances habit formation. *Journal of Neuroscience*, *26*, 3805–3812.

Nemeth-Coslett, R., & Griffiths, R. R. (1984a). Determinants of puff duration in cigarette smokers: I. *Pharmacology Biochemistry and Behavior*, *20*, 965–971.

Nemeth-Coslett, R., & Griffiths, R. R. (1984b). Determinants of puff duration in cigarette smokers: II. *Pharmacology Biochemistry and Behavior*, *21*, 903–912.

Nordquist, R. E., Voorn, P., Malsen, J., Joosten, R., Pennartz, C. M. A., &

Vanderschuren, L. (2007). Augmented reinforcer value and accelerated habit formation after repeated amphetamine treatment. *European Neuropsychopharmacology, 17*, 532–540.

Olmstead, M. C., Lafond, M. V., Everitt, B. J., & Dickinson, A. (2001). Cocaine seeking by rats is a goal-directed action. *Behavioral Neuroscience, 115*, 394–402.

Ostlund, S. B., & Balleine, B. W. (2008). The disunity of Pavlovian and instrumental values. *Behavioral and Brain Sciences, 31*, 456.

Padoa-Schioppa, C. (2007). Orbitofrontal cortex and the computation of economic value. In G. Schoenbaum, J. A. Gottfried, E. A. Murray, & S. J. Ramus (Eds.), *Annals of the New York Academy of Sciences: Vol. 1121. Linking affect to action: Critical contributions of the orbitofrontal cortex* (pp. 232–253). Oxford, UK: Blackwell.

Palfai, T. P. (2002). Positive outcome expectancies and smoking behaviour: The role of expectancy accessibility. *Cognitive Therapy and Research, 26*, 317–333.

Paredes-Olay, C., Abad, M. J. F., Gámez, M., & Rosas, J. M. (2002). Transfer of control between causal predictive judgments and instrumental responding. *Animal Learning & Behavior, 30*, 239–248.

Patton, J. H., Stanford, M. S., & Barratt, E. S. (1995). Factor structure of the Barratt Impulsiveness Scale. *Journal of Clinical Psychology, 51*, 768–774.

Pelloux, Y., Everitt, B. J., & Dickinson, A. (2007). Compulsive drug seeking by rats under punishment: Effects of drug taking history. *Psychopharmacology, 194*, 127–137.

Perkins, K. A. (2009). Does smoking cue-induced craving tell us anything important about nicotine dependence? *Addiction, 104*, 1610–1616.

Perkins, K. A., Broge, M., Gerlach, D., Sanders, M., Grobe, J. E., Cherry, C., et al. (2002). Acute nicotine reinforcement, but not chronic tolerance, predicts withdrawal and relapse after quitting smoking. *Health Psychology, 21*, 332–339.

Perkins, K. A., Epstein, L. H., Grobe, J., & Fonte, C. (1994). Tobacco abstinence, smoking cues, and the reinforcing value of smoking. *Pharmacology Biochemistry and Behavior, 47*, 107–112.

Rangel, A., Camerer, C., & Montague, P. R. (2008). A framework for studying the neurobiology of value-based decision making. *Nature Reviews Neuroscience, 9*, 545–556.

Rescorla, R. A. (1991). Associative relations in instrumental learning: The 18 Bartlett memorial lecture. *Quarterly Journal of Experimental Psychology Section B: Comparative and Physiological Psychology, 43*, 1–23.

Rescorla, R. A. (1994). Transfer of instrumental control mediated by a devalued outcome. *Animal Learning & Behavior, 22*, 27–33.

Robbins, S. J., & Ehrman, R. N. (1992). Designing studies of drug conditioning in humans. *Psychopharmacology, 106*, 143–153.

Rohsenow, D. J., Childress, A. R., Monti, P. M., Niaura, R. S., & Abrams, D. B. (1991). Cue reactivity in addictive behaviors: Theoretical and treatment implications. *International Journal of the Addictions, 25*, 957–993.

Rose, J. E. (2006). Nicotine and nonnicotine factors in cigarette addiction. *Psychopharmacology, 184*, 274–285.

Scherrer, J. F., Grant, J. D., Duncan, A. E., Sartor, C. E., Haber, J. R., Jacob, T., et al. (2009). Subjective effects to cannabis are associated with use, abuse and dependence after adjusting for genetic and environmental influences. *Drug and Alcohol Dependence, 105*, 76–82.

Schoenbaum, G., & Setlow, B. (2005). Cocaine makes actions insensitive to outcomes but not extinction: Implications for altered orbitofrontal-amygdalar function. *Cerebral Cortex, 15*, 1162–1169.

Schwabe, L., & Wolf, O. T. (2009). Stress prompts habit behavior in humans. *The Journal of Neuroscience, 29*, 7191–7198.

Schwabe, L., & Wolf, O. T. (2010). Socially evaluated cold pressor stress after instrumental learning favors habits over goal-directed action. *Psychoneuroendocrinology, 35*, 977–986.

Shiffman, S. (2009). Responses to smoking cues are relevant to smoking and relapse. *Addiction, 104*, 1617–1618.

Skinner, M. D., & Aubin, H.-J. (2010). Craving's place in addiction theory: Contributions of the major models. *Neuroscience & Biobehavioral Reviews, 34*, 606–623.

Stalnaker, T. A., Takahashi, Y., Roesch, M. R., & Schoenbaum, G. (2009). Neural substrates of cognitive inflexibility after chronic cocaine exposure. *Neuropharmacology, 56*, 63–72.

Stanford, M. S., Mathias, C. W., Dougherty, D. M., Lake, S. L., Anderson, N. E., & Patton, J. H. (2009). Fifty years of the Barratt Impulsiveness Scale: An update and review. *Personality and Individual Differences, 47*, 385–395.

Stoops, W. W., Lile, J. A., Robbins, C. G., Martin, C. A., Rush, C. R., & Kelly, T. H. (2007). The reinforcing, subject-rated, performance, and cardiovascular effects of d-amphetamine: Influence of sensation-seeking status. *Addictive Behaviors, 32*, 1177–1188.

Talmi, D., Dayan, P., Kiebel, S. J., Frith, C. D., & Dolan, R. J. (2009). How humans integrate the prospects of pain and reward during choice. *The Journal of Neuroscience, 29*, 14617–14626.

Talmi, D., Seymour, B., Dayan, P., & Dolan, R. J. (2008). Human Pavlovian–instrumental transfer. *The Journal of Neuroscience, 28*, 360–368.

Tiffany, S. T., Cox, L. S., & Elash, C. A. (2000). Effects of transdermal nicotine patches on abstinence-induced and cue-elicited craving in cigarette smokers. *Journal of Consulting and Clinical Psychology, 68*, 233–240.

Tiffany, S. T., & Drobes, D. J. (1991). The development and initial validation of a questionnaire on smoking urges. *British Journal of Addiction, 86*, 1467–1476.

Tiffany, S. T., Warthen, M. W., & Goedeker, K. C. (2007). The functional significance of craving in nicotine dependence. In A. R. Caggiuls & R. A. Bevins (Eds.), *The motivational impact of nicotine and its role in tobacco use* (Nebraska Symposium on Motivation) (pp. 1–27). New York, NY: Springer.

Tiffany, S. T., & Wray, J. (2009). The continuing conundrum of craving. *Addiction, 104*, 1618–1619.

Tricomi, E., Balleine, B. W., & O'Doherty, J. P. (2009). A specific role for posterior dorsolateral striatum in human habit learning. *European Journal of Neuroscience, 29*, 2225–2232.

Urban, R. (2010). Smoking outcome expectancies mediate the association between sensation seeking, peer smoking, and smoking among young adolescents. *Nicotine & Tobacco Research, 12*, 59–68.

Ursu, S., Clark, K. A., Stenger, V. A., & Carter, C. S. (2008). Distinguishing expected negative outcomes from preparatory control in the human orbitofrontal cortex. *Brain Research, 1227*, 110–119.

Valentin, V., Dickinson, A., & O'Doherty, J. P. (2007). Determining the neural

4. Vulnerabilities in drug dependence 101

substrates of goal-directed learning in the human brain. *The Journal of Neuroscience, 27*, 4019–4026.

Vanderschuren, L. J. M. J., & Everitt, B. J. (2004). Drug seeking becomes compulsive after prolonged cocaine self-administration. *Science, 305*, 1017–1019.

Vlaev, I., Seymour, B., Dolan, R. J., & Chater, N. (2009). The price of pain and the value of suffering. *Psychological Science, 20*, 309–317.

Volkow, N. D., Fowler, J. S., Wang, G. J., Baler, R., & Telang, F. (2009). Imaging dopamine's role in drug abuse and addiction. *Neuropharmacology, 56*, 3–8.

Volkow, N. D., Fowler, J. S., Wang, G. J., Telang, F., Logan, J., Jayne, M., et al. (2010). Cognitive control of drug craving inhibits brain reward regions in cocaine abusers. *NeuroImage, 49*, 2536–2543.

Wagner, F. A., & Anthony, J. C. (2002). From first drug use to drug dependence: Developmental periods of risk for dependence upon marijuana, cocaine, and alcohol. *Neuropsychopharmacology, 26*, 479–488.

Waters, A. J., Shiffman, S., Sayette, M. A., Paty, J. A., Gwaltney, C. J., & Balabanis, M. H. (2004). Cue-provoked craving and nicotine replacement therapy in smoking cessation. *Journal of Consulting and Clinical Psychology, 72*, 1136–1143.

Willner, P., Hardman, S., & Eaton, G. (1995). Subjective and behavioral-evaluation of cigarette cravings. *Psychopharmacology, 118*, 171–177.

Wise, R. A., & Rompre, P. P. (1989). Brain dopamine and reward. *Annual Review of Psychology, 40*, 191–225.

Yacubian, J., & Buchel, C. (2009). The genetic basis of individual differences in reward processing and the link to addictive behavior and social cognition. *Neuroscience, 164*, 55–71.

5 Context and extinction:

Mechanisms of relapse in drug self-administration

Mark E. Bouton, Neil E. Winterbauer, and Drina Vurbic

In a classic paper, Hunt, Barnett, and Branch (1971) examined relapse as a function of time since the end of treatment for heroin, alcohol, and tobacco abuse. The paper summarized data from 84 studies in a graph that showed the percentage of people who continued to abstain from each drug over the 12 months that followed quitting. The three curves were essentially identical. Each showed a steep and negatively accelerated decline to an asymptote of only about 30 percent abstaining after 6 and 12 months. Thus, for each drug, about 70 percent of the users were using the drug again within 6 months of quitting. Relatively recent studies of relapse over time have reported similar curves with similarly high relapse rates (e.g., Hughes, Keely, & Naud, 2004; Kirshenbaum, Olsen, & Bickel, 2009). It is clearly difficult for drug users to stay abstinent. A significant challenge to therapy, therefore, is to find ways to prevent relapse and promote long-term behaviour change.

Like many pathological behaviours, substance abuse is learned. Drug taking is an operant behaviour that is reinforced by its consequences (the effects of the drug). And like all operant learning, it takes place in the presence of many cues that both set the occasion for drug taking and are directly associated with the drug themselves (e.g., Stolerman, 1992). Through Pavlovian learning, the drug-associated cues may activate uncomfortable physiological processes (e.g., Siegel, 2008), approach behaviours, and/or motivational states or expectancies that motivate and invigorate the operant responding (e.g., Berridge & Robinson, 2003; Dickinson & Balleine, 1994; Hogarth, Dickinson, Wright, Kouvaraki, & Duka, 2007; Rescorla & Solomon, 1967; Stewart, de Wit, & Eikelboom, 1984). To change addictive behaviour, behavioural therapies would therefore benefit from considering and modifying both operant and Pavlovian learning processes.

For many years our laboratory has investigated extinction, one of the most fundamental behaviour change processes studied in all of learning theory. In operant learning, extinction is the reduction in the strength of behaviour that occurs when the reinforcer is no longer delivered after responding; in Pavlovian learning, extinction is the reduction in responding

Table 5.1 Four context and extinction phenomena that may provide mechanisms of relapse

Phenomenon	Description
Spontaneous recovery	Recovery of responding that occurs when the CS is tested after time has passed following extinction.
Renewal	Recovery of extinguished behaviour that can occur when the context is changed after extinction. Most often observed when the subject is returned to the original context of conditioning (ABA renewal). But it also depends in part on mere removal from the extinction context, as in ABC or AAB renewal.
Reinstatement	Recovery of behaviour that occurs when the subject is exposed to the US after extinction. Strongly controlled by contextual conditioning produced when the US is presented; hence, the phenomenon is strongest when the CS is tested in the context where the US has occurred.
Reacquisition	Recovery of responding that occurs when the CS is paired with the US (or reinforcer) again after extinction. Often rapid, especially when cues in the background renew conditioned performance (as above). Can be slow when the background cues retrieve extinction.

Note: CS = conditional stimulus; US = unconditional stimulus.
Source: Adapted from Bouton and Swartzentruber (1991), with permission.

to the conditional stimulus (CS) that occurs when the reinforcer with which it has been associated (the unconditional stimulus or US) is removed. Although there are other methods for weakening behaviours (e.g., **counter-conditioning** or the reinforcement of alternative behaviours), they all usually involve extinction. Extinction can therefore be regarded as one of the most ubiquitous ways to remove unwanted behaviours, as well as thoughts and emotions.

Although extinction looks like it destroys or erases the original learning, the results of a large number of laboratory studies suggest that it does not (e.g., Bouton, 1988). Instead, extinction involves new learning, the retrieval of which is remarkably dependent on the context in which extinction learning has occurred (see Bouton, 2004; Bouton & Woods, 2008, for recent reviews). This conclusion is clearly supported by research on Pavlovian fear and appetitive conditioning, which has identified at least four key phenomena that are summarized in Table 5.1. In the first, *spontaneous recovery*, extinguished responding may recover when time elapses after the end of extinction. In the second, *renewal*, extinguished responding may return when the context (the cues in the background, such as the room or apparatus or even internal mood state) is changed after extinction. In the third, *reinstatement*, extinguished responding recovers if the organism is exposed to the US – alone – after extinction. In the last, *reacquisition*, responding to the CS may be acquired more quickly than in original learning when the CS is paired with the US again after extinction.

All of the phenomena defined in Table 5.1 indicate that extinction is not the erasure or destruction of the original learning. They are all also context effects. The renewal effect clearly illustrates the idea that extinction is specific to the context in which it occurs. Spontaneous recovery can be viewed as the renewal effect that occurs when the CS is tested in a "temporal context" that is different from that of extinction (e.g., Bouton, 1988, 1993). And in reinstatement, the behaviour-returning effects of exposure to the US are almost entirely mediated by conditioning of the context that occurs when the US is presented. In fear conditioning, US presentations condition anxiety to the context that then triggers fear of an extinguished CS presented in it (e.g., Bouton, 1984). Rapid reacquisition may be a context effect too. The evidence suggests that the rapid recovery of responding occurs because early CS–US pairings during the reacquisition phase reintroduce part of the context of conditioning rather than of extinction (Ricker & Bouton, 1996; Bouton, Woods, & Pineño, 2004).

The Table 5.1 phenomena, and the inherent context-dependence of extinction performance, might readily contribute to the high rates of relapse that follow behaviour change (e.g., Hunt et al., 1971). As time after an extinction treatment goes by, spontaneous recovery may occur. Or the passage of time might also increase the likelihood of an encounter with the original context (causing renewal) or the US or reinforcer itself (causing reinstatement). Any of these phenomena could initiate a lapse, and thus new response–reinforcer pairings, and rapid reacquisition may then begin the spiral into full-blown relapse. In the present chapter, we examine implications of what we know about relapse phenomena like those listed in Table 5.1 for our understanding of drug abuse. We are mainly focused on extinction and relapse in drug self-administration experiments, where animals have learned to perform operant behaviours to receive drug reinforcers. For reviews providing more focus on the parallel effects in Pavlovian extinction, see Bouton (2002) or Bouton, Westbrook, Corcoran, and Maren (2006).

Pavlovian renewal effects with drugs

As just noted, the renewal effect has been amply demonstrated in Pavlovian learning, such as fear conditioning, where the CS is paired with mild footshock, and in appetitive conditioning, where the CS is paired with food pellets. It has also been demonstrated in other preparations, including taste aversion learning, where rats reject tastes that have been associated with illness (e.g., Rosas & Bouton, 1998), and in human contingency learning, where people estimate the predictive values of cues associated with various outcomes (e.g., Rosas, Vila, Lugo, & Lopez, 2001). It has also been shown in Pavlovian learning preparations in which drugs provide the US. For example, Parker, Limebeer, and Slomke (2006) found renewal in the conditioned place preference (CPP) paradigm, where animals learn to associate (and consequently prefer to stay in) places that are associated with drugs of abuse. In several experiments, rats were confined to compartments that had floors of different textures; exposure to one texture was paired with injections of a drug (cocaine or morphine), and exposure to the other was paired with injections of saline. These pairings occurred in the presence of either white or black contextual cues provided by the walls of the apparatus. Extinction trials, in which the rats were exposed to both types of floors in the absence of the drug, were then conducted in either the same or different context. Although exposure to the floor without the drug extinguished the conditioned floor preference, when the rats were returned to the original context, the original drug-conditioned preference returned. Responding in the group that received no context switch was not changed. Thus, extinction of the CS–cocaine or CS–morphine association was context-specific – and did not reflect erasure of the original learning.

Using a different method, Chaudhri, Sahuque, and Janak (2008) demonstrated renewal of responding to CSs associated with alcohol. After 30–36 days of drinking ethanol in the home cage that habituated the rats to the taste of alcohol, Chaudhri et al. paired an auditory CS with delivery of a small (0.2 ml) drink of 10 percent ethanol to a cup embedded in a wall of a Skinner box. This led the rat to investigate the cup at the sound of the CS. The CS was then presented repeatedly without ethanol delivery while the rat was in a Skinner box that differed from the first in the shading of the walls (clear vs. black), the nature of the floor (mesh vs. solid Plexiglas), and in ambient odour (strawberry vs. vinegar scent). There were 128 extinction trials distributed over a series of eight daily sessions. The extinction trials eliminated the cup investigation response. But in a final test conducted in the original conditioning context, the rats renewed their responding to the CS to a level that appeared similar to that observed at the end of conditioning. Once again, extinction did not erase the original learning, which was revealed in performance by context change.

There is preliminary evidence that extinction of responding to alcohol cues is also context-specific in humans. Collins and Brandon (2002) exposed undergraduate social drinkers to the sight and smell of beer, without the opportunity to drink, over a series of trials. Presumably, the sight and smell of beer had become associated with beer during the participants' previous real-world experience. Both salivation and a self-reported urge to drink decreased over trials. However, if participants were then tested in another room, both the salivation and the urge were renewed. It should be noted that other reports have had less success at observing renewal in alcoholics (Stasiewicz, Brandon, & Bradizza, 2007) or other human subjects (MacKillop & Lisman, 2008) in experiments that likewise defined "context" as different rooms in a university building. One issue is whether such rooms are different enough, or meaningful enough to human drinkers, to support contextual control over alcohol craving.

It is worth noting that although drugs can readily play the role of USs and reinforcers, they can also play the role of context. For example, the extinction of fear in rats given an injection of a benzodiazepine tranquilliser before extinction is renewed when testing occurs outside of the drug context (Bouton, Kenney, & Rosengard, 1990). Compatible results have been observed when fear extinction occurred in the presence of ethanol instead of a benzodiazepine (Cunningham, 1979; Lattal, 2007). Such results have at least two implications for relapse. First, if a drug is combined with extinction therapies for anxiety, we might observe a renewal of anxiety when the client stops taking the drug. The second implication concerns drug abuse. A person may be motivated to take a drug like valium or alcohol in order to reduce his or her anxiety – drug taking would thus be reinforced through anxiety reduction. Although the drug occasions reinforcement, it might also be a context that maintains the anxiety that motivates drug taking. Specifically, as a context, the drug would insulate the person from extinction that would otherwise naturally occur during exposure to the anxiety-evoking cues in the environment. When the person encounters the anxiety cues again outside the drug state, the anxiety is still there, ready to motivate continued drug taking, and thus initiating a vicious cycle.

Renewal of extinguished operant behaviour

There is little doubt that operant behaviour can also be renewed after extinction. Welker and McAuley (1978) were among the first to demonstrate that extinguished operant responses can return if contextual cues associated with the initial training are re-presented. This effect was more recently demonstrated by Nakajima, Tanaka, Urushihara, and Imada (2000). In the first of two experiments, hungry rats were trained to lever press for food pellets on a variable interval schedule of reinforcement. After a stable baseline of lever pressing was established, the rats were transferred to a different set of Skinner boxes where the lever press response was no longer reinforced. In a third phase, the rats were returned to the original training context for testing. Consistent with the numerous studies of Pavlovian renewal effects, there was significant recovery of lever pressing even though none of the responses was reinforced during this phase. Similar results have been found when nose-poking was reinforced with sucrose (Hamlin, Blatchford, & McNally, 2006).

Nakajima et al. (2000) also studied renewal with a discriminated operant method in which a second layer of stimulus control was introduced. As in the first experiment, rats were trained to lever press for food pellets and later subjected to extinction training in a different context. However, during the initial training phase the rats were only reinforced for lever pressing when a 30-s light cue was given, and no pellets were ever delivered in the absence of the light cue. The light became a discriminative stimulus (S^D) that set the occasion for the operant response. After the rats had learned this discrimination, they were given extinction training in which the light cue was presented, but the lever press response was never reinforced. Over the course of this phase, the light lost its ability to set the occasion for the lever press. But in a final test in which the rats were presented with the light cue in the original training context, the response reappeared. In this case, renewal suggests that contexts not only have the power to control operant behaviour directly, but also indirectly by modulating the power of other cues to do the same.

Until recently, a similar role for environmental contexts in drug self-administration had largely been overlooked. In the last few years, however, a number of studies have investigated contextual control of drug-seeking behaviour, and have shown that environmental contexts exert the same control over operant responding for drugs of abuse. Crombag, Grimm, and Shaham (2002) were among the first to demonstrate that contexts can renew responding for drugs. Using a modified version of the method described above, they investigated renewal of cocaine seeking. In one context, rats were trained to lever press for cocaine reinforcement that was delivered directly into the jugular vein through an intravenous catheter. Each drug infusion coincided with the onset of a 5-s light cue. After stable rates of drug self-administration were achieved, the lever press response was extinguished in an alternate context. During this phase, lever presses were followed by presentations of the light cue, but no cocaine was delivered. On a renewal test, rats that were returned to the original training context resumed lever pressing even though cocaine was not available. Similar results have been reported with alcohol (Marinelli, Funk, Juzytsch, Li, & Lê, 2007), heroin (Bossert, Gray, Lu, & Shaham, 2006; Bossert, Liu, Lu, & Shaham, 2004; Bossert, Poles, Wihbey, Koya, & Shaham, 2007), and a combination of cocaine and heroin (Crombag & Shaham, 2002). Kearns and Weiss (2007) demonstrated the renewal effect using a discriminated operant procedure. In the first phase, they trained rats to self-administer cocaine whenever a tone was present but not when it was absent. After learning the discrimination, extinction was conducted in a separate context in which neither responding in the presence or the absence of the tone was reinforced. The extinguished responding in the tone was renewed when the rats were returned to the training context. Renewal of cocaine-seeking was similarly found when the environmental context was the only stimulus that signalled availability and/or delivery of the drug (Fuchs et al., 2005). Similar results have been reported using an operant nose-poking response that resulted in the same type of cocaine delivery (Hamlin, Clemens, & McNally, 2008) or alcohol (Hamlin, Newby, & McNally, 2007). Thus, renewal of drug-seeking appears to be a relatively consistent and robust effect that can be obtained with various methods, owing to both the compulsive nature of drug use and the commanding role played by the context.

One interesting feature of the work on renewal in operant conditioning and drug self-administration learning is that the studies have generally focused on ABA renewal, in which conditioning, extinction, and testing occurred in Contexts A, B, and A, respectively. Two other forms of renewal have received less attention, and their status is less certain. These are AAB renewal and ABC renewal, in which conditioning, extinction, and testing occur in Contexts A, A, and B or A, B, and C (respectively). AAB and ABC renewal are theoretically important, because they indicate that mere removal from the extinction context, rather than removal plus return to the conditioning context, can be sufficient to cause a lapse in responding. Several operant experiments have notably reported no evidence of AAB renewal (Bossert et al., 2004; Crombag & Shaham, 2002; Nakajima et al., 2000), and ABC renewal has received little investigation. Zironi, Burattini, Aicardi, and Janak (2006) reported an ABC effect with a sucrose reinforcer, but not an ethanol reinforcer, but did not counterbalance contexts, leaving other explanations (e.g., differences between contexts in the ease with which the lever could be operated) possible. To further address the issue, Bouton, Todd, Vurbic, and Winterbauer (2011) recently reported several experiments in which lever pressing in rats was first reinforced with food pellets and then extinguished. Every rat was then tested in the context of extinction and in a second context in a counterbalanced order (i.e., using a within-subjects testing method). The results produced unequivocal evidence of all forms of renewal, that is, ABA, AAB, and ABC. Although the AAB and ABC effects were numerically weaker than ABA, across all experiments 89.6 percent of the rats tested in an AAB condition showed more responding in the renewal than the extinction context, and 93.75 percent of the ABC rats did. One hundred percent of the ABA rats also did. The results with our methods therefore indicate that extinction of an operant behaviour, like Pavlovian behaviour, can be relatively specific to the context in which it is learned.

Given the importance of both drug-associated environments and discrete CSs in drug-seeking behaviour, it has been suggested that renewal might be an especially relevant model for relapse outside of the laboratory. The findings may also help explain the shortcomings of cue exposure therapy in preventing relapse in humans. It is widely believed that cues present in the drug-taking environment, such as syringes and other drug paraphernalia, become endowed with motivational properties after repeated pairings with the subjective effects of drugs (Robbins, Ehrman, Childress, & O'Brien, 1999). Consistent with this view, clinical studies have shown that drug-associated cues can elicit powerful physiological and subjective reactions, including changes in heart rate and bouts of craving (Carter & Tiffany, 1999; Foltin & Haney, 2000; Hogarth, Dickinson, & Duka, 2010) that are presumed to motivate drug-seeking behaviour. Cue exposure therapy is aimed at reducing these conditioned responses through repeated exposures to drug-associated stimuli, and has been employed in relapse prevention efforts for a variety of drugs. In a typical cue exposure treatment session, patients may be asked to handle or view images of drug paraphernalia in a controlled environment to ensure that abstinence is maintained. The therapeutic benefit of cue exposure is derived from the extinction of the conditioned responses elicited by those cues. But as preclinical studies have clearly demonstrated, extinction treatments are heavily dependent on environmental context, and as a consequence, the therapeutic benefit of this strategy has been limited (see Conklin & Tiffany, 2002 for a review).

Interestingly, there is another reason why cue exposure treatments may not always be effective. Our studies of operant renewal (Bouton et al., 2011) also found that extensive direct extinction exposure to Context A during the extinction phase did not detectably weaken the strength of the ABA renewal effect. That result was consistent with the idea that Context A might be an S^D setting the occasion for the operant response, rather than a CS that had simply entered into an association with the reinforcer. Occasion setters may be difficult to extinguish by simple nonreinforced exposure to them (e.g., see Rescorla, 1986). The fact that cues that evoke drug taking might be occasion setters is a second reason why they may sometimes resist the effects of traditional extinction.

It should be mentioned that re-presentation of discriminative stimuli themselves can also produce renewal-like effects. For example, Ghitza, Fabbricatore, Prokopenko, Pawlak, and West (2003) trained rats to self-administer cocaine in the presence of a tone stimulus. Responses that occurred in the absence of the tone were never reinforced. The rats were then given 3–4 weeks with no exposure to cocaine, the conditioning chambers, or the experimental stimuli, and were subsequently returned to the chambers for a test session. During the first hour of the test session, no tones were presented, but rats were able to lever press. In the second hour, tones were presented using the same distribution as occurred during acquisition. Despite the fact that cocaine was never presented during testing, the tone had a dramatic effect upon lever pressing. It led to more than 10 times the number of presses while it was presented than in its absence. Like a context, a nonextinguished discriminative stimulus may thus continue to support drug self-administration following extended periods of abstinence (see also Grimm, Hope, Wise, & Shaham, 2001, discussed later in the chapter).

Reinstatement of extinguished operant behaviour

In operant experiments with food pellet and/or sucrose reinforcers, non-contingent presentation of the reinforcer after extinction can cause a robust return of extinguished responding. This is especially clear when the response lever is available at the same time as the reinforcer is being presented again (e.g., Baker, 1990; Baker, Steinwald, & Bouton, 1991; Delamater, 1997; Ostlund & Balleine, 2007; Reid, 1958; Rescorla & Skucy, 1969). When animals have been trained that one response leads to one outcome (e.g., pellet) and another response leads to a different outcome (e.g., sucrose), presentation of one reinforcer can specifically reinstate the behaviour that had been associated with it (Ostlund & Balleine, 2007). The results may depend on the fact that the reinforcer becomes a simple S^D for responding during training; its delivery sets the occasion for the next response (Ostlund & Balleine, 2007). However, as in Pavlovian learning, presentation of the reinforcer also conditions the context that is in the background when reinstating reinforcer presentations occur. And this context conditioning can also cause a reinstatement of extinguished responding when testing occurs 24 h or longer after reinforcer presentation, long after the S^D effect of the reinforcer would be gone (Baker et al., 1991). This longer term form of reinstatement is specific to the context in which reinforcer presentation has occurred, can be extinguished by repeated exposure to the context between reinforcer presentation and testing, and is reduced when the reinstating reinforcers are signalled by a CS, which would compete with (overshadow) conditioning of the context (Baker et al., 1991). The translational implications are that taking a drug after a period of abstinence can initiate relapse either by setting the occasion for more immediate drug taking (the immediate S^D effect) or, because of refreshment of the drug's association with the context, motivate relapse in that context when drug taking is possible even days later.

Operant research with drug reinforcers is consistent with these conclusions. Experiments on drug self-administration demonstrate that non-contingent, postextinction presentation of the reinforcer can likewise cause a return to performance of the operant response. For example, Gerber and Stretch (1975) showed that squirrel monkeys trained to self-administer d-amphetamine and then given extinction would perform the operant response again in sessions preceded by experimenter-administered d-amphetamine. De Wit and Stewart (1981, 1983) showed a similar effect in rats, where lever pressing for administration of cocaine or heroin was, following extinction, also reinstated by noncontingent infusion of the drug. Later studies have shown such reinstatement with a variety of drug reinforcers, including methylphenidate (Botly, Burton, Rizos, & Fletcher, 2008), methamphetamine (Kruzich & Xi, 2006; Moffett & Goeders, 2007), MDMA (Banks, Sprague, Czoty, & Nader, 2008), nicotine (Chiamulera, Borgo, Falchetto, Valerio, & Tessari, 1996; but see LeSage, Burroughs, Dufek, Keyler, & Pentel, 2004), alcohol (Chiamulera, Valerio, & Tessari, 1995; Lê et al., 1998), benzodiazepines (Weerts, Kaminski, & Griffiths, 1998), and a synthetic cannabinoid (Spano et al., 2004).

Interestingly, the presentation of a new drug other than the original reinforcer can sometimes reinstate extinguished drug seeking. Thus, extinguished cocaine-reinforced operant responses may be reinstated not only by presentation of cocaine, but also by amphetamine, methylphenidate, or caffeine (Schenk & Partridge, 1999; De Vries, Schoffelmeer, Binnekade, Mulder, & Vanderschuren, 1998; Schenk, Worley, McNamara, & Valadez, 1996). Similarly, heroin-reinforced operants may be reinstated not only by heroin and morphine (Stewart & Wise, 1992), but also by amphetamine or cocaine (De Vries et al., 1998). Cannabinoid-reinforced behaviour may be reinstated by heroin, although not by cocaine (Spano et al., 2004); and alcohol-reinforced lever presses are reinstated by corticotropin-releasing factor (CRF) and 8-OH-DPAT (Lê, Harding, Juzytsch, Fletcher, & Shaham, 2002), yohimbine (Marinelli, Funk, Juzytsch, Harding, et al., 2007), and the GABAergic modulator allopregnanolone (Nie & Janak, 2003). Such cross-reinforcer effects might suggest the role of a common neural reward system. Alternatively, the drug itself might be part of the context for responding; as we noted before, drugs can function as S^Ds as well as reinforcers. On this view, whether a drug will reinstate performance that had been reinforced by another drug will depend on how much the organism generalizes between the drugs. Such interdrug **generalization** occurs and can be influenced by a variety of pharmacological and psychological (i.e., learned) factors (e.g., for nicotine, see Bevins & Palmatier, 2004; Palmatier & Bevins, 2008; Smith & Stolerman, 2009). Note that, unlike reinstatement experiments with different drug reinforcers, experiments demonstrating reinforcer-specific reinstatement with nondrug reinforcers have involved explicit discrimination training with the different response–reinforcer combinations (Ostlund & Balleine, 2007).

Although reinstatement in drug self-administration is well established across a diverse set of drugs and species, much less attention has been devoted to the behavioural mechanisms that cause it. The range of actual experimental implementations of the phenomenon might allow multiple mechanisms to operate. For example, extinction, reinstatement, and testing are often collapsed into a single session (e.g., de Wit & Stewart, 1981, 1983; Schenk & Partridge, 1999), which might allow a role for the discriminative stimulus account. The same is true when extinction occurs in separate sessions prior to a session in which the reinstating drug is presented and the subject has the opportunity to respond (e.g., De Vries et al., 1998). In other cases, each phase is separated by at least 24 h outside of the experimental apparatus (e.g., Leri & Stewart, 2002); this might allow contextual conditioning contributions to relapse (e.g., Baker et al., 1991). It is also worth noting that some procedures might allow responding to increase because the drug generally activates behaviour. Nonselective effects can be ruled out if, during the test session, the animal has a second manipulandum (e.g., lever) available that has previously been associated with a different reinforcer. A general activation effect would lead to increased responding on both manipulanda. Many experiments instead employ an inactive control lever. However, often control lever data are not reported; other times, an increase in responding on the control lever is observed. For example, although Moffett and Goeders (2007) reported a reinstatement effect of methamphetamine, the pattern of activity on the inactive lever was quite similar to the pattern on the active lever. Larson and Carroll (2006) also reported a nonselective reinstatement effect. Both of these studies support the idea that reinstatement can sometimes result from general behavioural activation.

One interesting difference between reinstatement in the laboratory and the real world is that animals are given reinstating drug presentations regardless of (not contingent on) their behaviour. In contrast, human relapse usually occurs because the human takes the drug again via the usual routes – and thus resumes the original response–reinforcer pairings. Leri and Stewart (2002) examined the importance of the response–reinforcer contingency in a heroin reinstatement study. Rats lever pressed for the delivery of heroin infusion over seven daily sessions, were then extinguished over six daily sessions, and were next given one of several different kinds of reinstatement procedures in a single 1 h session. Testing then occurred 24 h later. Exposure to a saline infusion produced no reinstatement of test behaviour. However, if the subjects were allowed to respond (in extinction) during the reinstatement session, either response-contingent or response-noncontingent heroin caused high levels of behaviour the next day. In contrast, noncontingent heroin delivered in a session in which the rats were in the box but were not allowed to lever-press produced no reinstatement of behaviour the next day. Thus, presenting the drug in the context of lever pressing was necessary for reinstatement 24 h later, although the drug could be presented noncontingently. The finding may be consistent with the view that, in addition to other exteroceptive and interoceptive stimuli, behaviour itself may provide part of the "context" that can control extinction and relapse effects. There is, in fact, other evidence that behaviour can become part of the context that controls drug tolerance (e.g., Weise-Kelly & Siegel, 2001).

Stress-induced "reinstatement" of drug self-administration

In the animal learning literature, the term reinstatement has a restricted meaning that refers to the ability of a reinforcer presented following extinction to prompt a return of the response. Within the drug self-administration literature, the term is used more broadly to describe any of a variety of behavioural treatments that can cause extinguished behaviour to return. One of the most important of these is based on evidence that stress can play an important role in causing the onset of drug craving and physiological reactivity in humans (Sinha, Catapano, & O'Malley, 1999), which is believed to contribute to relapse of drug seeking. A multitude of animal studies have now shown that exposure to stressors can also reinitiate ("reinstate") extinguished operant responding for a variety of drugs, including cocaine (Erb, Shaham, & Stewart, 1996; Ahmed & Koob, 1997), heroin (Shaham & Stewart, 1995), alcohol (Lê, Harding, Juzytsch, Funk, & Shaham, 2005), and nicotine (Buczek, Lê, Wang, Stewart, & Shaham, 1999).

Early studies of stress-induced reinstatement found that a brief session of footshock exposure was sufficient to trigger relapse of extinguished lever pressing for heroin (Shaham & Stewart, 1995) and cocaine (Erb et al., 1996) even after prolonged drug-free periods. In both of these studies, rats were trained to self-administer the drug over multiple daily training sessions until they achieved a reliable rate of lever pressing. During the extinction phase, the training conditions were kept the same except that saline was delivered in place of the drug. When the animals had reached a low level of responding, they were given a 10-min session in which mild footshocks were presented on average every 45 s just before the lever was available in extinction. Exposure to this stressor immediately and powerfully reinstated lever pressing for the drug. In fact, the degree of reinstated responding was comparable to (or even greater than) that achieved by noncontingent injections of the drug itself. Four to six weeks later a second reinstatement test yielded a similar pattern of results, underscoring the ability of stress to trigger relapse even after periods of continuous abstinence.

Other studies have obtained similar results with other drugs of abuse. However, stress does not universally reinstate all appetitive behaviours. Using a method similar to Shaham and Stewart (1995) and Erb et al. (1996), Ahmed and Koob (1997) reported that intermittent footshocks failed to reinstate extinguished lever pressing that had been reinforced with food pellets instead of cocaine. Similarly, Buczek et al. (1999) were able to reinstate nicotine seeking, but not sucrose seeking, with shock in rats. These findings are inconsistent with the idea that stressors reinstate drug-seeking by inducing a general state of arousal or behavioural activation. Buczek et al. (1999) suggested that footshock stress may activate motivational systems that interfere with food-seeking behaviour. However, why stress contrastingly reactivates drug-seeking behaviour remains unclear (see below).

Although footshock is the most commonly used stressor in reinstatement studies, a number of different stressors can also induce reinstatement of drug seeking. Shalev, Highfield, Yap, and Shaham (2000) reported that one day of food deprivation reinstated lever pressing for heroin following 10–13 days of extinction. Using the CPP paradigm, Ribeiro Do Couto et al. (2006) found that mice subjected to defeat in a social encounter exhibited a reinstated preference for an extinguished context previously paired with the rewarding effects of morphine. Similar effects were found with tail pinch and physical restraint stress. Additionally, reinstatement of operant drug seeking has been reported following administration of the stress hormone corticotropin-releasing factor (Shaham et al., 1997) and the anxiogenic drug yohimbine (Lê et al., 2005).

As noted above, the behavioural mechanisms underlying stress-induced reinstatement are not entirely clear at present. Theories of addiction have generally appreciated the fact that both positive reinforcement (i.e., the pleasant or rewarding effects of the drug) and negative reinforcement (relief from stress or withdrawal symptoms) can be involved in relapse. Whereas Koob and Le Moal (1997) have proposed that stress serves as a primer that sensitizes the brain reward systems, Sinha (2001) has suggested that stress may function as a conditioned cue that elicits craving in humans. Humans often use drugs during stressful periods or life events. As a consequence, stress may become associated with drug taking, and subsequently work as a context setting the occasion for drug seeking or a CS that motivates behaviour. Stress may also resemble a withdrawal state that motivates drug seeking to relieve symptoms. Since rats in controlled laboratory environments have less obvious opportunity to associate stress with drugs and drug taking, it is less clear why stress reinstates extinguished drug seeking in the laboratory, although some version of the above mechanisms could be involved.

Spontaneous recovery

Operant behaviour, like Pavlovian behaviour, recovers as time elapses after extinction (e.g., Rescorla, 1997, 2004). Although spontaneous recovery is well known in animal learning, it has not been analyzed extensively in drug self-administration experiments. Peters, Vallone, Laurendi, and Kalivas (2008) recently trained rats to lever press for cocaine infusions for 7–12 daily 2-h sessions. There were then 14–19 daily 2-h extinction sessions in which lever pressing no longer produced cocaine. After a month (28 ± 4 days), the rats were returned to the Skinner boxes and allowed to lever press without cocaine. Reliable spontaneous recovery was observed. Di Ciano and Everitt (2002) also reported spontaneous recovery of extinguished cocaine self-administration. The interpretation of these studies is somewhat complicated by the fact that the rats received preliminary training with food pellet reinforcers (Peters et al., 2008) or that the test session involved presentation of the reinforcer contingent on lever pressing (Di Ciano & Everitt, 2002).

Time has other effects on drug self-administration, however. Grimm et al. (2001) had rats living in Skinner boxes. Twice daily, the lights in the box were turned on and a lever was inserted; the rats could then press the lever for intravenous cocaine. After 10 days of this training, the rats were left alone in the boxes, without the light or lever, for 1, 2, 4, 7, 15, 29, or 60 days. When the light discriminative stimulus was turned on, and the lever was reinserted, the rats lever pressed again (see also Ghitza et al., 2003). But interestingly, the longer the interval between training and testing, the more the rats pressed the lever. The strength of cocaine responding thus appeared to "incubate" as time elapsed after training (see also Lu, Grimm, Hope, & Shaham, 2004). The incubation effect also occurs with sucrose reinforcers (Lu et al., 2004). Thus, the passage of time is likely to have interesting effects on operant behaviour, just as it does in Pavlovian conditioning (Pickens, Golden, Adams-Deutsch, Nair, & Shaham, 2009).

Resurgence of extinguished operant responses

Another relapse phenomenon that has been studied in operant conditioning is known as "resurgence" (e.g., Epstein, 1983). In this paradigm, a target operant behaviour is extinguished at the same time a new alternative behaviour is reinforced. The new behaviour effectively replaces the old one. However, if the alternative behaviour is then itself extinguished, the first response frequently returns. This resurgence effect (see Cleland, Guerin, Foster, & Temple, 2001, for other uses of the term) suggests that people who stop taking drugs while being reinforced for alternative behaviours may return to the original behaviour if the alternative behaviour stops paying off.

The most widely studied form of resurgence is one developed by Leitenberg, Rawson, and colleagues (e.g., Leitenberg, Rawson, & Bath, 1970; Rawson, Leitenberg, Mulick, & Lefebvre, 1977), who used a simple three-phase procedure (cf. Epstein, 1983). In the first phase, the target behaviour (e.g., pressing a lever) was reinforced; in the second it was extinguished while a new behaviour (pressing a second lever) was reinforced; and in the final test, neither behaviour was reinforced. Over a number of studies, the original response returned during the final extinction test. We have systematically replicated these results in a series of experiments (Winterbauer & Bouton, 2010) that, among other things, found that resurgence is far stronger to a lever that had previously been reinforced than to one that had never been reinforced. Thus, like the phenomena listed in Table 5.1, resurgence is a relapse effect in which post-extinction recovery of a learned activity indicates that extinction – and the simultaneous learning of new alternative behaviours – does not erase the original learning.

Leitenberg et al.'s studies resulted in the hypothesis that reinforcement of the second behaviour suppresses the first behaviour, and thus effectively prevents it from being associated with extinction. Indeed, Rawson et al. (1977) demonstrated in rat lever pressing that resurgence that occurred when the second behaviour was extinguished was equivalent in strength to the effect of simply allowing the animal to respond again to a lever that had been removed from the apparatus for the same period of time. Thus, preventing the response either explicitly (by removing the lever) or implicitly (by providing an attractive alternative behaviour to engage in) caused the same return to responding at the final test. However, our recent experiments (Winterbauer & Bouton, 2010) produced evidence challenging the response prevention hypothesis. In experiments examining the effects of different reinforcement schedules on the second lever, we observed little correlation between the rate at which the target behaviour was suppressed during extinction and the subsequent level of resurgence. For example, even groups that responded more, rather than less, on the first lever than an extinction control during the second phase showed reliable resurgence during testing. Thus, regardless of whether resurgence groups stopped emitting the target response more quickly or more slowly than control groups undergoing simple extinction, the resurgence groups showed more elevation of original lever pressing during the test, contrary to the response prevention hypothesis.

The current evidence is instead consistent with the idea that resurgence is a special example of the renewal effect. Although the physical context never changes, the context provided by both presentation of reinforcers and the animal's own behaviour changes systematically across phases. Thus, the organism first learns to respond when no reinforced alternative is available, then enters a new context (provided by the reinforcement of the new behaviour) as the first behaviour is extinguished, and finally shifts to a test context in which the second behaviour is no longer reinforced and thus declines. The changes thus provide support for an "ABC" renewal effect, which (as described above) we have recently confirmed does occur after the extinction of operant learning (Bouton et al., 2011). The renewal mechanism may not apply as readily to a second resurgence paradigm in which the first behaviour is extinguished before the new behaviour is reinforced (Epstein, 1983; Lieving & Lattal, 2003, Experiment 1). However, in this case it is conceivable that resurgence of the first behaviour is due in part to reinstatement created by reinforcer presentations during training of the second response. Indeed, we recently confirmed this hypothesis in rats (Winterbauer & Bouton, 2011). We found, for example, that pellets that were presented either contingently on the new behaviour (as in resurgence) or in a yoked, noncontingent manner (as in reinstatement) caused an equivalent recovery of the extinguished first behaviour. Thus, resurgence may be due to general mechanisms already implicated by the Table 5.1 phenomena.

Resurgence has received relatively little attention thus far in the drug self-administration literature (but see Podlesnik, Jimenez-Gomez, & Shahan, 2006, who found resurgence of ethanol-reinforced behaviour in rats). The implications for drug-taking behaviour are nonetheless clear. Replacing unwanted behaviour with a newly reinforced behaviour is the main idea behind clinical treatments in which drug users are paid with vouchers that can be used to purchase retail items as long as the patient refrains from taking the drug (e.g., Higgins et al., 2006). Although the provision of such reinforcers successfully promotes drug abstinence, the resurgence phenomenon reminds us that relapse may be a possibility once the vouchers are no longer given after treatment. According to a renewal analysis of resurgence (Winterbauer & Bouton, 2010), the presentation of vouchers might be a part of the context that distinguishes the treatment (no drug) context from the original context in which drug taking was first acquired and maintained. A goal might therefore be to fade the delivery of reinforcers during treatment so as to reduce the discriminable change of context. Although there is evidence that increasing reward magnitude facilitates abstinence (see Stitzer & Petry, 2006, for a review of effects of this and other parameters of contingency management), and that dense schedules of reinforcement are more effective than sparse ones (e.g., Ghitza et al., 2007), we know of no systematic application of declining schedules of reinforcement over the course of treatment. The resurgence effect continues to suggest that maximizing the similarity of the treatment context to the post-treatment context is a highly desirable goal of any method of treating drug dependence.

Rapid reacquisition

Renewal, reinstatement, spontaneous recovery, and resurgence are all phenomena that would lead the drug user to take the drug again after a period of abstinence or extinction. They can cause a "lapse" that brings the person back into contact with the reinforcement contingency that led to drug use in the first place. Reacquisition – the recovery of responding that occurs when the CS or action is paired with the reinforcer again – is probably essential in converting a lapse into relapse.

In both Pavlovian and operant learning, reacquisition is often rapid (Bullock & Smith, 1953; Ricker & Bouton, 1996). That is, when CS–US pairings or response–reinforcer pairings occur again after extinction, the response returns quickly over trials. Although rapid reacquisition is another phenomenon indicating that the original learning is preserved through extinction, it is too simple to claim that reacquisition is rapid merely because of that preservation. That is because in Pavlovian conditioning, the reacquisition of responding when CS–US pairings occur again after extinction can actually be *slower* than the original conditioning (Bouton, 1986; Bouton & Swartzentruber, 1989), even though there is no question that the original learning has been preserved. We have suggested that when reacquisition is slow, it might be because the prevailing context continues to retrieve extinction. When reacquisition is rapid, it likely occurs because the return of CS–US pairings returns the organism to the context of acquisition, because the organism has learned that the CS is reinforced in sessions that are full of other CS–US pairings (Ricker & Bouton, 1996). It is thus a new example of ABA renewal in which Context A is provided by the memory of recent CS–US pairings. Consistent with this idea, reacquisition is rapid in those situations in which there have been many original CS–US pairings (see Ricker & Bouton, 1996), thus providing ample opportunity to learn about the connections between sequences of reinforced trials. Of course, the typical substance abuser likewise experiences a very large number of acquisition trials. The typical two-packs-a-day smoker smokes almost 15,000 cigarettes a year. According to our hypothesis, rapid reacquisition of smoking would be expected because smoking a few cigarettes would reintroduce cues that were a part of the original smoking context.

If rapid reacquisition in Pavlovian learning is caused by CS–US pairings reintroducing the original acquisition context, then it might be possible to slow it down by undermining the connection between CS–US pairings and additional reinforced trials. Bouton et al. (2004) reasoned that the occasional presentation of a CS–US pairings among a series of extinction (CS-only) trials would do exactly that. Rats were first given an extended series of CS–food pairings. Some groups then received ordinary extinction, in which the CS was repeatedly presented alone. Other groups received a "partial reinforcement" procedure in which the CS was occasionally but infrequently paired with food, so that the CS–food pairings were embedded among a string of CS-only trials. Although this procedure reduced but never quite eliminated conditioned responding, it significantly slowed down the return of responding that occurred when CS–US pairings were reintroduced in a final reacquisition phase. The groups that received only extinction showed a relatively fast recovery of conditioned responding. The groups that had received partial reinforcement were thus slower to change. Although these rats were quicker to reacquire responding than a group that had never received initial conditioning in Phase 1, the partial reinforcement procedure slowed the very rapid reacquisition – relapse – observed in the simple extinction groups.

Woods and Bouton (2007) extended this finding to operant conditioning. Rats were first trained to lever press on a VI (variable interval) 30-s schedule of reinforcement over several daily sessions. Then, in an extinction phase that occurred over a series of daily sessions, they received either simple extinction in which the lever press produced no further reinforcement (food pellets), or a partial reinforcement procedure in which the VI schedule was gradually lengthened from VI 4 min to VI 32 min (one reinforcer earned, on average, after 32 min with no reinforcers). Again, although partial reinforcement gradually and substantially reduced responding, it did not completely eliminate it. However, when the response was then reinforced again on a VI 8 min schedule, a slower return of responding was observed in the partially reinforced group than the extinction only group. The results were mainly apparent in the animal's reaction to each renewed response–reinforcer pairings in the reacquisition phase. For the simple extinction rats, there was a high level of responding for a period of time following each new response–reinforcer pairing. In contrast, the partially reinforced subjects showed a significantly lower level of responding after each successive response–reinforcer pairing. Thus, one way to think of the partial reinforcement's effect was to decrease the tendency for individual occasions when the response was reinforced again to return the rat to a high level of responding.[1]

To date, no one has investigated this procedure using self-administration methods in which animals are reinforced for responding with drugs such as nicotine, alcohol, heroin, or cocaine. Nonetheless, the implication is that allowing the user to take an occasional drink or "hit" of a drug may help defeat the reacquisition mechanism of relapse. Interestingly, a loosely analogous procedure may be effective in treating smoking in humans. Cinciripini et al. (1994) developed a "scheduled smoking" procedure in which smokers were allowed to smoke cigarettes at predetermined instants over a 3-week period before they quit. The cigarettes were allowed at increasing intervals (analogous to our increasing VI requirement). This procedure, which was also combined with standard cognitive behaviour therapy and relapse prevention, produced abstinence rates that were higher than that produced with a control treatment in which other participants were given information about quitting smoking. A follow-up study

(Cinciripini et al., 1995) replicated this finding and suggested that a treatment that allowed cigarettes at predetermined instants, even without reducing overall consumption, was also helpful. Both of the procedures separated the consumption of cigarettes from their usual contexts (the participants presumably smoked scheduled cigarettes outside of their ordinary contexts). Although there is more work to be done to understand these effects, there is evidence consistent with the idea that occasional response–reinforcer pairings during extinction can be a promising way to prevent human relapse (see also Marlatt & Witkiewitz, 2002; Sitharthan, Sitharthan, Hough, & Kavanagh, 1997 for examples with alcohol).

Methods for preventing relapse effects

The above method for reducing the rate of reacquisition is an example of a general strategy that all of our work suggests might be effective at preventing relapse. If the therapist can find those contextual cues that are most likely to initiate relapse (renewal) in a given individual, an effective treatment would be to conduct extinction directly in the presence of those cues. The studies just reviewed accomplish this by noting that a recent CS–US or action–reinforcer pairing can be such a context. In this way, one or two drinks or smokes may lead to many more by creating an ABA renewal effect.

Bouton, Woods, Moody, Sunsay, and García-Gutiérrez (2006) distinguished between two general strategies for preventing relapse as represented in the phenomena we have discussed. The use of occasional reinforcers to slow down rapid reacquisition (Bouton et al., 2004; Woods & Bouton, 2007) is an example of a "bridging" method, a treatment that accepts that extinction is highly context-specific and attempts to bridge extinction learning from the extinction context to contexts where relapse is possible. The most straightforward bridging method is to situate extinction procedures in the contexts that are going to be most problematic. Another bridging strategy is to give the client cues that he or she can use to help remind them of the therapy experience. The rationale is that the various relapse effects occur through a failure to retrieve extinction. Animal research in Pavlovian learning indicates that both renewal (Brooks & Bouton, 1994) and spontaneous recovery (Brooks, 2000; Brooks & Bouton, 1993) can be reduced if the animal is given a cue that has been a part of the extinction session or experience just before the test. Interestingly, Collins and Brandon (2002), in their demonstration discussed earlier of renewal in college sophomores exposed to beer cues, likewise found that the renewal effect could be weakened by presenting a stimulus (a distinctive clipboard on which participants responded to questions) that had also been featured in the extinction session. Retrieval cues can probably be built into any extinction treatment.

Another method that can be seen as a bridging treatment is conducting extinction in multiple contexts. For example, in the study of renewal to an alcohol-associated CS we described earlier, Chaudhri et al. (2008) found that a group that received the same number and temporal distribution of extinction trials in a rotating series of three contexts (rather than in just one context) did not show a renewal effect when the CS was returned to and tested in the original conditioning context. One interpretation of this finding is that contexts are made up of many different cues, and by conducting extinction in the presence of multiple contexts, one connects a broader range of contextual cues with the extinction experience, and thus increases the possibility that cues in a new (renewing) environment contain features that have been through extinction. Unfortunately, although the multiple-context effect has also been reported in fear conditioning (Gunther, Denniston, & Miller, 1998), it does not appear to be a universal result (e.g., Bouton, García-Gutiérrez, Zilski, & Moody, 2006; Neumann, Lipp, & Cory, 2007). The most recent evidence suggests that it is especially likely to occur in procedures that involve a very large number of extinction trials (Thomas, Vurbic, & Novak, 2009). This result might suggest that, instead of enhancing generalization across contexts (that presumably could occur with less extensive extinction training), the effect may be making extinction learning deeper and especially effective by reducing the amount of "protection from extinction" (e.g., Rescorla, 2003) produced by inhibitory conditioning of the context that might contribute to the renewal seen after extensive extinction in a single context.

The other general strategy for preventing relapse is to find ways to optimize or deepen the extinction learning (Bouton, Woods, et al., 2006). For example, although phenomena like renewal appear to survive a very large number of extinction trials (e.g., Bouton & Swartzentruber, 1989), there is evidence that "massive" exposure to the CS during extinction (800 extinction trials after 8 initial fear conditioning trials) may weaken renewal (Denniston, Chang, & Miller, 2003). Another behavioural method that might deepen extinction learning is suggested by the idea that extinction learning is driven by error correction, in which the learning system works to decrease the discrepancy between what the CS predicts (a US or reinforcer) and what actually occurs on an extinction trial (nothing). To increase the predictive error during extinction, several investigators have combined two or more CSs into a stimulus compound and presented the compound without a US. Theoretically, putting the CSs in a compound allows their separate predictions to summate, generating a greater prediction of a US and thus more error that needs correcting. There is consequently greater associative loss (Rescorla, 2000; Thomas & Ayres, 2004; Rescorla & Wagner, 1972). We do not know of any experiments that have tested the idea in a discriminated operant setting (i.e., examining the effects of combining two separately trained S^Ds during extinction). And it is important to note that in the one investigation of this hypothesis in humans, there was so little generalization between the extinguished compound stimulus and the single CS tested that there was an *increase* in responding when the CS was tested outside of the extinguished compound (Vervliet, Vansteenwegen, Hermans, & Eelen, 2007). Thus, adding an extra cue to extinction can backfire by creating a new context and producing a new kind of renewal effect.

Still other methods are available to deepen extinction learning. For example, there has been growing interest in d-cycloserine (DCS), a partial agonist of the NMDA receptor, as a potential adjunct to extinction therapy. Interest in DCS stems from the idea, advocated here and elsewhere, that extinction involves new learning. The NMDA receptor is critically involved in "long-term potentiation", a physiological process that facilitates the connection between neurons and is widely held to be a cellular model of new learning. Accordingly, numerous studies have established that DCS facilitates extinction learning in both animals (e.g., Walker, Ressler, Lu, & Davis, 2002) and humans (e.g., Ressler et al., 2004). Motivated by this evidence, a number of recent studies have investigated the use of DCS in extinction of drug-associated cues and drug-seeking behaviour. For example, Botreau, Paolone, and Stewart (2006) were able to show such a benefit of DCS in an appetitive situation using cocaine-induced CPP. After establishing a conditioned preference for the cocaine-paired context, rats were given several sessions of extinction in which they were exposed to the entire apparatus in the absence of the drug. DCS treatment was given after each extinction session in order to target the consolidation process that DCS is believed to enhance. Over the course of extinction, preference for the cocaine-paired context decreased more rapidly in rats treated with DCS. In a follow-up study the authors reported that the effect of DCS treatment persisted across a 2-week retention interval and, more remarkably, was resistant to cocaine-induced reinstatement (Paolone, Botreau, & Stewart, 2009). Similar effects on cocaine-induced CPP have been reported in mice (Thanos, Bermeo, Wang, & Volkow, 2009) and with rats in amphetamine-induced CPP (Sakurai, Yu, & Tan, 2007). Benefits of using DCS treatment during extinction have also been shown using operant procedures for food (Shaw et al., 2009), intravenous cocaine (Nic Dhonnchadha et al., 2010), and alcohol reinforcers (Vengeliene, Kiefer, & Spanagel, 2008). In the latter study, rats were trained to lever press for 10 percent alcohol, after which they were given multiple sessions in which both lever presses and a response-contingent auditory cue (conditioned reinforcer) that had also been associated with alcohol during training occurred without alcohol (i.e., were extinguished). Compared with saline-treated controls, rats that were treated with DCS showed faster extinction of alcohol seeking and less alcohol-induced reinstatement. It is interesting to note that all of the operant studies on DCS included extinction of an explicit conditioned reinforcer during the extinction phase, perhaps allowing DCS to facilitate *Pavlovian* extinction of that cue. We (Vurbic, Gold, & Bouton, 2011) have had less success uncovering a DCS effect on the extinction of an operant response reinforced by food that did not involve extinction of an explicit conditioned reinforcer. However, the results overall begin to suggest that DCS may have some clinical utility in the treatment of drug-seeking behaviour.

Another problem, of course, is that a drug that speeds up extinction learning will not necessarily change the context-specific nature of extinction. Consistent with this idea, we have shown that fear extinction learning facilitated by DCS is still context-specific, and thus vulnerable to relapse in the form of the renewal effect (Bouton, Vurbic, & Woods, 2008; Woods & Bouton, 2006). Moreover, a similar pattern emerged with another drug that has been considered as an adjunct to facilitate fear extinction – yohimbine (Morris & Bouton, 2007). Although combination of this drug with extinction training did facilitate the loss of fear, it did not eliminate the renewal effect. Rats extinguished with yohimbine showed strong renewal of fear when tested in the original fear conditioning context (ABA renewal) or in a third, neutral one (ABC renewal). The broad implication of the results of these studies seems clear. Although there is some evidence that DCS effects on extinction of a conditioned reinforcer associated with cocaine may transfer to some extent across contexts (Torregrossa, Sanchez, & Taylor, 2010), future studies investigating the effects of new compounds on extinction should take care to test the effects of an extinction enhancer on this and other relapse effects.

Other possibilities are suggested by the neuroscience of learning and memory. We know that recently learned memories are easy to disrupt before they are converted into a permanent memory or record in the brain. Memory "consolidation" requires the synthesis of new brain proteins, and can be blocked by injection of compounds that inhibit protein synthesis (e.g., anisomycin). Interestingly, if a learned and consolidated memory is *re*activated by presentation of a retrieval cue, reactivation returns the memory briefly to a vulnerable state that can also be blocked by protein synthesis inhibitors. Thus, a single presentation of the CS after a fear conditioning experience can allow the memory to be disrupted by anisomycin (e.g., Nader, Schafe, & LeDoux, 2000). That is, there is little evidence of fear when the CS is tested later; anisomycin is said to block "reconsolidation" of the fear memory. Propranolol, a β-adrenergic blocker, also blocks reactivated fear memories (e.g., Debiec & LeDoux, 2004), and parallel results have recently been reported in humans given fear conditioning. In this case, the presentation of propranolol during a reexposure to the CS eliminated signs of fear when the CS was tested later, although it did not eliminate self-reported knowledge of the CS–US contingency (Kindt, Soeter, & Vervliet, 2009). To our knowledge, no similar effects have been reported with CS–drug or operant–drug learning, but we suspect that investigations of them are coming soon. Importantly, as we have seen with extinction, it is essential to remember that the absence of a behaviour after treatment does not necessarily reflect the erasure of memory. There is evidence that fear of the CS that has been reduced by reconsolidation in mice returns over time (i.e., spontaneously recovers) (e.g., Lattal & Abel,

2004). Whether the reconsolidation procedure will eliminate the relapse processes identified in the laboratory is thus still an open and important research question.

Conclusion

There is ample evidence that learning can survive extinction and possibly other treatments (as identified, for example, in reconsolidation and resurgence). The return of conditioned behaviour after extinction can be viewed as an example of relapse. Basic laboratory research on Pavlovian and operant learning suggests a number of such relapse effects. We have argued that all are generally context effects that ultimately flow from the fact that extinction is a form of learning that is especially dependent on the context for retrieval. This perspective leads us to conclude that treatments that will be especially effective at preventing relapse will be the ones that somehow make extinction learning less context-specific, or connect extinction with contextual cues that are especially likely to initiate an individual's lapse and relapse.

Acknowledgements

Preparation of the manuscript was supported by Grant MH R01 MH064847 from the U.S. National Institute of Mental Health to MEB. We thank Travis Todd for his comments.

Note

1 It should be noted that response-independent (Woods & Bouton, 2007) and CS-independent (Bouton et al., 2004) reinforcers caused even stronger interference with reacquisition. Thus, if a clinician could arrange noncontingent reinforcers during extinction, even stronger protection against rapid reacquisition might be obtained.

References

Ahmed, S. H., & Koob, G. F. (1997). Cocaine- but not food-seeking behavior is reinstated by stress after extinction. *Psychopharmacology*, *132*, 289–295.

Baker, A. G. (1990). Contextual conditioning during free-operant extinction: Unsignaled, signaled, and backward-signaled noncontingent food. *Animal Learning & Behavior*, *18*, 59–70.

Baker, A. G., Steinwald, H., & Bouton, M. E. (1991). Contextual conditioning and reinstatement of extinguished instrumental responding. *The Quarterly Journal of Experimental Psychology*, *43B*, 199–218.

Banks, M. L., Sprague, J. E., Czoty, P. W., & Nader, M. A. (2008). Effects of ambient temperature on the relative reinforcing strength of MDMA using a choice procedure in monkeys. *Psychopharmacology*, *196*, 63–70.

Berridge, K. C., & Robinson, T. E. (2003). Parsing reward. *Trends in Neurosciences*, *26*, 507–513.

Bevins, R. A., & Palmatier, M. I. (2004). Extending the role of associative learning processes in nicotine addiction. *Behavioral and Cognitive Neuroscience Reviews*, *3*, 143–158.

Bossert, J. M., Gray, S. M., Lu, L., & Shaham, Y. (2006). Activation of group II metabotropic glutamate receptors in the nucleus accumbens shell attenuates context-induced relapse to heroin seeking. *Neuropsychopharmacology*, *31*, 2197–2209.

Bossert, J. M., Liu, S. Y., Lu, L., & Shaham, Y. (2004). A role of ventral tegmental area glutamate in contextual cue-induced relapse to heroin seeking. *The Journal of Neuroscience*, *24*, 10726–10730.

Bossert, J. M., Poles, G. C., Wihbey, K. A., Koya, E., & Shaham, Y. (2007). Differential effects of blockade of dopamine D1-family receptors in nucleus accumbens core or shell on reinstatement of heroin seeking induced by contextual and discrete cues. *Journal of Neuroscience*, *27*, 12655–12663.

Botly, L. C. P., Burton, C. L., Rizos, Z., & Fletcher, P. J. (2008). Characterization of methylphenidate self-administration and reinstatement in the rat. *Psychopharmacology*, *199*, 55–66.

Botreau, F., Paolone, G., & Stewart, J. (2006). D-cycloserine facilitates extinction of a cocaine-induced conditioned place preference. *Behavioural Brain Research*, *172*, 173–178.

Bouton, M. E. (1984). Differential control by context in the inflation and reinstatement paradigms. *Journal of Experimental Psychology: Animal Behavior Processes*, *10*, 56–74.

Bouton, M. E. (1986). Slow reacquisition following the extinction of conditioned suppression. *Learning and Motivation*, *17*, 1–15.

Bouton, M. E. (1988). Context and ambiguity in the extinction of emotional learning: Implications for exposure therapy. *Behaviour Research and Therapy*, *26*, 137–149.

Bouton, M. E. (1993). Context, time, and memory retrieval in the interference paradigms of Pavlovian learning. *Psychological Bulletin*, *114*, 80–99.

Bouton, M. E. (2002). Context, ambiguity, and unlearning: Sources of relapse after behavioral extinction. *Biological Psychiatry*, *52*, 976–986.

Bouton, M. E. (2004). Context and behavioral processes in extinction. *Learning & Memory*, *11*, 485–494.

Bouton, M. E., García-Gutiérrez, A., Zilski, J., & Moody, E. W. (2006). Extinction in multiple contexts does not necessarily make extinction less vulnerable to relapse. *Behaviour Research and Therapy*, *44*, 983–994.

Bouton, M. E., Kenney, F. A., & Rosengard, C. (1990). State-dependent fear extinction with two benzodiazepine tranquilizers. *Behavioral Neuroscience*, *104*, 44–55.

Bouton, M. E., & Swartzentruber, D. (1989). Slow reacquisition following extinction: Context, encoding, and retrieval mechanisms. *Journal of Experimental Psychology: Animal Behavior Processes*, *15*, 43–53.

Bouton, M. E., Todd, T. P., Vurbic, D., & Winterbauer, N. E. (2011). Renewal after the extinction of free operant behavior. *Learning & Behavior*, *39*, 57–67.

Bouton, M. E., Vurbic, D., & Woods, A. M. (2008). D-cycloserine facilitates context-specific fear extinction learning. *Neurobiology of Learning and Memory*, *90*, 504–510.

Bouton, M. E., Westbrook, R. F., Corcoran, K. A., & Maren, S. (2006). Contextual and temporal modulation of extinction: Behavioral and brain mechanisms. *Biological Psychiatry*, *60*, 352–360.

Bouton, M. E., & Woods, A. M. (2008). Extinction: Behavioral mechanisms and their implications. In J. H. Byrne, D. Sweatt, R. Menzel, H. Eichenbaum, & H. Roediger (Eds.), *Learning and memory: A comprehensive reference: Vol. 1. Learning theory and behaviour* (pp. 151–171). Oxford, UK: Elsevier.

Bouton, M. E., Woods, A. M., Moody, E. W., Sunsay, C., & García-Gutiérrez, A. (2006). Counteracting the context-dependence of extinction: Relapse and tests of some relapse prevention methods. In M. G. Craske, D. Hermans, & D. Vansteenwegen (Eds.), *Fear and learning: Basic science to clinical application* (pp. 175–196). Washington, DC: American Psychological Association.

Bouton, M. E., Woods, A. M., & Pineño, O. (2004). Occasional reinforced trials during extinction can slow the rate of rapid reacquisition. *Learning and Motivation*, *35*, 371–390.

Brooks, D. C. (2000). Recent and remote extinction cues reduce spontaneous recovery. *Quarterly Journal of Experimental Psychology*, *53B*, 25–58.

Brooks, D. C., & Bouton, M. E. (1993). A retrieval cue for extinction attenuates spontaneous recovery. *Journal of Experimental Psychology: Animal Behavior Processes*, *19*, 77–89.

Brooks, D. C., & Bouton, M. E. (1994). A retrieval cue for extinction attenuates response recovery (renewal) caused by a return to the conditioning context. *Journal of Experimental Psychology: Animal Behavior Processes*, *20*, 366–379.

Buczek, Y., Lê, A. D., Wang, A., Stewart, J., & Shaham, Y. (1999). Stress reinstates nicotine seeking but not sucrose solution seeking in rats. *Psychopharmacology*, *144*, 183–188.

Bullock, D. H., & Smith, W. C. (1953). An effect of repeated conditioning-extinction upon operant strength. *Journal of Experimental Psychology*, *46*, 349–352.

Carter, B. L., & Tiffany, S. T. (1999). Meta-analysis of cue-reactivity in addiction research. *Addiction*, *94*, 327–340.

Chaudhri, N., Sahuque, L. L., & Janak, P. H. (2008). Context-induced relapse of conditioned behavioral responding to ethanol cues in rats. *Biological Psychiatry*, *64*, 203–210.

Chiamulera, C., Borgo, C., Falchetto, S., Valerio, E., & Tessari, M. (1996). Nicotine reinstatement of nicotine self-administration after long-term extinction. *Psychopharmacology*, *127*, 102–107.

Chiamulera, C., Valerio, E., & Tessari, M. (1995). Resumption of ethanol seeking behaviour in rats. *Behavioural Pharmacology*, *6*, 32–39.

Cinciripini, P. M., Lapitsky, L., Seay, S., Wallfisch, A., Kitchens, K., & Vunakis, H. V. (1995). The effects of smoking schedules on cessation outcome: Can we improve on common methods of gradual and abrupt nicotine withdrawal? *Journal of Consulting and Clinical Psychology*, *63*, 388–399.

Cinciripini, P. M., Lapitsky, L. G., Wallfisch, A., Mace, R., Nezami, E., & Vunakis, H. V. (1994). An evaluation of a multicomponent treatment program involving scheduled smoking and relapse prevention procedures: Initial findings. *Addictive Behaviors*, *19*, 13–22.

Cleland, B. S., Guerin, B., Foster, T. M., & Temple, W. (2001). On terms: Resurgence. *The Behavior Analyst, 24,* 255–260.

Collins, B. N., & Brandon, T. H. (2002). Effects of extinction context and retrieval cues on alcohol cue reactivity among nonalcoholic drinkers. *Journal of Consulting & Clinical Psychology, 70,* 390–397.

Conklin, C. A., & Tiffany, S. T. (2002). Applying extinction research and theory to cue-exposure addictive treatments. *Addiction, 97,* 155–167.

Crombag, H. S., Grimm, J. W., & Shaham, Y. (2002). Effect of dopamine receptor antagonists on renewal of cocaine seeking by reexposure to drug-associated contextual cues. *Neuropsychopharmacology, 27,* 1006–1015.

Crombag, H. S., & Shaham, Y. (2002). Renewal of drug seeking by contextual cues after prolonged extinction in rats. *Behavioral Neuroscience, 116,* 169–173.

Cunningham, C. L. (1979). Alcohol as a cue for extinction: State dependency produced by conditioned inhibition. *Animal Learning & Behavior, 7,* 45–52.

Debiec, J., & LeDoux, J. E. (2004). Disruption of reconsolidation but not consolidation of auditory fear conditioning by noradrenergic blockade in the amygdale. *Neuroscience, 129,* 267–272.

Delamater, A. R. (1997). Selective reinstatement of stimulus-outcome associations. *Animal Learning & Behavior, 25,* 400–412.

Denniston, J. C., Chang, R. C., & Miller, R. R. (2003). Massive extinction treatment attenuates the renewal effect. *Learning and Motivation, 34,* 68–86.

De Vries, T. J., Schoffelmeer, A. N. M., Binnekade, R., Mulder, A. H., & Vanderschuren, L. J. M. J. (1998). Drug-induced reinstatement of heroin and cocaine-seeking behaviour following long-term extinction is associated with expression of behavioural sensitization. *European Journal of Neuroscience, 10,* 3565–3571.

de Wit, H., & Stewart, J. (1981). Reinstatement of cocaine-reinforced responding in the rat. *Psychopharmacology, 75,* 134–143.

de Wit, H., & Stewart, J. (1983). Drug reinstatement of heroin-reinforced respond- ing in the rat. *Psychopharmacology, 79,* 29–31.

Di Ciano, P., & Everitt, B. J. (2002). Reinstatement and spontaneous recovery of cocaine-seeking following extinction and different durations of withdrawal. *Behavioural Pharmacology, 13,* 397–405.

Dickinson, A., & Balleine, B. W. (1994). Motivational control of goal directed action. *Animal Learning & Behavior, 22,* 1–18.

Epstein, R. (1983). Resurgence of previously reinforced behavior during extinction. *Behaviour Analysis Letters, 3,* 391–397.

Erb, S., Shaham, Y., & Stewart, J. (1996). Stress reinstates cocaine-seeking behavior after prolonged extinction and a drug-free period. *Psychopharmacology, 128,* 408–412.

Foltin, R. W., & Haney, M. (2000). Conditioned effects of environmental stimuli paired with smoked cocaine in humans. *Psychopharmacology, 149,* 24–33.

Fuchs, R. A., Evans, K. A., Ledford, C. C., Parker, M. P., Case, J. M., Mehta, R. H., et al. (2005). The role of the dorsomedial prefrontal cortex, basolateral amygdala, and dorsal hippocampus in contextual reinstatement of cocaine seeking in rats. *Neuropsychopharmacology, 30,* 296–309.

Gerber, G. J., & Stretch, R. (1975). Drug-induced reinstatement of extinguished self- administration behavior in monkeys. *Pharmacology Biochemistry and Behavior, 3,* 1055–1061.

Ghitza, U. E., Epstein, D. H., Schmittner, J., Vahabzadeh, M., Lin, J. L., & Preston, K. L. (2007). Randomized trial of prize-based reinforcement density for simultaneous abstinence from cocaine and heroin. *Journal of Consulting and Clinical Psychology, 75*, 765–774.

Ghitza, U. E., Fabbricatore, A. T., Prokopenko, V., Pawlak, A. P., & West, M. O. (2003). Persistent cue-evoked activity of accumbens neurons after prolonged abstinence from self-administered cocaine. *Journal of Neuroscience, 23*, 7239–7245.

Grimm, J. W., Hope, B. T., Wise, R. A., & Shaham, Y. (2001). Incubation of cocaine craving after withdrawal. *Nature, 412*, 141–142.

Gunther, L. M., Denniston, J. C., & Miller, R. R. (1998). Conducting exposure treatment in multiple contexts can prevent relapse. *Behaviour Research and Therapy, 36*, 75–91.

Hamlin, A. S., Blatchford, K. E., & McNally, G. P. (2006). Renewal of an extinguished instrumental response: Neural correlates and the role of D1 dopamine receptors. *Neuroscience, 143*, 25–38.

Hamlin, A. S., Clemens, K. J., & McNally, G. P. (2008). Renewal of extinguished cocaine seeking. *Neuroscience, 151*, 659–670.

Hamlin, A. S., Newby, J., & McNally, G. P. (2007). The neural correlates and role of D1 dopamine receptors in renewal of extinguished alcohol-seeking. *Neuroscience, 146*, 525–536.

Higgins, S. T., Heil, S. H., Dantona, R., Donham, R., Matthews, M., & Badger, G. J. (2006). Effects of varying the monetary value of voucher-based incentives on abstinence achieved during and following treatment among cocaine-dependent outpatients. *Addiction, 102*, 271–281.

Hogarth, L., Dickinson, A., & Duka, T. (2010). The associative basis of cue elicited drug taking in humans. *Psychopharmacology, 208*, 337–351.

Hogarth, L., Dickinson, A., Wright, A., Kouvaraki, M., & Duka, T. (2007). The role of drug expectancy in the control of human drug seeking. *Journal of Experimental Psychology-Animal Behavior Processes, 33*, 484–496.

Hughes, J. R., Keely, J., & Naud, S. (2004). Shape of relapse curve and long-term abstinence among untreated smokers. *Addiction, 99*, 29–38.

Hunt, W. A., Barnett, L. W., & Branch, L. G. (1971). Relapse rates in addiction programs. *Journal of Clinical Psychiatry, 27*, 455–456.

Kearns, D. N., & Weiss, S. J. (2007). Contextual renewal of cocaine seeking in rats and its attenuation by the conditioned effects of an alternative reinforcer. *Drug and Alcohol Dependence, 90*, 193–202.

Kindt, M., Soeter, M., & Vervliet, B. (2009). Beyond extinction: Erasing human fear responses and preventing the return of fear. *Nature Neuroscience, 12*, 256–258.

Kirshenbaum, A. P., Olsen, D. M., & Bickel, W. K. (2009). A quantitative review of the ubiquitous relapse curve. *Journal of Substance Abuse Treatment, 36*, 8–17.

Koob, G. F., & Le Moal, M. (1997). Drug abuse: Hedonic homeostatic dysregulation. *Science, 278*, 52–58.

Kruzich, P., & Xi, J. (2006). Differences in extinction responding and reinstatement of methamphetamine-seeking behavior between Fischer 344 and Lewis rats. *Pharmacology Biochemistry and Behavior, 83*, 391–395.

Larson, E., & Carroll, M. (2006). Estrogen receptor α but not β mediates estrogens effect on cocaine-induced reinstatement of extinguished cocaine-seeking behavior in ovariectomized female rats. *Neuropsychopharmacology, 32*, 1334–1345.

Lattal, K. M. (2007). Effects of ethanol on the encoding, consolidation, and expression of extinction following contextual fear conditioning. *Behavioral Neuroscience, 121*, 1280–1292.

Lattal, K. M., & Abel, T. (2004). Behavioral impairments caused by injections of the protein synthesis inhibitor anisomycin after contextual retrieval reverse with time. *Proceedings of the National Academy of Sciences, 101*, 4667–4672.

Lê, A. D., Harding, S., Juzytsch, W., Fletcher, P. J., & Shaham, Y. (2002). The role of corticotropin-releasing factor in the median raphe nucleus in relapse to alcohol. *Journal of Neuroscience, 22*, 7844–7849.

Lê, A. D., Harding, S., Juzytsch, W., Funk, D., & Shaham, Y. (2005). Role of alpha-2 adrenoceptors in stress-induced reinstatement of alcohol seeking and alcohol self-administration in rats. *Psychopharmacology, 179*, 366–373.

Lê, A. D., Quan, B., Juzytch, W., Fletcher, P. J., Joharchi, N., & Shaham, Y. (1998). Reinstatement of alcohol-seeking by priming injections of alcohol and exposure to stress in rats. *Psychopharmacology, 135*, 169–174.

Leitenberg, H., Rawson, R. A., & Bath, K. (1970). Reinforcement of competing behavior during extinction. *Science, 169*, 301–303.

Leri, F., & Stewart, J. (2002). The consequences of different "lapses" on relapse to heroin seeking in rats. *Experimental and Clinical Psychopharmacology, 10*, 339–349.

LeSage, M. G., Burroughs, D., Dufek, M., Keyler, D. E., & Pentel, P. R. (2004). Reinstatement of nicotine self-administration in rats by presentation of nicotine-paired stimuli, but not nicotine priming. *Pharmacology Biochemistry and Behavior, 79*, 507–513.

Lieving, G. A., & Lattal, K. A. (2003). Recency, repeatability, and reinforcer retrenchment: An experimental analysis of resurgence. *Journal of the Experimental Analysis of Behavior, 80*, 217–234.

Lu, L., Grimm, J. W., Hope, B. T., & Shaham, Y. (2004). Incubation of cocaine craving after withdrawal: A review of preclinical data. *Neuropharmacology, 47*, 214–226.

MacKillop, J., & Lisman, S. A. (2008). Effects of a context shift and multiple context extinction on reactivity to alcohol cues. *Experimental and Clinical Psychopharmacology, 16*, 322–331.

Marinelli, P. W., Funk, D., Juzytsch, W., Harding, S., Rice, K. L., Shaham, Y., et al. (2007). The CRF 1 receptor antagonist antalarmin attenuates yohimbine-induced increases in operant alcohol self-administration and reinstatement of alcohol seeking in rats. *Psychopharmacology, 195*, 345–355.

Marinelli, P. W., Funk, D., Juzytsch, W., Li, Z., & Lê, A. D. (2007). Effects of opioid receptor blockade on the renewal of alcohol seeking induced by context: Relationship to c-fos mRNA expression. *European Journal of Neuroscience, 26*, 2815–2823.

Marlatt, G. A., & Witkiewitz, K. (2002). Harm reduction approaches to alcohol use: Health promotion, prevention, and treatment. *Addictive Behaviors, 27*, 867–886.

Moffett, M. C., & Goeders, N. E. (2007). CP-154,526, a CRF type-1 receptor antagonist, attenuates the cue- and methamphetamine-induced reinstatement of extinguished methamphetamine-seeking behavior in rats. *Psychopharmacology, 190*, 171–180.

Morris, R. W., & Bouton, M. E. (2007). The effect of yohimbine on the extinction of conditioned fear: A role for context. *Behavioral Neuroscience, 121*, 501–514.

Nader, K., Schafe, G. E., & LeDoux, J. E. (2000). Fear memories require protein synthesis in the amygdala for reconsolidation after retrieval. *Nature, 406,* 722–726.

Nakajima, S., Tanaka, S., Urushihara, K., & Imada, H. (2000). Renewal of extinguished lever-press responses upon return to the training context. *Learning and Motivation, 31,* 416–431.

Neumann, D. L., Lipp, O. V., & Cory, S. E. (2007). Conducting extinction in multiple contexts does not necessarily attenuate the renewal of shock expectancy in a fear-conditioning procedure with humans. *Behavior Research and Therapy, 45,* 385–394.

Nic Dhonnchadha, B. A., Szalay, J. J., Achat-Mendes, C., Platt, D. M., Otto, M. W., Spealman, R. D., et al. (2010). D-cycloserine deters reacquisition of cocaine self-administration by augmenting extinction learning. *Neuropsychopharmacology, 35,* 357–367.

Nie, H., & Janak, P. H. (2003). Comparison of reinstatement of ethanol- and sucrose-seeking by conditioned stimuli and priming injections of allopregnanolone after extinction in rats. *Psychopharmacology, 168,* 222–228.

Ostlund, S. B., & Balleine, B. W. (2007). Selective reinstatement of instrumental performance depends on the discriminative stimulus properties of the mediating outcome. *Learning & Behavior, 35,* 43–52.

Palmatier, M. I., & Bevins, R. A. (2008). Occasion setting by drug states: Functional equivalence following similar training history. *Behavioural Brain Research, 195,* 260–270.

Paolone, G., Botreau, F., & Stewart, J. (2009). The facilitative effects of D-cycloserine on extinction of a cocaine-induced conditioned place preference can be long lasting and resistant to reinstatement. *Psychopharmacology, 202,* 403–409.

Parker, L. A., Limebeer, C. L., & Slomke, J. (2006). Renewal effect: Context-dependent extinction of a cocaine- and a morphine-induced conditioned floor preference. *Psychopharmacology, 187,* 133–137.

Peters, J., Vallone, J., Laurendi, K., & Kalivas, P. W. (2008). Opposing roles for the ventral prefrontal cortex and the basolateral amygdala on the spontaneous recovery of cocaine-seeking in rats. *Psychopharmacology, 197,* 310–326.

Pickens, C. L., Golden, S. A., Adams-Deutsch, T., Nair, S. G., & Shaham, Y. (2009). Long-lasting incubation of conditioned fear in rats. *Biological Psychiatry, 65,* 881–886.

Podlesnik, C. A., Jimenez-Gomez, C., & Shahan, T. A. (2006). Resurgence of alcohol seeking produced by discontinuing non-drug reinforcement as an animal model of drug relapse. *Behavioural Pharmacology, 17,* 369–374.

Rawson, R. A., Leitenberg, H., Mulick, J. A., & Lefebvre, M. F. (1977). Recovery of extinction responding in rats following discontinuation of reinforcement of alternative behavior: A test of two explanations. *Animal Learning & Behavior, 5,* 415–420.

Reid, R. L. (1958). The role of the reinforcer as a stimulus. *British Journal of Psychology, 49,* 202–209.

Rescorla, R. A. (1986). Extinction of facilitation. *Journal of Experimental Psychology: Animal Behavior Processes, 12,* 16–24.

Rescorla, R. A. (1997). Response inhibition in extinction. *Quarterly Journal of Experimental Psychology, 50B,* 238–252.

Rescorla, R. A. (2000). Extinction can be enhanced by a concurrent exciter. *Journal of Experimental Psychology: Animal Behavior Processes, 26*, 251–260.

Rescorla, R. A. (2003). Protection from extinction. *Learning & Behavior, 31*, 124–132.

Rescorla, R. A. (2004). Spontaneous recovery. *Learning & Memory, 11*, 501–509.

Rescorla, R. A., & Skucy, J. C. (1969). Effect of response-independent reinforcers during extinction. *Journal of Comparative & Physiological Psychology, 67*, 381–389.

Rescorla, R. A., & Solomon, R. L. (1967). Two-process learning theory: Relationships between Pavlovian conditioning and instrumental learning. *Psychological Review, 74*, 151–182.

Rescorla, R. A., & Wagner, A. R. (1972). A theory of Pavlovian conditioning: Variations in the effectiveness of reinforcement and nonreinforcement. In A. H. Black & W. K. Prokasy (Eds.), *Classical conditioning II: Current research and theory* (pp. 64–99). New York, NY: Appleton-Century-Crofts.

Ressler, K. J., Rothbaum, B. O., Tannenbaum, L., Anderson, P., Graap, K., Zimand, E., et al. (2004). Cognitive enhancers as adjuncts to psychotherapy: Use of d-cycloserine in phobic individuals to facilitate extinction of fear. *Archives of General Psychiatry, 61*, 1136–1144.

Ribeiro Do Couto, B., Aguilar, M. A., Manzanedo, C., Rodriguez-Arias, M., Armario, A., & Miñarro, J. (2006). Social stress is as effective as physical stress in reinstating morphine-induced place preference in mice. *Psychopharmacology, 185*, 459–470.

Ricker, S. T., & Bouton, M. E. (1996). Reacquisition following extinction in appetitive conditioning. *Animal Learning & Behavior, 24*, 423–436.

Robbins, S. J., Ehrman, R. N., Childress, A. R., & O'Brien, C. P. (1999). Comparing levels of cocaine cue reactivity in male and female outpatients. *Drug and Alcohol Dependence, 53*, 223–230.

Rosas, J. M., & Bouton, M. E. (1998). Context change and retention interval can have additive, rather than interactive, effects after taste aversion extinction. *Psychonomic Bulletin & Review, 5*, 79–83.

Rosas, J. M., Vila, N. J., Lugo, M., & Lopez, L. (2001). Combined effect of context change and retention interval on interference in causality judgments. *Journal of Experimental Psychology: Animal Behavior Processes, 27*, 153–164.

Sakurai, S., Yu, L., & Tan, S. E. (2007). Roles of hippocampal N-methyl-D-aspartate receptors and calcium/calmodulin-dependent protein kinase II in amphetamine-produced conditioned place preference in rats. *Behavioural Pharmacology, 18*, 497–506.

Schenk, S., & Partridge, B. (1999). Cocaine-seeking produced by experimenter-administered drug injections: Dose–effect relationships in rats. *Psychopharmacology, 147*, 285–290.

Schenk, S., Worley, C. M., McNamara, C., & Valadez, A. (1996). Acute and repeated exposure to caffeine: Effects on reinstatement of extinguished cocaine-taking behavior in rats. *Psychopharmacology, 126*, 17–23.

Shaham, Y., Funk, D., Erb, S., Brown, T. J., Walker, C., & Stewart, J. (1997). Corticotropin-releasing factor, but not corticosterone, is involved in stress-induced relapse to heroin-seeking in rats. *Journal of Neuroscience, 17*, 2605–2614.

Shaham, Y., & Stewart, J. (1995). Stress reinstates heroin-seeking in drug-free animals: An effect mimicking heroin, not withdrawal. *Psychopharmacology, 119,* 334–341.

Shalev, U., Highfield, D., Yap, J., & Shaham, Y. (2000). Stress and relapse to drug seeking in rats: Studies on the generality of the effect. *Psychopharmacology, 150,* 337–346.

Shaw, D., Norwood, K., Sharp, K., Quigley, L., McGovern, S. F. J., & Leslie, J. C. (2009). Facilitation of operant behavior by D-cycloserine. *Psychopharmacology, 202,* 397–402.

Siegel, S. (2008). Learning and the wisdom of the body. *Learning & Behavior, 36,* 242–252.

Sinha, R. (2001). How does stress increase risk of drug abuse and relapse? *Psychopharmacology, 158,* 343–359.

Sinha, R., Catapano, D., & O'Malley, S. (1999). Stress-induced craving and stress response in cocaine dependent individuals. *Psychopharmacology, 142,* 343–351.

Sitharthan, T., Sitharthan, G., Hough, M. J., & Kavanagh, D. J. (1997). Cue exposure in moderation drinking: A comparison with cognitive-behavior therapy. *Journal of Consulting & Clinical Psychology, 65,* 878–882.

Smith, J. W., & Stolerman, I. P. (2009). Recognising nicotine: The neurobiological basis of nicotine discrimination. In J. E. Henningfield, E. D. London, & S. Pogun (Eds.), *Nicotine psychopharmacology* (pp. 295–333). Berlin: Springer-Verlag.

Spano, M. S., Fattore, L., Cossu, G., Deiana, S., Fadda, P., & Fratta, W. (2004). CB1 receptor agonist and heroin, but not cocaine, reinstate cannabinoid-seeking behaviour in the rat. *British Journal of Pharmacology, 143,* 343–350.

Stasiewicz, P. R., Brandon, T. H., & Bradizza, C. M. (2007). Effects of extinction context and retrieval cues on renewal of alcohol-cue reactivity among alcohol-dependent outpatients. *Psychology of Addictive Behaviors, 21,* 244–248.

Stewart, J., & Wise, R. A. (1992). Reinstatement of heroin self-administration habits: Morphine prompts and naltrexone discourages renewed responding after extinction. *Psychopharmacology, 108,* 79–84.

Stewart, J., de Wit, H., & Eikelboom, R. (1984). Role of unconditioned and conditioned drug effects in the self-administration of opiates and stimulants. *Psychological Review, 91,* 251–268.

Stitzer, M., & Petry, N. (2006). Contingency management for treatment of substance abuse. *Annual Review of Clinical Psychology, 2,* 411–434.

Stolerman, I. P. (1992). Drugs of abuse: Behavioral principles, methods and terms. *Trends in Pharmacological Sciences, 13,* 170–176.

Thanos, P. K., Bermeo, C., Wang, G. J., & Volkow, N. D. (2009). D-cycloserine accelerates the extinction of cocaine-induced conditioned place preference in C57bL/c mice. *Behavioural Brain Research, 199,* 345–349.

Thomas, B. L., & Ayres, J. J. B. (2004). Use of the ABA fear renewal paradigm to assess the effects of extinction with co-present fear inhibitors or excitors: Implications for theories of extinction and for treating human fears and phobias. *Learning and Motivation, 35,* 22–51.

Thomas, B. L., Vurbic, D., & Novak, C. (2009). Extensive extinction in multiple contexts eliminates the renewal of conditioned fear in rats. *Learning and Motivation, 40,* 147–159.

Torregrossa, M. M., Sanchez, H., & Taylor, J. R. (2010). D-cycloserine reduces the context specificity of Pavlovian extinction of cocaine cues through actions in the nucleus accumbens. *The Journal of Neuroscience, 30,* 10526–10533.

Vengeliene, V., Kiefer, F., & Spanagel, R. (2008). D-cycloserine facilitates extinction of conditioned alcohol-seeking behavior in rats. *Alcohol & Alcoholism*, *43*, 626–629.

Vervliet, B., Vansteenwegen, D., Hermans, D., & Eelen, P. (2007). Concurrent excitors limit the extinction of conditioned fear in humans. *Behaviour Research & Therapy*, *45*, 375–383.

Vurbic, D., Gold, B., & Bouton, M. E. (2011). Effects of D-cycloserine on extinction of appetitive operant learning. *Behavioural Neuroscience*, *125*.

Walker, D. L., Ressler, K. J., Lu, K. T., & Davis, M. (2002). Facilitation of conditioned fear extinction by systemic administration or intra-amygdala infusions of D-cycloserine as assessed with fear-potentiated startle in rats. *Journal of Neuroscience*, *22*, 2343–2351.

Weerts, E. M., Kaminski, B. J., & Griffiths, R. R. (1998). Stable low-rate midazolam self-injection with concurrent physical dependence under conditions of long-term continuous availability in baboons. *Psychopharmacology*, *135*, 70–81.

Weise-Kelly, L., & Siegel, S. (2001). Self-administration cues as signals: Drug self-administration and tolerance. *Journal of Experimental Psychology: Animal Behavior Processes*, *27*, 125–136.

Welker, R. L., & McAuley, K. (1978). Reductions in resistance to extinction and spontaneous recovery as a function of changes in transportational and contextual stimuli. *Animal Learning & Behavior*, *6*, 451–457.

Winterbauer, N. E., & Bouton, M. E. (2010). Mechanisms of resurgence of an extinguished instrumental behavior. *Journal of Experimental Psychology: Animal Behavior Processes*, *36*, 343–353.

Winterbauer, N. E, & Bouton, M. E. (2011). Mechanisms of resurgence II: Response-contingent reinforcers can reinstate a second extinguished behavior. *Learning and Motivation*, in press.

Woods, A. M., & Bouton, M. E. (2006). D-cycloserine facilitates extinction but does not eliminate renewal of the conditioned emotional response. *Behavioral Neuroscience*, *120*, 1159–1162.

Woods, A. M., & Bouton, M. E. (2007). Occasional reinforced responses during extinction can slow the rate of reacquisition of an operant response. *Learning and Motivation*, *38*, 56–74.

Zironi, I., Burattini, C., Aicardi, G., & Janak, P. H. (2006). Context is a trigger for relapse to alcohol. *Behavioural Brain Research*, *167*, 150–155.

6 Placebo and nocebo responses

Sibylle Klosterhalfen and Paul Enck

Introduction

The placebo response is the beneficial effect of a treatment with a drug or other medicinal tool that is thought to *not* be specific to the drug but rather to "unspecific" circumstances of the treatment. The nocebo response is the worsening of symptoms due to these unspecific factors. In clinical trials of new compounds, these effects are controlled for to not overestimate the efficacy of the new drug; in clinical routine, placebo and nocebo responses occur with any treatment, but cannot easily be separated from the specific effects.

Such "unspecific" treatment effects are believed to include predisposing individual factors on the side of the physician and the patient, e.g., training, empathy, suggestions on the one hand and expectancies, worries and concerns, previous illness experience, a history of successful or failed therapy, and health behaviours on the other. It also includes mechanisms based on their interaction, e.g., time, duration, and intensity of patient–doctor communication. Finally, the placebo response itself as well as other aspects of clinical trials in medicine and beyond are always also subject to cultural differences and influences. Hence, the placebo response may represent an ideal behavioural medicine paradigm to study the interaction between physiological and psychological properties of any medical treatment.

Mechanisms and current models of the placebo and nocebo response

A major insight from the recent publications on placebo (Klosterhalfen & Enck, 2008; Enck, Benedetti, & Schedlowski, 2008) and to a much lesser degree on nocebo (Benedetti, 2008; Benedetti, Amanzio, Vighetti, & Asteggiano, 2006; Benedetti, Lanotte, Lopiano, & Colloca, 2007) is that there seems not to be a single neurobiological or psychobiological mechanism that is able to explain placebo and nocebo phenomena in general. Instead, we have learned that different mechanisms exist by which placebo and nocebo responses are steered across diseases and experimental conditions; so far, placebo and nocebo responses have not been compared across diseases.

Mechanisms of the placebo response

It is generally agreed that many responses in the placebo arm of a clinical drug study are not "true" placebo responses but design and measurement errors that generate false responses ("regression to the mean"): they may be due to low sample sizes (Figure 6.1), design characteristics (crossover versus parallel group studies), recruitment biases (e.g., including of patients not matching inclusion criteria), drug/placebo characteristics (e.g., incomplete blinding), and whether efficacy assessment was done by patients or their doctors.

Beyond this, current psychological theories have proposed that placebo effects as seen in clinical trials are due to two distinct mechanisms: Pavlovian conditioning on the one hand and expectancy theory (e.g., Shapiro, 1981), signal-detection (e.g., Allan & Siegel, 2002), or "meaning"

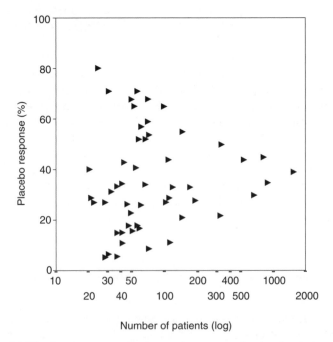

Number of patients (log)

Figure 6.1 Placebo response rates (percentage responder to placebo) across 50 clinical randomized trials in irritable bowel syndrome patients as a function of the size of the sample: the higher the number of patients studies, the less variable is the placebo response. Small sample sizes carry the risk of overestimating or underestimating the placebo response (adopted from Enck & Klosterhalfen, 2005).

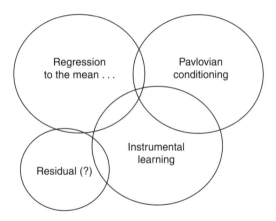

Figure 6.2 A model to explain the different mechanisms that contribute to the placebo and nocebo response. The degree of overlap between the mechanisms and the potential of other nonspecific mechanisms remain unclear.

(Moerman & Jonas, 2002) on the other to explain why patients respond with symptom improvement when they are told to receive an effective treatment for their symptoms and complaints. The relative contribution of Pavlovian conditioning has remained controversial (Montgomery & Kirsch, 1997; Flaten, Aasli, & Blumenthal, 2003).

As we will argue here, the two mechanisms behind placebo responses are *both* driven by learning theory: Pavlovian conditioning in the tradition of I. P. Pavlov (1849–1936), and instrumental learning in the tradition of E. L. Thorndike (1874–1949) and B. F. Skinner (1904–1990). Both contribute to placebo responses in clinical trials and both can be studied experimentally in the laboratory, either alone or in conjunction (Figure 6.2).

Mechanisms of the nocebo response

Compared with the placebo effect, much less is known about the nocebo effect, since the induction of a nocebo response represents a stressful and anxiogenic procedure, thus limiting its ethical investigation. The term nocebo ("I shall harm") was introduced in contraposition to the term placebo ("I shall please") by a number authors in order to distinguish the pleasing from the noxious effects of placebo (Kennedy, 1961; Hahn, 1985). If the positive psychosocial context, which is typical of the placebo effect, is reversed, the nocebo effect can be studied. Therefore, it is important to stress that the study of the nocebo effect relates to the negative psychosocial context surrounding the treatment, and its neurobiological investigation is the analysis of the effects of this negative context on the patient's brain and body. As for the placebo effect, the nocebo effect follows the administration of an inert substance, along with the suggestion that the subject will get worse. However, the term nocebo-related effect can also be used whenever symptom worsening follows negative expectations without the administration of any inert substance (Benedetti, 2008).

Most examples of nocebo responses therefore, derive from the investigation of adverse events that are apparent in the placebo arm of drug studies. These usually mimic the responses seen in the drug arm, and are therefore thought to be due to similar expectations patients have when receiving drug or placebo in a double-blind fashion: In both cases they have to sign informed consent that these events may eventually occur. However, other nocebo responses may be due to false diagnoses or to diagnostic and therapeutic interventions that may be misleading the patient with respect to the nature and severity of his/her disease.

Current thinking is that nocebo responses may as well be generated by the same two basic mechanisms, Pavlovian conditioning and negative expectancies, and may represent the opposite response to or the inverse of the placebo response. As we will argue here, the nocebo response may not only be conditioned by Pavlovian principles, but the negative expectancies also mimic some features of instrumental learning.

Reward mechanisms reflect "instrumental learning"

Most of our current knowledge is based on placebo responses with (experimental) pain, called "placebo analgesia", and most of the work is based on the expectancy model, i.e., the response of an individual following the information (or suggestion) that an intervention (a pill, cream, injection, etc.) will improve clinical or experimentally induced pain symptoms. The expected improvement thus operates as a potential "reward".

Both "analgesia" and "reward" have distinct central pathways that use opioids and dopamine as neurotransmitters. In a study by Scott et al. (2008) it was shown that both the endogenous opioid and the dopaminergic systems in different brain regions, including those involved in reward and motivational behaviour, are involved in placebo analgesia. Subjects underwent a pain challenge, in the absence and presence of a placebo with expected analgesic properties. It was found that placebo induced activation of opioid neurotransmission in the anterior cingulate, orbitofrontal and insular cortices, nucleus accumbens, amygdala, and periaqueductal grey matter. This assembly of brain areas has been called the "pain matrix".

Dopaminergic and opioid activity in this pain matrix were found not only during perceived effectiveness of the placebo intervention but already during the anticipation of a symptomatic improvement. In fact, the uncertainty of the reward increases the dopaminergic activation, which is maximized when the probability of reward is 0.5: At this stage nearly one third of dopaminergic cells in the prefrontal cortex are tonically activated (Fiorillo, Tobler, & Schultz, 2003). There is also phasic dopaminergic activation that takes place after reward, and this is stronger when the reward has come as a surprise. Therefore, uncertainty appears to heighten reward mechanisms in this brain reward circuitry model.

If so, the dopamine release during expectation of a symptom relief could – already – operate as reinforcing stimulus, as dopamine acts on many dendrites that transmit their signals into the periphery. Symptom improvement based on such expectations would then be perceived as attributable to the drug (or placebo) and would contribute to further improvement after drug/placebo intake. Such symptom improvement during the expectation of a presumed drug treatment has occasionally been noted in drug-free run-in phases of clinical trials of different drugs, e.g., in treatment of functional disorders (Enck, Vinson, Malfertheiner, Zipfel, & Klosterhalfen, 2009).

Investigators have found a correlation between the placebo responses and the monetary responses: The larger the nucleus accumbens responses to monetary reward, the stronger the nucleus accumbens responses to placebos (for a review see Lidstone, de la Fuente-Fernandez, & Stoessl, 2005). This strongly suggests that placebo responsiveness depends on the functioning and efficiency of the reward system, and would explain at least in part why some individuals respond to placebos whereas some others do not. Those who have a more efficient dopaminergic reward system would also be good placebo responders. Interestingly, the reward studies used an experimental approach that is typical of clinical trials, whereby the subjects know they have a 50 percent chance to receive either placebo or active treatment, and whereby no prior conditioning was performed.

In summary therefore, some features of the expectancy model of placebo reflect features of instrumental learning. However, it still needs to be shown whether – beyond reward – other principles of instrumental learning (immediacy, contingency, positive and negative reinforcement) also apply to the placebo response, before this conclusion can be drawn.

Does instrumental learning also apply to the nocebo response?

Brain-imaging techniques have been crucial to understanding the neurobiology of negative expectations, and most of this research has been performed in the field of pain. Overall, negative expectations may result in the amplification of pain (Dannecker, Price, & Robinson, 2003) and several brain regions, like the anterior cingulate cortex, the prefrontal cortex, and the insula have been found to be activated during the anticipation of pain (Keltner et al., 2006).

It has been shown that expectations of a positive outcome (pain decrease in a placebo analgesia experiment) activate endogenous opioid neurotransmission, whilst expectation of a negative outcome (hyperalgesia) activates central cholecystokinin (CCK) receptors. This neurochemical view implies that two opposite systems are activated by opposite expectations about pain. This is supported by the fact that CCK antagonists potentiate placebo-induced analgesia, probably due to the blockade of the anti-opioid action of CCK (Benedetti, 1996).

The involvement of CCK in nocebo hyperalgesia is likely to be mediated by anxiety, as benzodiazepines have been found to block both nocebo-induced hyperalgesia and the typical anxiety-induced hypothalamus–pituitary–adrenal hyperactivity. Conversely, the CCK antagonist, proglumide, has been found to prevent nocebo hyperalgesia but not the hypothalamus–pituitary–adrenal hyperactivity, which suggests two independent biochemical pathways activated by nocebo suggestions and anxiety (Benedetti, Amanzio, Casadio, Oliaro, & Maggi, 1997).

It is conceivable that a biochemical response to *expected* worsening of symptoms (nocebo response), e.g., an increased CCK release acts as negative reinforcement (punishment) by increasing symptoms prior to drug administration or another medical intervention, and that this symptomatic response is attributed to the intervention to further act as nocebo enhancing stimulus. In summary, therefore, some features of the nocebo response may as well be explained by the instrumental learning paradigm. As with placebo responses, however, final proof that instrumental learning is the basis of (some) nocebo responses needs to show that the laws of instrumental conditioning (e.g., immediacy, contingency) are also in effect.

Pavlovian learning of placebo and nocebo responses

The other model that has been used to study placebo mechanisms is learning of symptoms by Pavlovian conditioning. In this case, previous illness experience co-determines the response to a medical intervention. Pavlovian learning has been shown to contribute to the placebo response in a number of clinical symptoms, including pain, motor functions (e.g., in Parkinson's disease), and in immune and endocrine responses.

In the Pavlovian learning model of placebo responses, a successful medical intervention (the unconditioned stimulus, US) needs to be paired repetitively with a conditioned stimulus (CS), e.g., the application pathway of a drug (cream, pill, injection, etc.), its colour, environmental conditions (sight, smell, sound of the room), or other stimuli present. It has been shown that the patient's blood pressure tends to be higher when measured by the doctor (usually wearing a white coat) than during ambulatory measurements at home – this phenomenon has been called the "white coat effect".

In Parkinson's disease (PD), a successful treatment option is deep brain implantation of a pacemaker into the striatum, the area where dopamine is released and where PD patients have a deficit in dopamine production. During implantation surgery, Benedetti et al. (2004a) could show sham switching on and off of the simulator will decrease and increase the firing rate of single neuronal cells, associated with improved and worsened motor rigidity in the periphery. Such conditioned placebo responses of motor functions in PD can be found in patients with chronic brain stimulation for many years after surgery.

Long-term experimental studies that would prove the efficacy of Pavlovian conditioning on placebo responses are difficult to perform. In a set of experiments, however, Colloca and Benedetti (2006) demonstrated that prior experience is able to shape placebo analgesia over the course of a few days: Subjects that were conditioned to experience placebo analgesia in an acute paradigm would demonstrate reduced pain experiences for up to 7 days later, and would exhibit reduced extinction of responses in the range of minutes. Repetition of a negative (painful) procedure after one week would result in reduced placebo analgesia.

This work emphasizes that previous experience with successful or unsuccessful treatment of pain will have lasting effects on how a second or subsequent treatment of the same conditions is perceived. The analogy to clinical conditions is evident, but relative: While experimental pain is phasic and acute, clinical pain is usually chronic and long-lasting. Whether and to what degree previous pain treatment contributes to experience of placebo analgesia in a clinical trial – usually one sixth of the effect size of what was achieved in experimental pain conditions (Vase, Riley, & Price, 2002) – remains to be shown.

It is puzzling to realize that – beyond the laws of Pavlovian learning studied for almost a century by now – there is basically no model available that allows predicting the maintenance of a strong placebo response in a clinical trial that may last for a year or longer. In such trials, the CS is presented many times without further association with a US, but extinction seems not to occur at all, and previous experience with this drug (or a similar compound) that could have shaped the response cannot have happened. Hence, one may speculate that if conditioning (learning) would be part of this placebo response, it cannot be of Pavlovian nature.

The number of studies that report Pavlovian conditioning of nocebo responses is limited, and they are mostly in the pain area. In a series of experiments we showed, however, that also gastrointestinal symptoms such as nausea can be conditioned using a rotation chair as US in motion sickness susceptible subjects (Klosterhalfen et al., 1999, 2000), and that principles of Pavlovian learning, e.g., latent inhibition and overshadowing (Klosterhalfen et al., 2005; Klosterhalfen, Hausmann, Stockhorst, Hall, & Enck, 2002), can also be used to prevent the occurrence of conditioned nausea (see the chapter by Symonds & Hall, this volume).

In a more recent experiment (Klosterhalfen et al., 2009) we compared this conditioned nocebo response to one induced by verbal suggestion of symptom worsening and found the conditioning procedure to be substantially more effective (Figure 6.3), but differentially affecting men and women.

While we postulate that across clinical conditions the placebo and nocebo response is generated by these two distinct mechanisms, Pavlovian and instrumental learning, the relationship of these two remains unclear and

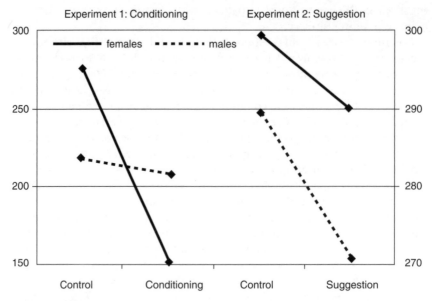

Figure 6.3 Tolerance towards rotation (RT, in s) in a conventional rotation chair in men (dashed line) and women (solid line) in two experiments, one using Pavlovian conditioning (left Y-axis) and one using verbal suggestion (right Y-axis) of symptom worsening following a salient taste stimulus. The graph compares the experimental group to the respective control group (adopted from Klosterhalfen et al., 2009). Note that the response is stronger with conditioning, but only in females, while for suggestions, the response is stronger in men than in women.

was subject to some debate in the past: According to Montgomery and Kirsch (1997) verbal information reversed the effect of conditioning trials on both placebo expectancies and placebo responses, and the magnitude of the placebo effect increased significantly over extinction trials. Contrary to these authors, Flaten et al. (2003) found that strong expectations about the effects of a common drug (caffeine) do not generate placebo responses after consumption of decaffeinated coffee. However, Benedetti et al. (2003) could show that Pavlovian conditioning is able to override suggested responses, but that suggestions are not able to manipulate conditioned responses (CRs) – at least in experimental pain and with motor function in PD (Figure 6.4). Whether this holds true for other medical and experimental conditions, remains open at this stage. Other explanations have been put forward, such that expectancies, achieved through verbal instructions, might also be seen as conditioning stimuli (CS) that reactivate earlier stimulus association, or that expectations may themselves be a product (CR) of previous conditioning.

Other questions that need to be addressed and yet need an answer are whether placebo responses follow a dose–response function (with more

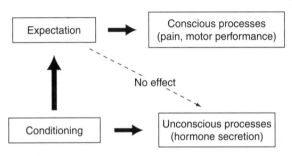

Figure 6.4 Association between conditioned and expected placebo responses (adopted from Benedetti et al., 2003): Conditioned responses may override expectancies, while expectancies may not modulate conditioned responses.

US–CS pairing inducing higher responses), whether and how they are generalized to other clinical conditions, and how long they may last.

Pavlovian conditioning of placebo effects: Neuroimmune and endocrine responses

One relatively new example of clinical application of Pavlovian learning in the understanding of physiological phenomena and their potential clinical use derives from neuroimmunology and neuroendocrinology, as outlined below. Other examples may be taken, e.g., from the chapter by Symonds and Hall and others in this volume.

The behavioural conditioning of immune responses is based on the intense crosstalk between the central nervous system (CNS) and the peripheral immune system (Tracey, 2007). Commonly, in these approaches, experimental animals are presented with a novel taste (e.g., saccharin) as CS in the drinking water, and subsequently injected with an agent that produces changes in immune status US. When the CS (saccharin solution) is presented at a subsequent time point, the animals avoid drinking the saccharin, which is termed "conditioned taste aversion" (CTA) (Garcia, Kimeldorf, & Koelling, 1985). Concomitantly, the animals demonstrate a modification of immune parameters that commonly mimics the actual US effect (Ader, 2003). Ader and Cohen (1975) demonstrated conditioned suppression of antibody production for the first time. Experimental evidence over the last 25 years has shown behaviourally conditioned effects in rodents, both in humoral and cellular immunity, with behavioural conditioning able to re-enlist changes in lymphocyte circulation and proliferation, cytokine production, natural killer (NK) cell activity, and endotoxin tolerance.

A number of studies have meanwhile demonstrated the clinical relevance of conditioned changes in immune function. Specifically, the morbidity and mortality of animals with autoimmune disease was abated via conditioning using cyclophosphamide (Ader & Cohen, 1982) or with cyclosporine (Klosterhalfen & Klosterhalfen, 1990) as the US and, in addition, behavioural conditioning prolonged the survival of heterotopic heart allograft and significantly inhibited the contact hypersensitivity reaction (Exton et al., 2000). The experiments by Klosterhalfen and Klosterhalfen (1990) have also shown that the autoimmune disease could be diminished by conditioned cyclosporine effects *without* resulting in CTA.

Experimental evidence also suggests that behavioural conditioning of immunopharmacological drug effects is possible in humans. Conditioned cyclosphosphamide-induced leucopenia has been reported (Giang et al., 1996), along with a conditioned immune response to the cytokine interferon-γ (Longo et al., 1999), as well as conditioned suppression of the *ex vivo* production and mRNA expression of interleukin-2 and interferon-γ, and of the proliferation of peripheral lymphocytes (Goebel et al., 2002). Allergic reactions have been shown to be affected by behavioural conditioning and emotional status. However, more recently, it was demonstrated that the antihistaminergic properties of the H_1-receptor antagonist desloratadine can be behaviourally conditioned in patients suffering from allergic house-dust-mite rhinitis, as analyzed by subjective symptom score, skin prick test and decreased basophile activation (Goebel, Meykadeh, Kou, Schedlowski, & Hengge, 2008). These data support earlier observations indicating that conscious physiological pain and motor mechanisms are mainly affected by patients' conscious expectations, whereas unconscious physiological processes, such as hormone release or immune functions, appear to be mediated by behavioural conditioning (Benedetti et al., 2003).

Similar conditioning mechanisms have been found in the endocrine system. In a study aimed at differentiating the effects of conditioning and expectation, Benedetti et al. (2003) showed that verbal suggestions alone of hormone increase and decrease did not have any effect on both hormones. However, when drug application associated with an effective CS were used to condition hormone secretion, significant effects were shown after placebo (CS) administration alone. These conditioned effects occurred regardless of the direction (increase or decrease) of verbal suggestions the subjects received (see above, Figure 6.4). It can be assumed that in this case the CS was represented by the act of injecting the pharmacological agent (i.e., the context around the treatment).

This experimental evidence demonstrates the potential applicability of such behavioural conditioning protocols in clinical practice. Recent clinical studies even demonstrated efficacy of a Pavlovian conditioning procedure to reduce medication in psoriasis patients during corticosteroid therapy (Ader et al., 2010), and in attention-deficit hyperactivity disorder (ADHD) children during amphetamine therapy (Sandler, Glesne, & Bodfish, 2010).

However, in future studies it will be necessary to analyze the kinetics of the behaviourally conditioned immuno-pharmacological and endocrine response and to elucidate whether and to what extent these CRs can be re-conditioned on multiple occasions. Only with this information and more detailed knowledge of the mechanisms behind the CNS–immune system and CNS–endocrine system interaction will it be possible to design conditioning protocols that can be employed in clinical situations to the patients' advantage.

Placebo and nocebo responses in clinical trials

Ever since the dawn of the first randomized placebo-controlled trials testing new drugs and treatments in the middle of the last century, and even before (Hill, 1990), placebo responses in clinical trials have given rise to discussion and concern regarding their mechanisms, and have usually been regarded as a nuisance or a barrier to a rational approach in modern drug development.

Attempts to unravel the mechanisms of the placebo response in clinical trials have used meta-analytic approaches of the placebo arm of trials – with mixed results. The placebo effect in randomized controlled trials has been reported to be around 40 percent in functional disorders (Enck & Klosterhalfen, 2005) but lower in depression (29 percent), bipolar mania (31 percent), and migraine (21 percent). The reasons for these variable placebo response rates a number of variables that have been discussed above. Meta-analyses can come to opposite conclusions on the same data set, e.g., with respect to the direction of the effects of the number of study visits on the placebo effect size, but this may be due to data extraction errors that lead to false findings and conclusions (Gøtzsche, Hróbjartsson, Maric, & Tendal, 2007). Hróbjartsson and Gøtzsche (2001, 2004) came to conclude that the placebo response appears to be powerful only because of a lack of "no treatment" control groups in most studies. They recently showed that when "no treatment" groups were included into a meta-analysis, both spontaneous improvement *and* effect of placebo contributed importantly to the observed treatment effect, and both were closely related to each other (Krogsboll, Hróbjartsson, & Gøtzsche, 2009) (Figure 6.5).

Because of the difficulties to reliably identify placebo responders and predicting placebo response rates in clinical trials, different methodological attempts have been made to the way (novel) drugs are tested against placebo.

In experimental laboratory research, a number of experimental designs have been employed that may help to identify predictors of the placebo response in the future. The so-called "balanced placebo design" (BPD) was traditionally used in the testing for placebo effects of frequently consumed everyday drugs such as caffeine, nicotine, and alcohol. While one half of the study sample receives placebo and the other half the drug, half of each group is receiving correct information while the other half is receiving false information on the nature of their study condition (drug or placebo) immediately prior to drug testing, thus allowing to differentiate between the "true" drug effect (those receiving the drug but are told they received

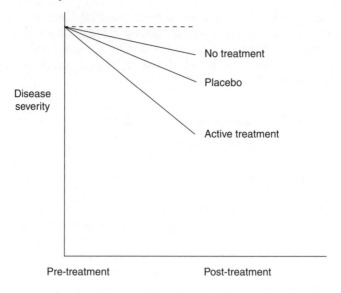

Figure 6.5 Relative contribution of spontaneous symptom course, placebo effect, and active treatment to symptom change during a drug trial (adopted from Krogsboll et al., 2009); the model is based on a meta-analysis of placebo-controlled depression trials that included a no-treatment arm.

placebo) and the true placebo effect (those receiving placebo but are told they received the drug) (Figure 6.6). As is evident, the BPD implies "deception" of the subjects (Miller, Wendler, & Swartzman, 2005) that limits its suitability and acceptance outside the laboratory and in patients for ethical reasons (Ehni & Wiesing, 2008).

Hidden treatment (HT) or covert treatment is another option that may be specifically useful for the test of drug effects in acute and highly symptomatic conditions such as with postoperative pain (Levine, Gordon, Smith, & Fields, 1981), anxiety, and motor dysfunction in PD (Lanotte et al., 2005). In case of HT, the patient may receive a drug unnoticed in terms of timing and dosage, and the drug effect (or its missing action) can be determined independent of the patient's expectations. Benedetti and colleagues demonstrated that under these circumstances drugs commonly believed to have analgesic properties such as CCK-antagonists failed to show any antinociceptive effects (Colloca, Lopiano, Lanotte, & Benedetti, 2004). Evidently, HT can only be applied with the patient agreeing prior to the test that she/he may or may not receive a drug at all, which may raise other ethical concerns especially with the test of novel compounds of unknown properties.

Finally, a free-choice paradigm (FCP), which may be regarded as a modification of the adaptive response design, the early-escape design, or the human variant of the two-bottle test in CTA may offer an alternative

		Information	
		Medication	**Placebo**
Application	**Medication**	true positive	false negative
	Placebo	false positive	true negative

Figure 6.6 The balanced placebo design. Half of the subjects in each group (drug, placebo) are misinformed prior to testing about the drug they will receive, thus allowing to separate drug and placebo responses in the drug arm of the study.

approach to common drug test procedures. FCP allows the patient to choose between two pills, of which one is the drug and one the placebo, at medication-dispensing time; it is, however, essential that the patient does not take both pills at the same time (hence, a technical or administrative modus has to be implemented to prevent this, and to prevent overdosage, etc.), and that he/she may switch to the other condition at any time (hence, the pharmacodynamics of the compound under investigation have to be appropriate, e.g., the speed of action, the feasibility of on-demand medication, etc.). It would, on the other hand, allow assessment of drug efficacy via the choice behaviour rather than with symptomatic endpoints. The FCP has been used occasionally in optimizing dosage of drugs in clinical trials. It bypasses many of the ethical concerns against the use of placebos (Ehni & Wiesing, 2008), but its methodology and statistics in assessing drug superiority over placebo have not been validated (Zhang & Rosenberger, 2006).

In contrast to these experimental models that allow a clear separation of placebo and drug responses, randomized and placebo-controlled clinical trials usually mix both under the assumption that drug and placebo effects are additive in the drug arm of the study (Figure 6.7), and subtracting the placebo response would allow to assess the "true" drug efficacy.

This model has, however, been questioned (Kirsch, 2000): While high intercorrelations between the response rates in drug and placebo arms of medication studies provide an argument for low drug effectiveness in favour of the additive model, separate analyses for predicting variables for responses in study arms often generate different factors and variables responsible (e.g., Enck et al., 2009) that clearly argue against the additive model (Enck, Weimer, Horing, Klosterhalfen, & Zipfel, 2011). Other arguments against the additive model are incomplete blinding with many drugs, so that patients may be aware of the experimental condition by taking adverse events into account.

In contrast to placebo effects, nocebo effects in clinical trials are usually referred to as adverse events (side effects) occurring in the placebo arm of a drug study and that can, but need to lead to study termination by the

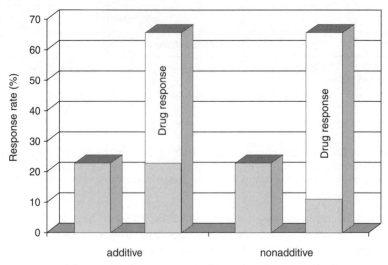

Figure 6.7 The "additive" and the "nonadditive" model of the response to drugs in a placebo-controlled trial (adopted from Kirsch, 2000): The assumption in the additive model is that the placebo response is the same in both arms and needs to be subtracted from the response in the drug arm to identify the true drug response. This view is challenged in the nonadditive model where the drug response can be independent of the placebo response in the other arm.

individual. Usually, the type of adverse events is closely mimicking those occurring in the drug arm, but often they are less prevalent or severe. They are thought to be due to the information about potential side effects a patient receives when signing the informed consent form. Patients that subsequently experience any symptoms during a drug study are more likely to attribute these to the drug if these symptoms are listed in the patient information sheet. Hence, nocebo responses during a clinical trial are a good example for the potential effect of suggestions and expectations. Whether they are due to Pavlovian or instrumental learning, or both, needs to be determined individually.

Summary and conclusion

In summary, both placebo and nocebo phenomena in the laboratory as well as in clinical practice resemble features of Pavlovian and instrumental learning; however, whether all the respective laws of learning (e.g., contingency, immediacy) are in effect still needs to be shown, as needs to be demonstrated whether and how they can operate in conjunction, and whether other (e.g., genetic) mechanisms beyond learning are present.

Besides the profound implications of placebo research for a better understanding of human biology, some practical aspects should not be forgotten. For example, placebo and nocebo phenomena are a major hurdle in the development and validation of new treatments, as high placebo responses sometimes distort the effects of a therapy. If we can identify in more detail the major mechanisms involved in placebo responsiveness, we could also develop strategies aimed at minimizing placebo effects, thereby uncovering the real effect of a therapy. Likewise, nocebo effects can be a serious drawback, as negative reactions to drugs are sometimes due to psychological effects rather than to specific negative effects of the drug itself. Therefore, research aimed at investigating nocebo mechanisms would enable us to disentangle the negative effects of the drug from those of the psychological state of the patient. In addition, a better understanding of the neurobiology of the placebo and nocebo responses will form the basis for designing behavioural protocols that can be employed as supportive therapy together with standard pharmacological regimen; the aim being to maximize the therapeutic outcome for the patient's benefit.

The experimental work on the neurobiological and neuropsychological mechanisms of the placebo/nocebo response from the last decade has impressively increased our knowledge of this long known phenomenon. It became clear that these approaches will not only help us to better understand human physiology but might have many practical consequences such as on the design of clinical studies, our health care systems, in particular the doctor–patient relationship as well as the education of medical care professionals. However, there are still numerous open questions that urgently need to be addressed in future studies.

References

Allan, L. G., & Siegel, S. (2002). A signal detection theory analysis of the placebo effect. *Evaluation and the Health Professions, 25*, 410–420.

Ader, R., & Cohen, N. (1975). Behaviorally conditioned immunosuppression. *Psychosomatic Medicine, 37*, 333–340.

Ader, R., & Cohen, N. (1982). Behaviorally conditioned immunosuppression and murine systemic lupus erythematosus. *Science, 215*, 1534–1536.

Ader, R. (2003). Conditioned immunomodulation: Research needs and directions. *Brain, Behavior and Immunity, 17* (Suppl. 1), S51–S57.

Ader, R., Mercurio, M. G., Walton, J., James, D., Davis, M., Ojha, V., et al. (2010). Conditioned pharmacotherapeutic effects: A preliminary study. *Psychosomatic Medicine, 72*, 192–197.

Benedetti, F. (1996). The opposite effects of the opiate antagonist naloxone and the cholecystokinin antagonist proglumide on placebo analgesia. *Pain, 64*, 535–543.

Benedetti, F. (2008). Mechanisms of placebo and placebo-related effects across diseases and treatments. *Annual Review of Pharmacology and Toxicology, 48*, 33–60.

Benedetti, F., Amanzio, M., Casadio, C., Oliaro, A., & Maggi, G. (1997). Blockade of nocebo hyperalgesia by the cholecystokinin antagonist proglumide. *Pain, 71*, 135–140.

Benedetti, F., Amanzio, M., Vighetti, S., & Asteggiano, G. (2006). The biochemical and neuroendocrine bases of the hyperalgesic nocebo effect. *Journal of Neuroscience, 26*, 12014–12022.

Benedetti, F., Colloca, L., Lanotte, M., Bergamasco, B., Torre, E., & Lopiano, L. (2004b). Autonomic and emotional responses to open and hidden stimulations of the human subthalamic region. *Brain Research Bulletin, 63*, 203–211.

Benedetti, F., Colloca, L., Torre, E., Lanotte, M., Melcarne, A., Pesare, M., et al. (2004a). Placebo-responsive Parkinson patients show decreased activity in single neurons of subthalamic nucleus. *Nature Neuroscience, 7*, 587–588.

Benedetti, F., Lanotte, M., Lopiano, L., & Colloca, L. (2007). When words are painful – Unraveling the mechanisms of the nocebo effect. *Neuroscience, 147*, 260–271.

Benedetti, F., Pollo, A., Lopiano, L., Lanotte, M., Vighetti, S., & Rainero, I. (2003). Conscious expectation and unconscious conditioning in analgesic, motor, and hormonal placebo/nocebo responses. *Journal of Neuroscience, 23*, 4315–4323.

Colloca, L., & Benedetti, F. (2006). How prior experience shapes placebo analgesia. *Pain, 124*, 126–133.

Colloca, L., Lopiano, L., Lanotte, M., & Benedetti, F. (2004). Overt versus covert treatment for pain, anxiety, and Parkinson's disease. *The Lancet Neurology, 3*, 679–684.

Dannecker, E. A., Price, D. D., & Robinson, M. E. (2003). An examination of the relationships among recalled, expected, and actual intensity and unpleasantness of delayed onset muscle pain. *Journal of Pain, 4*, 74–81.

Ehni, H. J., & Wiesing, U. (2008). International ethical regulations on placebo-use in clinical trials: A comparative analysis. *Bioethics, 22*, 64–74.

Enck, P., Benedetti, F., & Schedlowski, M. (2008). New insights into the placebo and nocebo responses. *Neuron, 59*, 195–206.

Enck, P., & Klosterhalfen, S. (2005). The placebo response in functional bowel disorders: Perspectives and putative mechanisms. *Neurogastroenterology & Motility, 17*, 325–331.

Enck, P., Vinson, B., Malfertheiner, P., Zipfel, S., & Klosterhalfen, S. (2009). Placebo effects in functional dyspepsia – reanalysis of trial data. *Neurogastroenterology & Motility, 21*, 370–377.

Enck, P., Weimer, K., Horing, B., Klosterhalfen, S., & Zipfel, S. (2011). Placebo effects in clinical trials: More questions than answers. *Philosophical Transactions of the Royal Society, Series B, 366*, 1889–1895.

Exton, M. S., Elfers, A., Jeong, W. Y., Bull, D. F., Westermann, J., & Schedlowski, M. (2000). Conditioned suppression of contact sensitivity is independent of sympathetic splenic innervation. *American Journal of Physiology, 279*, R1310–R1315.

Fiorillo, C. D., Tobler, P. N., & Schultz, W. (2003). Discrete coding of reward probability and uncertainty by dopamine neurons. *Science, 299*, 1898–1902.

Flaten, M. A., Aasli, O., & Blumenthal, T. D. (2003). Expectations and placebo responses to caffeine-associated stimuli. *Psychopharmacology (Berlin), 169*, 198–204.

Garcia, J., Kimeldorf, D. J., & Koelling, R. A. (1985). Conditioned aversion to saccharin resulting from exposure to gamma radiation. *Science, 122*, 157–158.

Giang, D. W., Goodman, A. D., Schiffer, R. B., Mattson, D. H., Petrie, M., Cohen, N., et al. (1996). Conditioning of cyclophosphamide-induced leukopenia in humans. *Journal of Neuropsychiatry and Clinical Neurosciences, 8*, 194–201.

Goebel, M. U., Trebst, A. E., Steiner, J., Xie, Y. F., Exton, M. S., Frede, S., et al.

(2002). Behavioral conditioning of immunosuppression is possible in humans. *Journal of the Federation of American Societies for Experimental Biology, 16,* 1869–1873.

Goebel, M. U., Meykadeh, N., Kou, W., Schedlowski, M., & Hengge, U. R. (2008). Behavioral conditioning of anti-histamine effects in patients with allergic rhinitis. *Psychotherapy and Psychosomatics, 77,* 227–234.

Gøtzsche, P. C., Hróbjartsson, A., Maric, K., & Tendal, B. (2007). Data extraction errors in meta-analyses that use standardized mean differences. *JAMA, 298,* 430–437.

Hahn, R. A. (1985). A sociocultural model of illness and healing. In L. White, B. Tursky, & G. E. Schwartz (Eds.), *Placebo: Theory, research, and mechanisms* (pp. 332–350). New York, NY: Guilford.

Hill, A. B. (1990). Suspended judgment: Memories of the British streptomycin trial in tuberculosis. The first randomized clinical trial. *Controlled Clinical Trials, 11,* 77–79.

Hróbjartsson, A., & Gøtzsche, P. C. (2001). Is the placebo powerless? An analysis of clinical trials comparing placebo with no treatment. *New England Journal of Medicine, 344,* 1594–1602.

Hróbjartsson, A., & Gøtzsche, P. C. (2004). Is the placebo powerless? Update of a systematic review with 52 new randomized trials comparing placebo with no treatment. *Journal of Internal Medicine, 256,* 91–100.

Keltner, J. R., Furst, A., Fan, C., Redfern, R., Inglis, B., & Fields, H. L. (2006). Isolating the modulatory effect of expectation on pain transmission: A functional magnetic resonance imaging study. *Journal of Neuroscience, 26,* 4437–4443.

Kennedy, W. P. (1961). The nocebo reaction. *Medicina Experimentalis: International Journal of Experimental Medicine, 95,* 203–205.

Kirsch, I. (2000). Are drug and placebo effects in depression additive? *Biological Psychiatry, 47,* 733–735.

Klosterhalfen, S., Braun, S., Kellermann, S., Kowalski, A., Schrauth, M., Zipfel, S., et al. (2009). Gender and nocebo response following conditioning and expectancy. *Journal of Psychosomatic Research, 66,* 323–328.

Klosterhalfen, S., & Enck, P. (2008). Neurophysiology and psychobiology of the placebo response. *Current Opinion in Psychiatry, 21,* 189–195.

Klosterhalfen, S., Hausmann, S., Stockhorst, S., Hall, G., & Enck, P. (2002). Behavioural interventions are effective to reduce (experimental) nausea. *Gastroenterology, 122,* A-553f.

Klosterhalfen, S., Kellermann, S., Stockhorst, U., Wolf, J., Kirschbaum, C., Hall, G., et al. (2005). Latent inhibition of rotation-chair induced nausea in healthy male and female volunteers. *Psychosomatic Medicine, 67,* 335–340.

Klosterhalfen, S., & Klosterhalfen, W. (1990). Conditioned cyclosporine effects but not conditioned taste aversion in immunized rats. *Behavioral Neuroscience, 104,* 716–724.

Klosterhalfen, S., Rüttgers, A., Krumrey, E., Otto, B., Riepl, R. L., Stockhorst, U., et al. (2000). Pavlovian conditioning of taste aversion using a motion sickness paradigm. *Psychosomatic Medicine, 62,* 671–677.

Krogsboll, L. T., Hróbjartsson, A., & Gøtzsche, P. C. (2009). Spontaneous improvement in randomised clinical trials: Meta-analysis of three-armed trials comparing no treatment, placebo and active intervention. *BMC Medical Research Methodology* doi: 10.1186/1471-2288-9-1.

Lanotte, M., Lopiano, L., Torre, E., Bergamasco, B., Colloca, L., & Benedetti, F. (2005). Expectation enhances autonomic responses to stimulation of the human subthalamic limbic region. *Brain, Behavior, and Immunity, 19*, 500–509.

Levine, J. D., Gordon, N. C., Smith, R., & Fields, H. L. (1981). Analgesic responses to morphine and placebo in individuals with postoperative pain. *Pain, 10*, 379–389.

Lidstone, S. C., de la Fuente-Fernandez, R., & Stoessl, J. (2005). The placebo response as a reward mechanism. *Seminars in Pain Medicine, 3*, 37–42.

Longo, D. L., Duffey, P. L., Kopp, W. C., Heyes, M. P., Alvord, W. G., Sharfman, W. H., et al. (1999). Conditioned immune response to interferon-[gamma] in humans. *Clinical Immunology, 90*, 173–181.

Miller, F. G., Wendler, D., & Swartzman, L. C. (2005). Deception in research on the placebo effect. *PLoS Medicine, 2*:e262.

Moerman, D. E., & Jonas, W. B. (2002). Deconstructing the placebo effect and finding the meaning response. *Annals of International Medicine, 136*, 471–476.

Montgomery, G. H., & Kirsch, I. (1997). Classical conditioning and the placebo effect. *Pain, 72*, 107–113.

Sandler, A. D., Glesne, C. E., & Bodfish, J. W. (2010). Conditioned placebo dose reduction: A new treatment in attention-deficit hyperactivity disorder? *Journal of Developmental & Behavioral Pediatrics, 31*, 369–375.

Shapiro, D. A. (1981). Comparative credibility of treatment rationales: Three tests of expectancy theory. *British Journal of Clinical Psychology 20*, 111–122.

Scott, D. J., Stohler, C. S., Egnatuk, C. M., Wang, H., Koeppe, R. A., & Zubieta, J. K. (2008). Placebo and nocebo effects are defined by opposite opioid and dopaminergic responses. *Archives of General Psychiatry, 65*, 220–231.

Tracey, K. J. (2007). Physiology and immunology of the cholinergic antiin-flammatory pathway. *The Journal of Clinical Investigation, 117*, 289–296.

Vase, L., Riley, J. L., & Price, D. D. (2002). A comparison of placebo effects in clinical analgesic trials versus studies of placebo analgesia. *Pain, 99*, 443–452.

Zhang, L., & Rosenberger, W. F. (2006). Response-adaptive randomization for clinical trials with continuous outcomes. *Biometrics, 62*, 562–569.

7 Depressive realism?

Sadly not wiser

Andrew G. Baker, Rachel M. Msetfi, Neil Hanley, and Robin A. Murphy

The role of dysfunctional cognitions in maintaining or contributing to symptoms is central to most theories of depression. The nature of the dysfunction however, is controversial. Beck (1967) emphasizes the presence of negative schemas, others a depressogenic attributional style (Abramson, Metalsky, & Alloy, 1989). Paired with an enabling stressor, dysfunctional cognitions encourage negatively biased beliefs about the self, contributing to depressive symptomatology (for detailed reviews see Coyne & Gotlib, 1983; Gotlib, Kurtzman, & Blehar, 1997; Teasdale & Barnard, 1993; Williams, Watts, MacLeod, & Mathews, 1997). However, there is other evidence that, when evaluating certain causal scenarios, depressed people are more accurate than their nondepressed counterparts (Alloy & Abramson, 1979). This *depressive realism* stands in sharp contrast to a dysfunctional cognitions view of depression. The most compelling evidence for depressive realism comes from studies that examine learning (Ackermann & DeRubeis, 1991). We discuss here how contemporary learning theory provides insight into the depressive realism phenomenon. We also show how an appreciation of the principles of learning, involving associations and basic motivational states, undermines the argument that depressed people have more realistic cognitions than the nondepresssed. We propose that the data from learning tasks are actually consistent with a cognitive bias and reduced motivation account of depression. Moreover, we argue that both depressed and non-depressed people react the same way to traditional associative and behavioural manipulations but that the depressed have different sensitivities to these manipulations. Specifically we examine two aspects of learning that are different in depression, namely context exposure and motivation, and examine how depressed mood relates to these variables.

Depression and cognitive theories

Depression is a disorder with psychological and somatic symptoms that range from subjective feelings of sadness, depression, and guilt to objective changes in overt behaviour including sleeping and eating patterns and, at its most severe, thoughts and behaviours related to suicide (American

Psychiatric Association, 1994). Depression is one of the most common disorders with estimates suggesting that one out of every six people will experience an episode of major depression at some point in their lives (Bierut et al., 1999). The symptoms pervade almost all aspects of daily life and impair functioning as much as or more than most other medical or psychiatric conditions (Gotlib & Lee, 1989; Wells et al., 1989). In spite of the availability of medical and psychological treatments, depression is often chronic and is characterized by relapse and recurrence (Kessler, McGonagle, Swartz, & Blazer, 1993). This has led to the suggestion that some individuals have traits that constitute an enduring vulnerability to suffering from the disorder.

The vulnerability view has been embraced by cognitive theories of depression, of which Beck's (1967) theory has been the most influential, particularly in relation to therapeutic intervention. Indeed, therapies based on this theory are among the recommended first lines of treatment for mild to moderate depression in the UK (National Institute for Clinical Excellence [NICE], 2009). According to this view, people possess internal models or schemata of themselves and their world that guide how incoming information is perceived and the meaning that is assigned to it. People who are vulnerable to depression have schemata containing negative core beliefs about the self in relation to the world and the future, such as "I am helpless" and "I am unloveable". Once activated by a congruent event, negatively biased thoughts influence how an individual feels and behaves. In other words the symptoms of depression are, in part, a consequence of cognitive distortions involving negative views of the self, the world, and the future, and are triggered by experience. This is a common theme running through most cognitive theories of depression (e.g., Abramson et al., 1989; Beck, 1967).

Depressive realism

Depressive realism as a characterization of the cognitions of depressed people is controversial since the cornerstone of therapy relates to the assumption that depression involves cognitive distortions. It is easy to see how this does not sit well with an idea that finds the depressed as having a less biased self-perception. The therapeutic repercussions for patients believing themselves to be more accurate than the nondepressed are obvious and concerning. In spite of some variability in the strength of the finding, there is a strong evidence base. Studies have examined depressive realism using different methodologies which include estimating the frequency of reinforcement (e.g., Nelson & Craighead, 1977), perception of performance feedback (e.g., DeMonbreun & Craighead, 1977), expert versus observer judgements (e.g., Lewinsohn, Mischel, Chaplin, & Barton, 1980), judgement of health risk (Keller, Lipkus, & Rimer, 2002), and the likelihood of answering general knowledge questions correctly (Stone, Dodrill, & Johnson, 2001). Although it is common to find differences in the experimental judgements between depressed and nondepressed on various tasks, knowing which of the two groups is more realistic is itself a subjective enterprise (Murphy, Vallée-Tourangeau, Msetfi, & Baker, 2005). Just what is realistic is hard to establish as it is never unambiguous what objective standard participants might recruit (for a discussion on this point see Ackermann & DeRubeis, 1991).

One experimental procedure that, more than others, involves an objective standard is a task in which people are required to learn statistical relationships. The objective measure present in these tasks is the statistical norm. In one of these contingency judgement tasks, participants judge the relationship between a simple action (e.g., pressing a button) and an outcome (e.g., the flash of a light). Since the experimenter controls the presentation of the statistical correlation or contingency between the action and the outcome, judgements can be studied in relation to this objective scale. Alloy and Abramson (1979) carried out several experiments using this method from which they concluded that depression was related to more accurate contingency judgements. Their influential "sadder but wiser" study, along with findings from other similar studies (Alloy, Abramson, & Kossman, 1985; Benassi & Mahler, 1985; Martin, Abramson, & Alloy, 1984; Vasquez, 1987), has been viewed as the strongest evidence for depressive realism (Ackermann & DeRubeis, 1991). In order to understand these findings in depth and to explore how learning theory might inform their interpretation, we first describe the methodology in some detail. We will pay particular attention to the difference between statistical contingency and outcome frequency effects.

Contingency learning and depressive realism

In every day experience, people make judgements about how accurately events and actions predict subsequent outcomes. The events or actions might be as simple as preparing to walk across a street at a green light or as complex as using bad economic news to sell investments in anticipation of a fall in stock prices; all causal and signalling relations involve some degree of contingency. The experimental work on this ability involves programming either action-contingent or event-contingent outcomes and asking participants to judge the degree to which the action or the event predicts the occurrence of the outcome. Action–outcome contingencies involve instrumental behaviour in which the participant is an actor in the contingency whereas event–outcome contingencies involve passively observing the signalling or predictive relationship of the event. The experimenter programmes the degree of contingency by calculating one of several similar contingency metrics with which participants' judgements are compared (see Allan, 1980; and Crocker, 1981 for a discussion of appropriate measures).

The action–outcome contingency judgement task used by Alloy and Abramson can be summarized as follows. Participants were given multiple

Table 7.1 Three 2 × 2 contingency tables showing the four possible combinations of action–outcome information

	Outcome	
Action	present	absent
Present	A	B
Absent	C	D

ΔP = 0: Low outcome density				ΔP = 0: High outcome density			
	Outcome				Outcome		
Action	present	absent		Action	present	absent	
Present	5	15	P(O|A) = 0.25	Present	15	5	P(O|A) = 0.75
Absent	5	15	P(O|NoA) = 0.25	Absent	15	5	P(O|NoA) = 0.75

Notes: The upper table shows generic information from which ΔP is calculated, where A, B, C, and D refer to the frequencies of such information. Note: $\Delta P = A/(A+B) - C/(C+D)$. The two lower tables show examples of two contingency conditions in which ΔP is zero, with a low outcome density condition on the left and a high outcome density condition on the right. P(O|A) refers to the conditional probability of the outcome given the presence of the action and P(O|NoA) refers to the conditional probability of the outcome given the absence of the action.

opportunities to press (or not press) a button, which could produce an outcome (e.g., light onset) according to a programmed degree of contingency. If the light switches on more often following the action than in its absence, participants might be expected to learn that their actions have some control over the light. There are four possible types of action–outcome conjunctions and these can be summarized in a 2 × 2 contingency table (see Table 7.1, top).

The values in this table can be used to calculate the overall contingency metric. The frequency of Cell A corresponds to the number of co-occurrences of the action and the outcome (Outcome|Action) ([O|A]), Cell B is the occurrence of the action without the outcome (Outcome|No Action) [(O|NoA)]. The conditional probability, A/(A+B), provides a measure of the P(O|A). The frequency of Cell C reflects the outcomes that occur in the absence of the action, while Cell D refers to the number of times neither the action nor the outcome occurred. This conditional probability reflects the likelihood of outcomes in the absence of the action P(O|NoA). Both Cells A and D represent the conjunctions of events or nonevents that contribute to evidence for a positive relation between the two events while Cells B and C contribute evidence that a negative or preventive relationship exists. For example, if event X predicts Y one would expect many co-occurrences of these events (Cell A) and if X is not present one would also expect Y to be absent (Cell D). Moreover the presence of either X or Y alone (Cells B and C) is evidence against a positive relationship between the two variables. However, if X is negatively related to, or prevents, Y one would expect a high frequency of Cell B and Cell C conjunctions and fewer Cell A or B conjunctions.

A common overall measure of contingency, delta P (ΔP), can be calculated by taking the difference between the two probabilities of the outcome conditional upon the occurrence or absence of the action [contingency = $\Delta P = P(O|A) - P(O|NoA) = A/(A+B) - C/(C+D)$]. ΔP varies between +1 and −1. Positive values reflect contingencies in which the action increases the likelihood of the outcome and negative values those where the action decreases the likelihood of the outcome. Zero values are consistent with an equal probability of outcome regardless of whether or not the action occurred and thus reflect the absence of control. Zero contingencies are particularly important for the depressive realism story since these are the contingencies to which depressed people are supposedly more sensitive. Alloy and Abramson (1979) found that depressed people judged some zero contingencies as closer to zero on the judgement scale than did the nondepressed.

A further feature of the contingency task is that the contingency is somewhat independent of the specific event frequencies. The same level of contingency can be represented with different configurations of cell frequencies. The two conditions shown in the lower pane of Table 7.1 illustrate two zero contingencies. In both cases the conditional probabilities are equal and the action does not control the outcome, so they are identical in their level of contingency. However, these examples differ in terms of the relative frequency or density of outcome occurrence. The outcome occurs on 25 percent of all trials in the low-density condition (left) and on 75 percent of trials in the high-density condition (right). Interestingly, from the perspective of this discussion, the correct judgement in both conditions should be that the action has no influence on the likelihood of the outcome.

Alloy and Abramson (1979) used these two conditions, which are described in the lower panel of Table 7.1, in one key experiment that demonstrated depression realism. They found that nondepressed people's judgements increased with the number of outcomes, although the programmed degree of contingency was ostensibly the same in both conditions. This might be thought of as an optimistic bias (e.g., Taylor & Brown, 1988). One explanation for this bias with nondepressed persons is that with higher outcome densities come more outcome events (i.e., more Cell A and C events). If it is assumed though that Cell A events – pairings of the action and the outcome – are particularly salient or more easily learned, then people may be more likely to mistakenly believe they are in control of the outcome. Depressed persons showed no such judgement bias, their judgements did not increase with higher levels of outcome density and were more consistent with the programmed zero contingency. This null effect was argued to reflect a tendency to be more realistic. Thus they were said to be sadder but wiser.

This differential density effect with zero contingencies has been demonstrated several times (high outcome density conditions: Alloy et al., 1985; Benassi & Mahler, 1985; Martin et al., 1984; Vasquez, 1987). However, studies have shown that with positive contingencies, in which the participant does have control over the outcome, both depressed and nondepressed participants are equally accurate in their judgements (Alloy et al., 1985; Carson, 2001; Cobbs, Critelli, & Tang, 1990; Ee, 1994; Lennox, Bedell, Abramson, Raps, & Foley, 1990; Vasquez, 1987). Thus "depressive realism" seems to be restricted to a narrow range of possible contingencies. In addition, no differences have been reported in conditions where the action is replaced by a passively experienced predictive event (Alloy et al., 1985).

According to Alloy and Abramson (Alloy & Abramson, 1979; Alloy et al., 1985), the pattern of optimism and realism in zero contingency control scenarios, but not positive contingencies or predictive scenarios, is linked to a motivational difference between groups and conditions. People who are not depressed are motivated to maintain their self-esteem. The feelings that accompany the lack of control experienced with noncontingent actions are simply incompatible with the motivation to maintain self-esteem. Judgements are a product of this conflict and are inflated to protect self-esteem. On the other hand, depressed people have little motivation to maintain their self-esteem and assess the situation accurately. This logic does not apply to positive contingencies or predictive scenarios. So this modified depressive realism explanation fits the empirical result that the differences found are only found with zero contingencies.

Outcome density effects

It seems then that the effect of relative outcome frequency, or more simply outcome density, on contingency learning is not as simple as a general tendency for most people to overestimate their own abilities (e.g., Alloy & Tabachnik, 1984). This certainly becomes clearer when a wider range of contingencies, configurations of events, and scenarios are tested than in the original depressive realism studies that often involved only high outcome density zero contingencies with actions and not passively experienced events.

One important factor that affects the prevalence of the outcome density effects in the general population is whether the contingency scenario involves actions or observations (Vallée-Tourangeau, Murphy, & Baker, 2005). The difference between active and passive scenarios is clearly illustrated in two studies in which the procedure and scenarios were similar but one version of the task was active and one was passive. Allan and Jenkins (1980, 1983) asked their participants to judge the relationship between the movement of a joystick and the appearance of a visual stimulus. Participants were able to move the joystick themselves in the active task (1R-I condition: Allan & Jenkins, 1980) but only observed its movement in the passive version (1R/1O condition: Allan & Jenkins, 1983). Among others, five zero contingency conditions were tested in which outcome density varied from .10, in which the outcome occurred on 10 percent of all trials, to .90, in which the outcome occurred on 90 percent of trials. Participants judged that the contingency was substantially stronger with higher levels of outcome density in the passive condition but not in the active condition. These data suggest that passive contingencies are more sensitive to outcome density effects than *active* contingencies, at least in the general population. This is certainly not consistent with theories that invoke motivation to maintain self-esteem to explain outcome density effects.

Allan and Jenkins's finding of a difference between active and passive contingencies is not isolated. Data from some of our own studies mirror their findings. Wasserman and his co-workers (Wasserman, Elek, Chatlosh, & Baker, 1993) used an active action–outcome procedure to examine judgements of multiple positive, negative, and zero contingency conditions. Like Allan and Jenkins, there was no evidence that people perceived a stronger degree of contingency with higher levels of outcome density. In fact, with nonzero positive and negative contingencies, more frequent outcomes were associated with a somewhat weaker perception of contingency. As it is unlikely that participants were depressed, this begs the question as to why some active tasks do not show the density effects described by Alloy and Abramson (1979). In contrast, our work involving passive contingencies produces consistent evidence for strong outcome frequency effects. Moreover, the passive outcome frequency effect seems to be more general than the active one. We have presented participants with contingencies between fictitious symptoms and diseases (Vallée-Tourangeau, Hollingsworth, & Murphy, 1998) and fictitious viruses and diseases (Vallée-Tourangeau, Murphy, Drew, & Baker, 1998). In these studies, participants observed numerous patient records, each of which could contain any combination of the event outcome conjunctions mentioned in Table 7.1 (e.g., virus present/disease present; or virus absent/disease present, etc.). They were asked to judge the causal relationship between the virus or symptom and the disease. The participants consistently reported that there was a stronger causal relationship in conditions where the disease occurred more frequently. Again, this body of work suggests that judgements made by the general population about passive contingencies are more likely to be influenced by outcome frequency than judgements made about active contingencies.

This result is of particular relevance to the topic of depressive realism. Alloy and colleagues reported that their nondepressed participants' judgements were influenced by the optimistic bias or outcome frequency effect in active zero contingencies (Alloy & Abramson, 1979). It was this optimistic bias that generated the difference between the judgements of the depressed and nondepressed. However, when they later used a passive scenario, in which we and others find the strongest evidence for an outcome-density bias, they found the density bias but no difference between depressed and nondepressed people (Alloy et al., 1985). Their conclusion was that "nondepressives were no more likely than depressives to exhibit an illusion of prediction" (p. 240).

The difference between active and passive situations is not unprecedented. For example, animal learning theorists have traditionally studied both active and passive learning tasks. Pavlovian conditioning involves passive learning and instrumental conditioning active learning in a manner analogous to the active and passive contingency tasks used with human participants. Although by no means a universal conclusion, one view is that the associative connections and the rules that govern the acquisition of those associations during learning obey the same associative principles regardless of whether acquired passively or actively (Mackintosh, 1983). However, one of the questions following on from this research is whether active instrumental learning provides the animal with a qualitatively different experience or whether learning is fundamentally about the association of stimuli, responses and outcomes with stimuli, and responses only differing with respect to the type of stimulation they excite.

Outcome density and mood effects in active and passively experienced contingencies

The following experiment directly compared the density effect in a zero contingency task using a within-subjects design in which the same participants learned both predictive (that is, passive) and active contingency event–outcome contingencies. We predicted that predictive tasks would show the standard density effect of higher judgements with increased outcome frequency but that active tasks would not show this effect. We screened participants for mood to look for evidence of the depressive realism effect since it is possible that previous work on density effects may have sampled different levels of depression.

As in Alloy and Abramson's original research, university students ($N = 43$) completed the Beck Depression Inventory (Beck, Ward, Mendelson, Mock, & Erbaugh, 1961) and were assigned to the depressed (BDI > 9: $n = 21$) or nondepressed group (BDI < 9: $n = 22$). Participants then completed active and passive versions of the contingency judgement task with low and high outcome density zero contingencies (see Table 7.1). The active scenario involved a computerized version of Alloy and Abramson's (1979) "light-bulb" task, in which participants were asked to judge the extent of their control over a light switching on. The passive scenario required participants to judge the predictive relationship between the results of a blood test (positive, negative) and a urine test (positive, negative) shown as individual

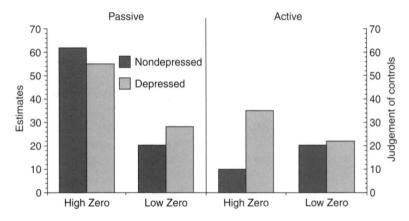

Figure 7.1 Judgements by depressed and nondepressed students of high-density and low-density zero contingencies on passive and active judgement task.

patient records. Each condition involved 40 trials and the timing of both procedures was identical. After each set of 40 trials in both procedures, participants were presented with a 0 (no control or no prediction) to 100 (total control or total prediction) judgement scale and were asked to make a judgement about the relationship between each event (button press, results of blood test) and its outcome (light onset, results of urine test).

The results are presented in Figure 7.1 and indicated a number of interesting findings. First, predictive tasks produce strong outcome density effects, regardless of mood state. The low-density zero contingency treatments were judged significantly lower than the high outcome density treatment. The active task showed a much weaker outcome density effect and, puzzlingly, only for the depressed sample.

Like Alloy, Abramson and Kosman's (1985) findings, these results suggest that predictive tasks do not support differences in the mood groups but that active tasks do. However, in this experiment, depressed participants unexpectedly showed a larger rather than a smaller bias. Rather than considering the two tasks as involving different notions of personal instrumentality and their differential effect on personal self-esteem, we considered the temporal differences in stimulus exposure that the two types of task generate. In spite of the emphasis of task type (predictive/active) our recent work suggests that these mood effects are more likely to be related to sensitivity to differences in the temporal or motivational characteristics of the two tasks.

These findings allow us to comment on Alloy et al.'s (1985) conclusions about, what they termed, the illusions of control and prediction. They argued that the nondepressed were more likely to display an illusion of control than the depressed because of their optimistic bias but no more likely to display an "illusion of prediction". They reasoned that contingencies between neutral, nonpersonal events would not be a subject for optimism. Our findings are not compatible with explanations based purely on self-esteem.

One significant difference, however, between our task and the one conducted by Alloy and Abramson relates to the temporal intervals between trials. Whilst standard associative theory treats stimuli and responses as quite similar in how they enter into association with the outcome, the theory can produce quite different predictions for the two tasks if temporal relationships between the associated events differ. We now consider how associative theory can predict density effects from these differences.

Associative theory and contingency learning

Associative learning theory explains the process of learning about contingencies through the development of associations between active or passively experienced events and subsequent outcomes (e.g., Rescorla & Wagner, 1972). Active experience does not itself produce a different type of associated event (Dickinson & Balleine, 1994; although see Blaisdell, Sawa, Leising, & Waldmann, 2006). Mental associations gradually develop and become stronger when such events and outcomes occur repeatedly at around the same time. The event–outcome association is directly strengthened by co-occurrences (Cell A) and weakened by the occurrence of the event on its own (Cell B). Indirect influences take place when the outcome occurs unaccompanied (Cell C) or when neither of them happen (Cell D). So all four of the events in a contingency table, including absent ones, affect the development of an association between an event and an outcome. The indirect influences occur as a function of changes in the associative strength of the hypothesized contextual cues that accompany the event under consideration.

Every stimulus present, including the stimuli composing the context in which events take place, will enter into an association with the outcome. The change in all of these associations at any given point in time can be understood in terms of the following equation: $\Delta V_n = \alpha\beta(\lambda - \Sigma V_n)$. This equation formalizes this idea in that the change in the strength of an association (ΔV_n) is determined by the discrepancy between maximum possible strength (λ) and the current strength of all the other associations combined (ΣV_n). This means that if one association grows in strength, there is less of the possible association (λ) to be shared around between all the other stimuli present. Finally, the parameters α and β determine learning speed and are related to the associability and salience of events and outcomes, respectively. Rather surprisingly, this model (Rescorla & Wagner, 1972) can not only describe the process of contingency learning but can also account for outcome density effects, how they are dependent on specific scenarios and why this might differ in those who are depressed.

If we consider a high-density zero contingency scenario, involving an action and a light flash, like that used in Alloy and Abramson's depressive

Table 7.2 A contingency table showing how the presence and absence of actions and outcomes affect the strength of the context–outcome association

| | Light flash | |
	Present	Absent
Action and context stimuli present	15 × Cell A Action stronger Context stronger	5 × Cell B Action weaker Context weaker
Only context stimuli present	15 × Cell C Context stronger Action weaker	5 × Cell D Context weaker Action stronger

realism experiments then action and light flash take place within a context so both the action and the context become associated with the flash as shown in Table 7.2. However, the events that make the context stronger (Cells A and C) are much more frequent than those that make the action stronger (Cells A and D) and events that make the action weaker (Cells B and C) are twice as frequent as those that make the context weaker (Cells B and D). The net result of this is that the context becomes strongly associated with the flash and any action–flash association that might have begun its initial development is extinguished back to zero. Thus, if all events are considered to be equally salient, then the asymptotic predictions of the Rescorla–Wagner model are identical to ΔP (Chapman & Robbins, 1990).

However, it is often the case that the four events shown above are not of equal salience. For example, Wasserman, Dorner, and Kao (1990) found that participants weight contingency events unequally. As one might expect, trials where the outcome occurs (Cells A and C) are weighted more highly than those in which it doesn't (Cells B and D). In terms of the associative model, this means that the value assigned to the learning rate parameter, β, that specifies the salience of the outcome, should reflect this difference. Therefore, β_1 that reflects the presence of the outcome should be set to be greater than β_0 that reflects its absence. This generates predictions of stronger associations in lower than higher outcome density nonzero contingencies but no density effects with zero contingency conditions. Importantly, this is consistent with data mentioned earlier, showing no outcome density effects with active zero contingencies (Allan & Jenkins, 1980; Wasserman et al., 1993) and negative density effects in nonzero contingencies (Wasserman et al., 1993). Interestingly, the reverse parameter manipulation ($\beta_0 > \beta_1$) generates the kind of positive density effect reported here and elsewhere (e.g., Vallée-Tourangeau, Murphy, et al., 1998) in passively experienced contingencies and in the depressive realism literature with nondepressed participants (e.g., Alloy & Abramson, 1979). Therefore factors that promote the salience and thus associability of outcomes determine the presence or absence of outcome density effects. Our studies have shown that three factors are of particular relevancy here – temporal contiguity, context, and motivation. We will discuss each of these in turn in relation to outcome density effects and in relation to depression.

Contiguity

Temporal contiguity is critical to associative learning and the outcome must follow the predictive event in close temporal succession. Events and outcomes that occur closely spaced in time are seen as more highly related than those with identical contingencies but between which there is a delay (Shanks, Pearson, & Dickinson, 1989). One reason for this is that delayed outcomes are likely to be less salient to the participant and so Cell A events will be less effective in increasing associative strength (Vallée-Tourangeau et al., 2005). In fact, delayed outcomes could reduce β_1 so much that $\beta_1 > \beta_0$ and, as described above, positive density effects could ensue.

So is there any evidence that poor temporal contiguity might be related to the different judgement patterns seen in passive compared to active contingencies? Of course, the delay was programmed to be the same in the active and passive tasks described earlier in this chapter. In all conditions, the task was structured such that there was a 3 s time window during which the passively experienced event was exposed or the participant could make the action and this was followed by the occurrence of the outcome. The delay between the occurrence of the passive event and the outcome was therefore always 3 s. However, the delay in the active task was likely to be considerably less. In the active task participants were given a signal that the 3 s "button press opportunity" had arrived and it usually took around 2 s for them to make that action. This would result in a delay of only around 1 s, and considerably improved temporal contiguity. Our previous studies have shown that even a small improvement in contiguity from 1 s to 0.5 s can make a substantial difference to outcome density effects (Vallée-Tourangeau et al., 2005). This suggests that $\beta_{1\ active}$ is considerably greater than $\beta_{1\ passive}$ and explains why our nondepressed participants only displayed outcome effects in the passive task and not the active one. However, this does not account for nondepressed outcome density effects in Alloy and Abramson's experiment because their delay was identical to that in our experiments.

Context

In order to investigate why Alloy and Abramson's experiments produced such strong outcome density effects under similar delay conditions, we studied the effect of a further factor that distinguished their procedures from others (Msetfi, Murphy, Simpson, & Kornbrot, 2005; Msetfi, Murphy, & Simpson, 2007). This was the duration of the empty interval programmed to occur between experimental trials – the intertrial interval (ITI). Previous studies of active contingency judgements in which outcome density (OD) effects were not observed tended to involve either no programmed ITI (Allan & Jenkins, 1980) or quite short intervals of around 1 s between experimental trials (Wasserman, Chatlosh, & Neunaber, 1983; Wasserman et al., 1993). In contrast, the depressive realism contingency task used ITIs of 14 s on average. This is important because ITIs are periods of time in which the participant is exposed to the experimental context in the absence of the occurrence of the outcome and this might be perceived as a sequence of Cell D events. These long periods of context exposure in the absence of any outcomes would weaken or extinguish context–outcome associations. This would allow the response to acquire associative strength, particularly in high-density conditions where there are more event–outcome pairings. In fact no matter how the model parameters are set, including the ITIs into the model as context–no outcome trials generates predictions of OD effects, such that higher levels of OD will result in stronger associations that should elicit more positive judgements (Baker, Murphy, Vallée-Tourangeau, & Mehta, 2001). An intriguing implication of this is that the depressed, who are not reported to display OD effects in experiments with long ITIs, are not sensitive to context exposure and extinction in the same manner as the nondepressed.

We tested this hypothesis in a series of experiments in which we exposed depressed and nondepressed students to active low or high OD zero contingencies under conditions with short (3 s) or long (15 s) ITIs (Msetfi et al., 2005, 2007). The results are shown in Figure 7.2.

As we predicted, judgements made by the nondepressed were strongly influenced by ITI length and OD. Long ITI conditions produced OD

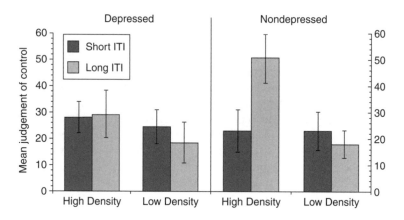

Figure 7.2 Mean judgements of control in a zero contingency condition as a function of intertrial interval (ITI) length, outcome density, and mood (error bars correspond with the standard error of the mean).

effects, like those reported by Alloy and Abramson. However, judgements made under short ITI conditions were very similar to those in the previous experiment reported here with no evidence of OD effects. On the other hand, depressed people's judgements did not change significantly with either ITI length or OD. The depressed group, just as in the previous experiment, were more likely to show the density bias with the short ITI conditions. The only evidence for so-called realism was in the condition with long ITIs and high OD. We have also observed similar patterns in studies of positive contingencies and negative contingencies (Msetfi et al., 2007). The general conclusion about depression and its effect on contingency learning from this set of experiments is that the depressed are not sensitive to changes in the information provided by the experimental context. In some limited circumstances, this produces judgements that may appear to be realistic. Though when depressed people's judgements are studied over a larger range of conditions and scenarios, there is little evidence of realism, merely inflexibility in terms of their response to what might be beneficial information.

Motivation

In addition to negative cognitions, people with depression commonly display behavioural manifestations of the disorder. As we have mentioned in our review at the start of the chapter, depressed people often seem less motivated than the nondepressed. Among the possible consequences of this low motivation is a marked reduction in the tendency to initiate action or a general passivity. Moreover, the depressed seem to be less sensitive to motivational effects of reinforcers in general (Buchwald, 1977). Either or both of these factors might be predicted to influence the experience of the participants in an active contingency judgement task.

The focus of these next experiments was to test a rather simple hypothesis generated by the self-serving motivational hypothesis. Koenig, Clements, and Alloy (1992) suggested that persons who are not depressed may perceive contingencies objectively, but their motivation to maintain their self-esteem at an adaptive level causes them to report higher control than they actually have. Depressed persons, who have little self-esteem to protect, both perceive and report the actual contingency. It follows from this explanation of the phenomenon that if motivation to report control accurately is increased, or if accuracy was made more relevant to self-esteem, then the nondepressed should give more accurate estimates. Depressed participants under the same circumstances should presumably maintain their *accurate* reports of control.

In order to test this prediction, we carried out an experiment in which participants in four different groups, two depressed and two not, were given a judgement of control task much like those we have already described. One depressed and one nondepressed group received incentives and were told that they would be paid for the accuracy of their estimates whereas the two other groups, as in the experiments reported earlier and most depressive realism studies, did not receive incentives. The assumption was that the motivational manipulation would have little effect on depressed people's judgements of high-density zero contingencies but that reinforcement might make the people who are not depressed more "realistic".

In this experiment, more stringent criteria were used to assign participants to the depressed and nondepressed groups. Only those who scored below 10 and above 17 on the BDI-II (Beck, Steer, & Brown, 1996) were invited to participate in the experiment. Volunteers scoring between 11 and 16 were excluded, as were those who reported that they were taking antidepressant medication. All remaining participants completed a number of active contingency judgement tasks in which they were told that they would need to push a computer space bar that might influence the appearance of a coloured circle (analogous to the light in previous experiments).

Each task involved a different contingency with different levels of OD. There was a moderate-density positive contingency [$\Delta P = .5$, $P(O|A) = .75$; $P(O|NoA) = .25$], and a moderate-density negative contingency [$\Delta P = -.5$, $P(O|A) = .25$; $P(O|NoA) = .75$]. There were also three zero contingencies that were a low-density zero contingency [$P(O|A) = .25$, $P(O|NoA) = .25$], a moderate-density zero contingency [$P(O|A) = .5$, $P(O|NoA) = .5$], and a high-density zero contingency [$P(O|A) = .75$, $P(O|NoA) = .75$]. The low- and high-density zero contingencies are the same as those used in the previous experiments reported here. The incentive groups, labelled low and high motivation, received the same contingencies except that they were informed in the instructions that they would be paid for the accuracy of their estimates of control once they had completed the five tasks.

Each game consisted of 50 trials. An individual trial consisted of the 2 s presentation of a trial marker (a small circle on the left side of the computer screen) during which participants could respond or not. In the following 1.5 s, the outcome circle would occur on outcome-present trials. The outcome was a larger circle presented on the right hand side of the screen. If there was no outcome the screen remained blank for this period. After each task, participants were asked to judge their control over the circle using a -100 to $+100$ rating scale. Negative scores mean the participants believe they are able to prevent the circle from illuminating and thus also represent impressions of control. In addition, based on responses made during each task, we calculated the exact contingency experienced by each participant and the deviation between the experienced contingency and the judged contingency (bias scores).

The judgements for the depressed and nondepressed women in the high and low motivation treatments are shown in the top panel of Figure 7.3.

It is quite clear that judgements made by both the depressed and nondepressed groups distinguished the positive and negative contingencies from the three zero contingencies and that the motivational manipulation had

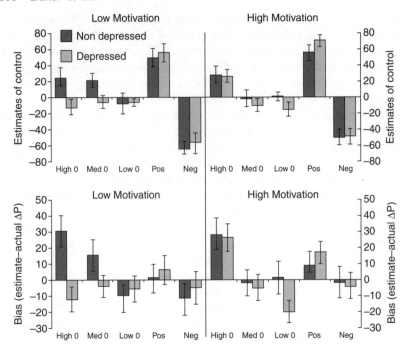

Figure 7.3 The upper panel shows contingency estimates made by depressed and nondepressed students in the high- and low-motivation conditions. The lower panels show the mean bias scores for the five contingencies (error bars are the standard errors of the mean).

very little influence on judgements of the positive and negative contingencies. As is usually the case, both groups made fairly *accurate* judgements of the positive and negative contingencies although in this example there appears a slight, but nonreliable, tendency for the depressives to judge the contingencies more negatively. However, there were reliable differences in how the groups judged the different density zero contingencies. In fact, the low motivation groups showed a fairly conventional *depressive realism* effect. That is to say participants who were not depressed showed a pronounced density bias in the high-density zero contingency. The depressed students, however, did not show this bias and in fact showed fairly equal, although slightly negative, estimates of all three zero contingencies.

Our original prediction was that if the self-serving motivational hypothesis was correct then increasing motivation by rewarding accuracy should reduce any bias and perhaps eliminate the difference between depressed and nondepressed students. As Figure 7.3 shows, increasing motivation did not reduce the high-density bias effect in the nondepressed group. However, it did have the effect of reducing the difference between the depressed and the nondepressed but did so, rather ironically, by generating a density bias in the depressed group that was at least as pronounced as that in those who were not depressed.

These findings are also clearly documented in the bias measure shown in the lower panel of Figure 7.3. Bias scores represent deviations between judgements of control and the contingencies experienced in light of response levels [e.g., judgement – (experienced $\Delta P \times 100$)], where positive values indicate overestimates and negative values underestimates. Generally in the low motivation condition, the biases of the depressed were quite close to zero, indicating they tracked the contingencies accurately. The non-depressed were quite accurate with all contingencies except the high-density zero contingency. In the high motivation condition, both the depressed and nondepressed groups showed a high-density bias and, if anything, the depressed group show a negative bias in the low-density condition.

There is a great deal of data in these experiments so it is beyond the scope of this chapter to report the results of the statistical analyses here. However, suffice it to say that the results support the observations made in the preceding paragraph that depressed students acted differently from those who were not depressed but not because they were fundamentally more accurate or *realistic*. Rather it seems that, when they are less motivated, the normal high-density bias is suppressed. It would seem that this result indicates that the manifestation of depressive realism is, at least partially, of motivational rather than simply cognitive origin. This is consistent with the widely held belief that depressed people are less motivated than others and that this impacts on their cognitions.

Given that motivation acts on the cognitions of depressed students can we say anything about possible mechanisms for these effects? Our data do give us some hints about this. Figure 7.4 shows the number of trials on which the participants in the four groups pressed the space bar in an attempt to illuminate the circle. It is quite clear from this figure that, in the low motivation condition, depressed students pushed the space bar on a lower proportion of trials across all contingencies. The effect of increasing motivation was to eliminate this difference and again this impression was confirmed by the statistical analysis.

This suggests that it is possible that at least part of the effect of mood on depressive realism is modulated by differences in response rates generated by the mood manipulation. Depressed participants respond at relatively low rates but how could this lead to a smaller density bias in these students? Differences in response rates generate differences in the frequency of the event conjunctions in a standard contingency table. Higher response rates lead to more response–outcome pairings (high Cell A) and more occur-rences of the response alone (Cell B), whereas low response rates lead to high Cell C and Cell D rates. Research in the past has shown that people believe that Cells A and B are more important in determining contingency than Cells C and D (this in itself is, of course, a bias). So it is possible that the lower level of Cell A and Cell B events might lead to the lower estimates

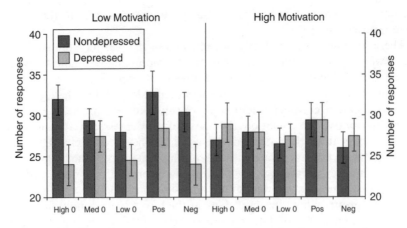

Figure 7.4 Number of responses for each contingency for depressed and nondepressed students on the two motivation levels (errors bars are standard errors of the mean).

in the high-density zero contingency for depressives. To test this, we correlated all participants' estimates for all contingencies with the number of occurrences of events in each cell. Not surprisingly these correlations were all reliable but, interestingly, the absolute values of the Pearson correlations for Cells A and B (.64 and −.61) were materially higher than those of Cells C and D (−.39 and .31). Remember that Cells A and D vary positively with contingency and Cells B and C vary negatively. This analysis is consistent with the fact that people put more weight on Cells A and B and that all other things being equal this could relate to the fact that depressives make lower estimates of the high-density zero contingency.

We did a similar correlational analysis on estimates of the zero contingencies and found that for the nondepressed in both motivation conditions and for the depressed group in the high motivation condition, Cells A and B were correlated with judgements (minimum absolute $r = .39$). Interestingly, depressed women did not show a correlation between Cell A and B maximum $r = .07$ in the low motivation condition. This result should be taken with great caution, however, because the variability of zero contingency estimates in that group is quite low, which should lead to lower correlations. The pattern for Cells C and D was similar but because of the small number of observations and the already documented tendency for lower correlations with Cells C and D fewer of these correlations were reliable.

Just as in the previous experiments on context manipulation, here too we can eliminate the difference between the depressed and nondepressed. Moreover there is a compelling hint that the mechanism for this motivational effect might be through the effect of motivation on response rates. Depressed students respond less often and thus experience fewer Cell A and

B events and consequently show a lower bias in high-density zero contingencies where this effect should be dominant.

We have argued that motivation seems to influence response rates in this task and that these higher response rates might influence estimates. However, this conclusion is based on correlations so we have carried out a preliminary experiment designed to determine whether an independent nonmotivational manipulation of response rates could influence estimates. To do this, we asked two groups of depressed ($n = 28$, BDI-II > 11) and nondepressed students ($n = 36$, BDI-II < 12) to complete a high-density and a low-density zero contingency task with no reward for accuracy. However, before doing the task we asked half of the students to respond (press the space bar in an attempt to illuminate the circle) on either a low (25 percent) or a high (75 percent) proportion of the trials. Other than that, the task was identical to the previous task. Following each task, the participants made estimates of their control on a –100 to + 100 scale and a bias measure was calculated.

The response manipulation was effective in generating different proportions of responses (response rates) in the high (range of mean proportion .63 to .83 trials with a response, target = .75) and the low response rate conditions (range of proportions .30 to .35). For all participants, there was a tendency to be more accurate in the low response conditions. High responders tended to attribute more positive control (mean bias = .33) to the high-density zero contingency than did the low responders (mean bias = .16). The high responders also reported the low-density contingency to be slightly more negative (bias –.19 versus –.11). Thus this experiment provides independent evidence that responding on a high proportion of trials biases not only high-density zero contingencies but possibly also low-density ones.

Figure 7.5 shows the mean bias scores for the depressed and non-depressed high and low responders for the two contingencies.

This figure shows quite clearly that relative bias of high responders in both the high- and low-density contingencies is, if anything, more pronounced in the more depressed students. In fact, considering the order of means in the high-density condition (i.e., where depressive realism is usually found), the means in the low response condition are consistent with depressive realism. The depressed are slightly less biased than the non-depressed but this pattern is reversed in the high response rate condition. However, the statistical analysis only confirms that all the students with the high response instructions on average made higher estimates of control in the high-density zero contingency than those who had received low response instructions. The difference in the low-density zero condition was not reliable.

The preceding is a summary of the results of a more complex analysis of these data including order effects and there were some interactions involving mood. Nonetheless at no point does it contradict the conclusion

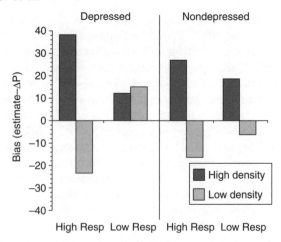

Figure 7.5 Bias of estimates of depressed and nondepressed students following high and low response suggestions on high- and low-density zero contingencies.

that people instructed to respond on a higher proportion of trials made more biased estimates and this included the participants in the sample who were most depressed.

Thus, we can conclude, as we did following the earlier experiments, that in general both depressed and nondepressed people are generally quite accurate at judging their control in active instrumental contingency tasks but that both groups show some biases particularly with high-density contingencies. As in the earlier experiments, these two experiments demonstrated that depressed people are not generally more accurate than the nondepressed and that standard manipulations of variables from learning theory, in this case motivational and behavioural manipulations, lawfully influence the biases of depressed and nondepressed students in a similar way. Moreover this experiment provides a hint that at least part of the mechanism for the influence of that effect in clinically depressed people may be through the direct effect of motivation on response activation. We showed that increasing motivation reduced differences in response rates between our depressed and nondepressed women but it also generated similar cognitive biases. We then showed that a nonmotivational manipulation of response rate directly influenced bias in a similar manner. It is well known that depressed people experience apathy. This may not just be an effect of the motivational and biochemical causes of depression but it also might be part of the causal mechanism of depression. Passivity changes individuals' interactions with their environment and this change in the simple instrumental interactions with the features and objects of their lives may influence their cognitions just as our manipulation, that changed the proportion of our participants' experiences with the cells of a contingency table, influenced their perception of control.

Concluding comments

It is always attractive to report a paradoxical finding or double dissociation in which someone suffering from a disorder, in spite of all the difficulties that it entails, is actually better at something than those without the disorder. Depressive realism seemed like just such a case. The depressed are better judges than the nondepressed because they can exercise their cognitions about self-control unencumbered by a drive for self-esteem. The depressed are sadder but wiser.

The research we have documented here shows that this conclusion was premature. We have shown that depressed people are not always more accurate than those who are not depressed – often they are less accurate. Moreover, we have shown that their reactions to a number of standard behavioural and motivational manipulations are similar to those of the nondepressed although their sensitivity to those manipulations may differ. Furthermore, our results are consistent with and provide independent support for many of the common assumptions of the cognitive behavioural theories of depression. Our work on the effects of the intertrial interval and its possible mechanism through perception of Cell D is consistent with the notion that people with depression have trouble with sustained attention. Our work on motivation and response rate is consistent with the claim that depressives are motivationally flat and passive. This is consistent with the notion of a vicious cycle in which depression generates passiveness that then feeds back and generates more depression.

Finally, we come to the issue of therapy. Our results do not suggest a new therapeutic approach, rather they encourage a traditional view that emphasises cognitive restructuring and behavioural activation interventions that encourage interactions with contingencies and rewards in the environment. Although we believe we have shown that the depressed person is not more realistic than persons who are not depressed, the therapist can be encouraged by the fact that at a fundamental level depressives are susceptible to cognitive interventions and if these interventions are applied judiciously, then a client with depressive symptoms can come to behave similarly to the nondepressed. The therapist is dealing with someone who is sadder but not necessarily wiser.

That being said, one very important issue must be acknowledged before concluding. The hypothesized negative psychological correlates and consequences of distortions in the perception of control come almost entirely from a Western cultural perspective. Indeed, it is this individualistic perspective, which focuses on individuality and self determination, that emphasizes perceived control as a key factor in influencing psychological well-being. Collectivist cultures, on the other hand, have a very different dynamic emphasizing interdependence with little emphasis on personal control (see Markus & Kitayama, 1991 for an extensive discussion). Moreover, cross-cultural comparisons show that there are differences in the perceived importance of personal control and even the strength of judgements that people make in different contingency situations (Ji, Peng, & Nisbett, 2000). Until a better understanding of such cultural effects exists, therapists must take nothing for granted and treat culture and personal control as a possible wild card in their formulations.

References

Abramson, L. Y., Metalsky, G. I., & Alloy, L. B. (1989). Hopelessness depression: A theory based subtype of depression. *Psychological Review, 96*, 358–372.

Ackermann, R., & DeRubeis, R. J. (1991). Is depressive realism real? *Clinical Psychology Review, 11*(5), 565–584.

Allan, L. G. (1980). A note on measurement of contingency between two binary variables in judgment tasks. *Bulletin of the Psychonomic Society, 15*(3), 147–149.

Allan, L. G., & Jenkins, H. M. (1980). The judgment of contingency and the nature of the response alternatives. *Canadian Journal of Psychology, 34*(1), 1–11.

Allan, L. G., & Jenkins, H. M. (1983). The effect of representations of binary variables on judgment of influence. *Learning and Motivation, 14*(4), 381–405.

Alloy, L. B., & Abramson, L. Y. (1979). Judgement of contingency in depressed and nondepressed students: Sadder but wiser? *Journal of Experimental Psychology: General, 108*(4), 441–485.

Alloy, L. B., Abramson, L. Y., & Kossman, D. A. (1985). The judgement of predictability in depressed and nondepressed college students. In F. R. Brush & J. B. Overmier (Eds.), *Affect, conditioning and cognition: Essays on the determinants of behaviour* (pp. 229–246). Hillsdale, NJ: Lawrence Erlbaum Associates, Inc.

Alloy, L. B., & Tabachnik, N. (1984). Assessment of covariation by humans and animals: The joint influence of prior expectations and current situational information. *Psychological Review, 91*(1), 112–149.

American Psychiatric Association (1994). *Diagnostic and statistical manual of mental disorders* (4th ed.). Washington, DC: American Psychiatric Publishing.

Baker, A. G., Murphy, R. A., Vallée-Tourangeau, F., & Mehta, R. (2001). Contingency learning and causal reasoning. In R. R. Mowrer & S. B. Klein (Eds.), *Handbook of contemporary learning theories* (pp. 255–306). Mahwah, NJ: Lawrence Erlbaum Associates, Inc.

Beck, A. T. (1967). *Depression: Clinical, experimental and theoretical aspects.* London, UK: Staples Press.

Beck, A. T., Steer, R. A., & Brown, G. K. (1996). *Manual for the Beck Depression Inventory – II.* San Antonio, TX: Psychological Corporation.

Beck, A. T., Ward, C. H., Mendelson, M., Mock, J., & Erbaugh, J. (1961). An inventory for measuring depression. *Archives of General Psychiatry, 4*, 561–571.

Benassi, V. A., & Mahler, H. I. M. (1985). Contingency judgements by depressed college students: Sadder but not always wiser. *Journal of Personality and Social Psychology, 49*(5), 1323–1329.

Bierut, L. J., Heath, A. C., Bucholz, K. K., Dinwiddie, S. H., Madden, P. A. F., Statham, D. J., et al. (1999). Major depressive disorder in a community based twin sample. *Archives of General Psychiatry, 56*, 557–563.

Blaisdell, A. P., Sawa, K., Leising, K. J., & Waldmann, M. R. (2006). Causal reasoning in rats. *Science, 311*, 1020–1022.

Buchwald, A. M. (1977). Depressive mood and estimates of reinforcement frequency. *Journal of Abnormal Psychology, 86*(4), 443–446.

Carson, R. C. (2001). *Depressive realism: Continuous monitoring of contingency judgements among depressed outpatients and nondepressed controls.* Doctoral dissertation, Vanderbilt University, Nashville, TN. *Dissertation Abstracts International, 62,* 1070.

Chapman, G. B., & Robbins, S. J. (1990). Cue interaction in human contingency judgement. *Memory and Cognition, 18,* 537–545.

Cobbs, D. L., Critelli, J. W., & Tang, C. S. (1990). *Judgement of contingency in clinical depressives.* Unpublished manuscript, University of North Texas, Denton, TX, USA.

Coyne, J. C., & Gotlib, I. H. (1983). The role of cognition in depression: A critical appraisal. *Psychological Bulletin, 94*(3), 472–505.

Crocker, J. (1981). Judgment of covariation by social perceivers. *Psychological Bulletin, 90*(2), 272–292.

DeMonbreun, B. G., & Craighead, E. (1977). Distortion of perception and recall of positive and neutral feedback in depression. *Cognitive Therapy and Research, 1*(4), 311–329.

Dickinson, A., & Balleine, B. (1994). Motivational control of goal-directed action. *Animal Learning & Behavior, 22*(1), 1–18.

Ee, J. S. C. (1994). *Judgment of contingency in hospitalized depressives.* PhD theses, University North Texas, Denton, TX, USA. *Dissertation Abstracts International: Section B. The Sciences and Engineering.* pp. 4385.

Gotlib, I. H., Kurtzman, H. S., & Blehar, M. C. (1997). Cognition and depression: Issues and future directions. *Cognition & Emotion, 11*(5–6), 663–673.

Gotlib, I. H., & Lee, C. M. (1989). The social functioning of depressed patients: A longitudinal assessment. *Journal of Social and Clinical Psychology, 8*(3), 223–237.

Ji, L., Peng, K., & Nisbett, R. E. (2000). Culture, control, and perception of relationships in the environment. *Journal of Personality and Social Psychology, 78*(5), 943–955.

Keller, P. A., Lipkus, I. M., & Rimer, B. K. (2002). Depressive realism and health risk accuracy: The negative consequences of positive mood. *Journal of Consumer Research, 29*(1), 57–69.

Kessler, R. C., McGonagle, K. A., Swartz, M., & Blazer, D. G. (1993). Sex and depression in the National Comorbidity Survey: I. Lifetime prevalence, chronicity and recurrence. *Journal of Affective Disorders, 29*(2), 85–96.

Koenig, L. J., Clements, C. M., & Alloy, L. B. (1992). Depression and the illusion of control: The role of esteem maintenance and impression management. *Canadian Journal of Behavioural Science, 24*(2), 233–252.

Lennox, S. S., Bedell, J. R., Abramson, L. Y., Raps, C., & Foley, F. W. (1990). Judgement of contingency: A replication with hospitalized depressed, schizophrenic and normal samples. *Journal of Social Behavior and Personality, 5*(4), 189–204.

Lewinsohn, P. M., Mischel, W., Chaplin, W., & Barton, R. (1980). Social competence and depression: The role of illusory self-perceptions? *Journal of Abnormal Psychology, 89,* 203–212.

Mackintosh, N. J. (1983). *Conditioning and associative learning.* Oxford, UK: Oxford University Press.

Markus, H. R., & Kitayama, S. (1991). Culture and the self: Implications for cognition, emotion and motivation. *Psychological Review*, *98*(2), 224–253.

Martin, D. J., Abramson, L. Y., & Alloy, L. B. (1984). Illusion of control for self and others in depressed and nondepressed college students. *Journal of Personality and Social Psychology*, *46*(1), 125–136.

Msetfi, R. M., Murphy, R. A., & Simpson, J. (2007). Depressive realism and the effect of the intertrial interval on judgements of zero, positive and negative contingencies. *Quarterly Journal of Experimental Psychology*, *60*(3), 461–481.

Msetfi, R. M., Murphy, R. A., Simpson, J., & Kornbrot, D. E. (2005). Depressive realism and outcome density bias in contingency judgements: The effect of context and the inter-trial interval. *Journal of Experimental Psychology: General*, *134*(1), 10–22.

Murphy, R. A., Vallée-Tourangeau, F., Msetfi, R. M., & Baker, A. G. (2005). Signal–outcome contingency, contiguity and the depressive realism effect. In A. Wills (Ed.), *New directions in associative learning* (pp. 193–220). Mahwah, NJ: Lawrence Erlbaum Associates, Inc.

National Institute for Clinical Excellence (2009). *Depression: The treatment and management of depression in adults, National clinical practice guideline no. 90.* London, UK: British Psychological Society.

Nelson, E., & Craighead, E. (1977). Selective recall of positive and negative feedback, self-control behaviors, and depression. *Journal of Abnormal Psychology*, *86*(4), 379–388.

Rescorla, R., & Wagner, A. (1972). A theory of Pavlovian conditioning: Variations in the effectiveness of reinforcement and non-reinforcement. In A. Black & W. Prokasy (Eds.), *Classical conditioning II: Theory and research* (pp. 64–99). New York, NY: Appleton-Century-Crofts.

Shanks, D., Pearson, S. M., & Dickinson, A. (1989). Temporal contiguity and the judgment of causality by human subjects. *Quarterly Journal of Experimental Psychology Section B: Comparative and Physiological Psychology*, *41*(2), 139–159.

Stone, E. R., Dodrill, C. L., & Johnson, N. (2001). Depressive cognition: A test of depressive realism versus negativity using general knowledge questions. *Journal of Psychology*, *135*(6), 583–602.

Taylor, S. E., & Brown, J. D. (1988). Illusion and well-being – a social psychological perspective on mental-health. *Psychological Bulletin*, *103*(2), 193–210.

Teasdale, J. D., & Barnard, P. J. (1993). *Affect, cognition and change: Remodelling depressive thought.* Hillsdale, NJ: Lawrence Erlbaum Associates, Inc.

Vallée-Tourangeau, F., Hollingsworth, L., & Murphy, R. A. (1998). 'Attentional bias' in correlation judgments? Smedslund (1963) revisited. *Scandinavian Journal of Psychology*, *39*(4), 221–233.

Vallée-Tourangeau, F., Murphy, R. A., & Baker, A. G. (2005). Contiguity and the outcome density bias in action–outcome contingency judgements. *Quarterly Journal of Experimental Psychology: Comparative and Physiological Psychology*, *58b*, 177–192.

Vallée-Tourangeau, F., Murphy, R. A., Drew, S., & Baker, A. G. (1998). Judging the importance of constant and variable candidate causes: A test of the power PC theory. *Quarterly Journal of Experimental Psychology Section A: Human Experimental Psychology*, *51*(1), 65–84.

Vasquez, C. (1987). Judgement of contingency: Cognitive biases in depressed and nondepressed subjects. *Journal of Personality and Social Psychology, 52*(2), 419–431.

Wasserman, E. A., Chatlosh, D. L., & Neunaber, D. J. (1983). Perception of causal relations in humans: Factors affecting judgments of response–outcome contingencies under free-operant procedures. *Learning and Motivation, 14*(4), 406–432.

Wasserman, E. A., Dorner, W. W., & Kao, S. F. (1990). Contributions of specific cell information to judgments of interevent contingency. *Journal of Experimental Psychology: Learning Memory and Cognition, 16*(3), 509–521.

Wasserman, E. A., Elek, S. M., Chatlosh, D. L., & Baker, A. G. (1993). Rating causal relations: Role of probability in judgments of response–outcome contingency. *Journal of Experimental Psychology: Learning, Memory, and Cognition, 19*(1), 174–188.

Wells, K. B., Stewart, A., Hays, R. D., Burnam, A., Rogers, W., Daniels, M., et al. (1989). The functioning and well-being of depressed patients: Results from the medical outcomes study. *Journal of the American Medical Association, 262*(7), 914–919.

Williams, J. M. G., Watts, F. N., MacLeod, C., & Mathews, A. (1997). *Cognitive psychology and emotional disorders* (2nd ed.). Oxford, UK: John Wiley and Sons.

8 An associative analysis of Tourette syndrome

Andrew J. D. Nelson, Ebrahim Kantini, and Helen J. Cassaday

The clinical problem

Tourette syndrome (TS) has been described as a developmentally regulated neurological disorder characterized by involuntary, repetitive, stereotyped movements (Albin & Mink, 2006; Chang, Tu, & Wang, 2004; Jankovic, 2001; Mink, 2003; Spencer et al., 1998). The Tourette Syndrome Classification Study Group (1993) has formulated a set of criteria for the diagnosis of TS. These include motor and vocal tics that cannot be explained by other medical conditions, lasting in excess of 1 year and with an onset during childhood (specifically before the age of 21). The cause of such tics is poorly understood but from the perspective of the sufferer they can have an apparent cause in the form of a prodrome. In other words, they are perceived as having been initiated by an urge or a sensation, and may increase during periods of stress. In particular, motor and phonetic tics are often preceded by premonitory sensations (such as burning sensation of the eye before an eyeblink tic, or a sore throat sensation before grunting), which are alleviated by the performance of the tic (Jankovic, 2001).

The frequency of tics is variable over time. They may occur many times a day (usually in bouts), nearly every day or intermittently. Fortunately, they can also stop altogether. In form, tics may be simple motor (e.g., eyeblinks or nose twitches), simple vocal (e.g., grunts or throat clearing), complex motor (e.g., touching, hitting, or scratching), or complex vocal (the repeated uttering of obscenities or coporolalia, though this is not, as commonly believed, the most typical feature of TS). The type of tic generally displayed in any one individual can also change over time. This variability makes the diagnosis of TS difficult clinically because, for some individuals, the tics may go unnoticed, or be diagnosed as somatic tics. From a research perspective, this variability also raises issues: the same participant with diagnosed TS could arrive at the experiment with high levels of symptoms or relatively symptom-free. Thus, although clearly symptomatic of TS, the assumption has to be that tics are the (variable) manifestation of some underlying difference in the nervous system. Evidence on this point is provided by the established techniques of neuropsychology and cognitive neuroscience: postmortem analyses of brain tissue; structural and functional imaging; and controlled behavioural experimentation.

The neural bases of TS

With regard to the likely neurological basis of TS, a number of studies, both structural and functional, have noted abnormalities in the dopamine (DA) system, basal ganglia, and the striatum in particular. For example, Minzer et al. (Minzer, Lee, Hong, & Singer, 2004) reported postmortem changes in TS, including increased density of D2 receptors in prefrontal cortex, together with increased concentration of the DA metabolite (homovanillic acid, HVA) in the putamen. Similarly, another postmortem analysis of brain tissue from TS confirmed this evidence for increased DA D2 receptor density in five of six frontal lobe regions examined (Yoon, Gause, Leckman, & Singer, 2007). The same authors also reported another measure of DA abnormality: the DA transporter (that would normally promote DA reuptake) was elevated in TS (Yoon et al., 2007). However, these studies were each based on only three individuals diagnosed with TS and notably a total of three of the individuals included were over 60 years old and only one was under 20. Individuals who continue to suffer with TS in adulthood may not be typical (see below). Moreover, neuroleptic use over protracted periods could well explain these changes in DA function. Thus whilst indicative, postmortem studies of this kind are necessarily inconclusive.

Structural imaging studies in living patients point to more subtle differences in the brains of those with TS. For example, dysfunction in TS could also arise in relation to atypical laterality in key brain structures. Yazgan et al. (Yazgan, Peterson, Wexler, & Leckman, 1995) compared the performance of 11 TS participants on neuropsychological tests for lateralization of function (e.g., line bisection) with their level of basal ganglia asymmetry (as determined by volumetric assessment). The participants with TS demonstrated both basal ganglia asymmetry (left greater volume than right) and a reduction in normal functional lateralization on three of the four neuropsychological measures.

Functional neuroimaging studies have indicated that the normal role of the basal ganglia is to organize voluntary movements and inhibit other interfering movements (Mink, 2003; Wang et al., 2007). Thus, from a clinical perspective, disorder in the basal ganglia would be entirely consistent with motor symptoms of the kind shown in TS. The frontal lobe has also been implicated in the pathology of TS. With respect to the level of TS symptoms displayed, fMRI has shown a distinctive pattern of activation during tic suppression: significantly increased activity in the (right) frontal cortex; increased activity in the right caudate nucleus; along with reduced activity in the globus pallidus, the putamen, and the thalamus (Peterson et al., 1998). However, it is unclear whether tic generation involves the same pattern of neural activation as seen during tic suppression.

Frontal compensation in TS

This neuropsychological evidence raises the possibility that there is functional compensation in the frontal lobes of TS sufferers. Since the disorder is neurodevelopmental and the frontal cortex is known to show late developmental changes (e.g., Sowell, Thompson, Holmes, Jernigan, & Toga, 1999), it is quite plausible that such compensation could be triggered by the need to suppress tics. One mechanism for functional compensation could be increased interactions between key cortical areas, developed to allow the inhibition of inappropriate motor responses. Serrien and colleagues have found support for this conjecture in the form of EEG evidence: coherent firing across a cortical network including dorsolateral prefrontal, premotor, sensorimotor, superior parietal, and supplementary motor cortical areas was seen whilst TS participants suppressed tics or voluntary movement during a Go–NoGo task (Serrien, Orth, Evans, Lees, & Brown, 2005).

Such findings suggest the hypothesis that, over time, the long-term use of frontal pathways to suppress tics could result in generally increased cognitive control. Indeed, experimentally, G. M. Jackson and colleagues have shown that, despite their general difficulties with inhibition, TS participants show paradoxically enhanced volitional control in suppressing established stimulus–response (S–R) associations. Specifically, this deficit was in suppressing automatic visual saccades to salient peripheral cues upon switching from a prosaccade test, where participants were allowed to attend to the peripheral cue, to an antisaccade test, where participants were required to look away from the peripheral cue. This task relies on executive processes to show the required flexibility when the response requirement is changed. "Switching" procedures are ideal for this purpose in that they require participants to inhibit the prepotent response that has first been performed in the task, and to produce an alternate response. In normal participants, this generates a switch cost – measured as an increased number of errors, particularly when the required switch is unpredictable. However, the switch cost is not seen to the same extent in TS participants, irrespective of the predictability with which the switch is required (Mueller, Jackson, Dhalla, Datsopoulos, & Hollis, 2006; Mueller, Swainson, & Jackson, 2007). These findings suggest that TS participants who remain susceptible to unwanted tics can nonetheless show enhanced cortical inhibition. Such enhanced cortical inhibition would be expected to have wide-ranging effects including improved performance on certain kinds of cognitive tests in TS and in particular on tasks that are believed to depend on frontal function. However, the persistence of unwanted tics in TS patients despite compensatory mechanisms in frontal cortex is consistent with the known basal ganglia abnormalities in TS and points to the relative autonomy of S–R learning from executive control.

TS as dysfunctional S–R habit learning?

Habitual responses are ready-assembled routines that link sensory cues in the environment with motor action and are carried out in the absence of conscious thought or without awareness of the goal of the action. They allow us to perform seemingly complex behaviours such as driving effort-lessly and automatically. The ability of stimuli in the environment to elicit these complex sequences of actions maps onto the theoretical suggestion that habit learning depends on the development of S–R associations. Habits are enormously adaptive as they free up cognitive resources and allow attention to be directed to the attainment of other goals. However, the notion of "bad" habits has long formed part of folk psychology and it is clear that as complex repertoires of actions come to be triggered by the mere presence of stimuli in the environment, behaviour can become inappropriate and maladaptive. Action slips (the performance of actions that are unattended or inappropriate in response to a stimulus in the environment) is a frustrating but arguably innocuous example of this phenomenon.

Similarly, TS is defined by the production of seemingly purposeless, involuntary, and repetitive behaviours that usually resemble aspects of normal behaviour. Tics, like habits, are coordinated ensembles of action that can be triggered by both internal and external stimuli. As discussed above, tics are often preceded by premonitory urges or internal sensations that build up and produce stress that is relieved by the expression of the tic. Seen in this context, tics can be viewed as a form of operant conditioning with premonitory urges acting as discriminative stimuli that lead to tic production and the resultant reduction in stress serving as negative reinforcement of the tic response according to classical S–R reinforcement learning theory. This phenomenological similarity between tics and habits has led to the suggestion that the repetitive behaviours seen in TS could represent a form of aberrant and dysfunctional S–R habit learning (e.g., Leckman & Riddle, 2000; Graybiel, 2008).

Tics and S–R habit learning – same neural substrates?

There is good, albeit indirect, evidence to suggest that the same brain systems responsible for the development of S–R habits may also underpin the production and maintenance of tics. As reviewed above, evidence from various sources including imaging and postmortem studies has implicated abnormalities in cortico–striato–thalamo–cortical (CSTC) loops and dopa-minergic systems in the neurobiology of TS (e.g., Singer & Minzer, 2003) (see Figure 8.1). S–R habit learning has similarly been shown to depend on neural plasticity within the basal ganglia and prefrontal cortex (Jog, Kubota,

Connolly, Hillegaart, & Graybiel, 1999; Killcross & Coutureau, 2003; Yin & Knowlton, 2006). This evidence comes in part from studies that have dissociated implicit S–R learning within the dorsal striatum from explicit forms of learning mediated by hippocampal and medial temporal cortical systems as well as from stimulus–stimulus (S–S) learning in limbic structures such as the amygdala (Packard & Knowlton, 2002). Furthermore, our understanding of the neuroanatomical and neuropharmacological basis of S–R habit learning has been greatly advanced in recent years through the application of modern behavioural assays of instrumental performance that allow the underlying associative structure of behaviour to be probed.

Behavioural studies in rodents have shown that instrumental performance can be controlled by two dissociable associative processes, as indexed by the sensitivity of instrumental response to outcome devaluation (changing the value of the instrumental outcome so that it is no longer motivationally significant or desirable for the animal). Early on in acquisition, instrumental responding is goal-directed and selectively sensitive to changes in outcome value (i.e., outcome devaluation leads to a decline in instrumental performance) but as training proceeds animals' instrumental performance becomes habitual, stimulus-bound, and no longer guided by the current value of the reinforcer (Adams & Dickinson, 1981; Adams, 1982). Lesion studies combined with outcome devaluation procedures have highlighted a critical role for the infralimbic region of the prefrontal cortex and dorsolateral striatum (the rat analogue of the putamen) in the performance of habitual lever press responding in rats (Killcross & Coutureau, 2003; Yin, Knowlton, & Balleine, 2004). Conversely, plasticity within the prelimbic prefrontal cortex and dorsomedial striatum (the rat analogue of the caudate nucleus) appears to underpin the performance of goal-directed instrumental action (Killcross & Coutureau, 2003; Yin, Knowlton, & Balleine, 2005). These findings reveal the importance of interactions between prefrontal and striatal systems in the control of habitual behaviour. It is likely that the same brain regions are involved in the expression of tics (Leckman & Riddle, 2000). Indeed, findings from an fMRI study – showing that tic suppression requires activation of the caudate nucleus and deactivation of the putamen – parallel evidence that these structures are critical to the expression of goal-directed and habitual responding in rodents (Peterson et al., 1998).

Consistent with putative dopaminergic abnormalities in TS, there is good evidence for dopaminergic modulation of the development of S–R habits. For example, lesions to the nigrostriatal DA pathway, the major dopaminergic input into the striatum, have been shown to disrupt habit formation (Faure, Haberland, Conde, & El Massioui, 2005). Similarly, repeated exposure to the indirect catecholamine agonist amphetamine appears to accelerate habit formation such that amphetamine-sensitized animals display habit-based goal-insensitive instrumental performance even after limited amounts of training (Nelson & Killcross, 2006). Significantly,

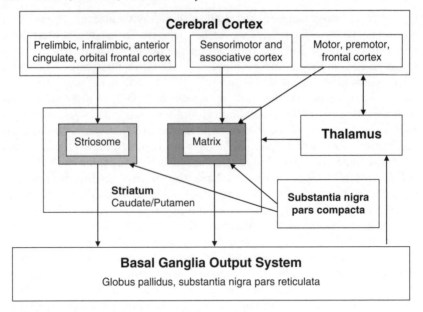

Figure 8.1 Simplified schematic representation of cortico–striato–thalamo–cortical loops implicated in tic expression and the development of S–R (stimulus–response) habits.

amphetamine exposure leads to the preferential activation of the striosomal compartment (see Figure 8.1) of the striatum (Graybiel, Moratalla, & Robertson, 1990) and this activation has been directly related to the occurrence of psychostimulant-induced stereotypies (Canales & Graybiel, 2000). Such stereotypies include a range of repetitive tic-like head and paw movements that resemble the motoric tics that occur in TS. It has been proposed that the changes in neuronal activity within the striosomal and matrix system associated with the production of behavioural stereotypies may also underpin the development of S–R habits (Canales, 2005; Nelson & Killcross, 2006). Moreover, these data have led to the suggestion that imbalances in the functional activity of striosome and matrix neurons may be related to the repetitive aimless behaviours seen in TS (Leckman & Riddle, 2000; Saka & Graybiel, 2003).

S–R learning in TS and therapeutic implications

The conceptualization of TS in terms of dysfunctional S–R habit learning is not only supported by the possibility of common neurobiological mechanisms but also by evidence that S–R learning is deficient in patients with TS. Studies have shown that both children and adult sufferers of TS are impaired in the acquisition of probabilistic classification tasks (Kéri, Szlobodnyik, Benedek, Janka, & Gádoros, 2002; Marsh et al., 2004).

Probabilistic classification tasks involve learning the relationship between combinations of cues and outcomes. Task acquisition relies not on explicit declarative memory, but rather on a general sense of the rules acquired over numerous trials, and may therefore depend on the gradual learning of S–R associations. TS patients' performance on such tasks does not improve over time and they show higher latencies and fewer correct responses compared with controls. Significantly, in both the aforementioned studies, symptom severity was negatively correlated with task performance indicating that participants with more severe tic symptoms were proportionally more impaired in S–R learning (Keri et al., 2002; Marsh et al., 2004). Furthermore, Marsh and colleagues (2005) found no evidence of deficits in the same cohort of TS patients on two perceptual-motor skill tasks (the pursuit rotor task and the mirror tracing task), suggesting that deficits seen on the probabilistic classification task cannot be explained in terms of impaired motor learning. The finding of intact motor learning in TS patients mirrors evidence that TS patients are unimpaired on Go–NoGo tasks that rely on the inhibition of pre-potent motor responses (Serrien et al., 2005; Roessner, Albrecht, Dechent, Baudewig, & Rothenberger, 2008). These preserved abilities may be due to compensatory mechanisms within frontal cortex (see above) and the authors suggest that deficits in their probabilistic classification task may relate to specific abnormalities within CSTC circuits that subserve S–R habit learning (Marsh et al., 2005). However, although not identified as important, S–S associations are also likely to play a role in performance on the probabilistic learning task described by these authors. The role of S–S associations in TS is returned to below.

Of course, the ultimate goal of translational research is to ameliorate the clinical condition. Pharmacological interventions have proven effective in treating the symptoms of TS but are often associated with unwanted side effects (especially neuroleptics) and hence the need for psychological therapies is ever present (Leckman & Riddle, 2000; Singer, 2005). In this respect, the conceptualization of TS in terms of dysfunctional S–R learning has proven most promising as habit reversal therapy is becoming increasingly popular as a behavioural alternative to pharmacological treatment. Habit reversal therapy involves changing the contingency between the urges and sensations that precede tics and interfering with the production of the tic through the introduction of competing incompatible responses (Azrin & Peterson, 1988). Significantly, habit reversal therapy has been shown to substantially reduce tic severity compared with supportive psychotherapy and the beneficial effects of this behavioural intervention appear to be long lasting (Deckersbach, Rauch, Buhlman, & Wilhelm, 2006; Wihelm et al., 2003).

Disinhibited behaviour and TS

The changes in spontaneous behaviour diagnostic of TS also point to a problem with inhibitory mechanisms that would normally prevent these kinds of outbursts. Therefore, a number of researchers have hypothesized that TS is the result of dysfunction in behavioural and/or cognitive inhibition (Gilbert et al., 2004; Ozonoff, Strayer, McMahon, & Filloux, 1998; Sheppard, Bradshaw, Purcell, & Pantelis, 1999). In addition to the standard Go–NoGo test variants, where subjects are instructed to respond to certain cues and withhold responding to other cues, "purer" tests of cognitive inhibition have also been developed. For example, in a negative priming task which measured the ability to inhibit the processing of irrelevant distractor stimuli presented on a visual display, it has been reported that TS participants with the most severe symptoms and presenting with comorbid ADHD or OCD showed deficits (Ozonoff et al., 1998).

Gilbert et al. (2004) investigated the relationship between motor cortex inhibition and tic severity in TS (and related disorders). This was done using transcranial magnetic stimulation (TMS) to produce motor-evoked potentials, measured using electrodes on the muscles, to manipulate the threshold for a stimulus-driven response: specifically cortical inhibition was measured through short interval intracortical inhibition (SICI). Gilbert et al. found that the level of symptom severity in TS (and ADHD, see also the section below on related disorders) was inversely related to cortical inhibition as indexed by SICI. This suggests that hyperactive or impulsive behaviours as seen in TS appear in consequence of diminished motor cortex inhibition (see also Sheppard et al., 1999, for review of other pathways involved).

S–S learning in TS and therapeutic implications

S–S associations provide a mechanism through which environmental events can act as symptom triggers and moreover provide some explanation of the variability in frequency of symptoms and time course. This kind of analysis has furthered our understanding of a number of disorders (Ferguson & Cassaday, 1999; Lishman, 1987; Siegel, 1977; Stewart, de Wit, & Eikelboom, 1984; Watson, 1924). In TS, a variety of associative triggers for tics have been documented, for example a person's cough or gesture (Jankovic, 2001; Leckman, 2003; Leckman, Walker, & Cohen, 1993; The Tourette Syndrome Classification Study Group, 1993; Prado et al., 2008). Likewise premonitory urges in the form of somatic sensations, for example "burning" of the eye before a eyeblink tic, sore throat preceding grunting, and the every day life events and emotional variables that affect pre-tic urges and sensations (Leckman et al., 1993; Conelea & Woods, 2008), provide a source of stimuli that could become associated with tic-generated stimuli through S–S associations. Moreover, controlled experimental studies have demonstrated that repeatedly reinforcing tic suppression in the presence of a particular antecedent discriminative stimulus results (as would be expected by operant learning theory) in that stimulus acquiring some control over tic expression (Woods, Walther, Bauer, Kemp, & Conelea, 2009). Thus, a chain of antecedents – providing both classically conditioned and (ultimately) discriminative stimuli – may be important in the triggering of a particular tic response, which can thus depend on other aspects of the environment beyond the immediately preceding stimulus. Such an associative chain reaction would be fully consistent with the triggering of the compulsive ideas which often accompany the urge to tic. Only recently have such environmental stimuli been targeted in behavioural treatments for TS: through extinction of the excitatory association (Verdellen et al., 2008); and in their capacity as discriminative stimuli in relation to tic reinforcement (Woods et al., 2009).

A role for Pavlovian inhibition in TS?

The variety of inhibitory deficits that have been reported in TS subsume a range of inhibitory mechanisms, some of which as we have seen are already under intensive investigation. For example, motor impulsivity is measured as reaction time in a variety of discrimination learning procedures that show excellent translational validity with human task variants (Robbins, 2002; Eagle & Robbins, 2003).

The common feature of these tasks is that they measure the participants' ability to inhibit a prepotent response in the presence of an environmental cue that means it will not be reinforced. Formally, in Pavlovian procedures the equivalent "conditioned inhibition" is demonstrated when the meaning of one signal (conditioned stimulus, CS) is qualified by another (conditioned inhibitor, CI). Whilst the CS presented alone reliably predicts the outcome (unconditioned stimulus, US), when presented in conjunction with the CI the otherwise expected US will not occur. In other words, humans and other animals learn a discrimination that is shown within-subjects and this discrimination can be improved or impaired in the animal model.

Conditioned inhibition thus provides a mechanism through which the chain of antecedents to a tic, or any other unwanted behavioural or cognitive response, for which S–S associations provide an underlying mechanism, could be broken. In human studies, Cassaday and colleagues have demonstrated that individual variation in conditioned inhibition can be predicted from personality characteristics, themselves predictive of predisposition to disorder (Migo et al., 2006). The likely relevance of impaired conditioned inhibition in producing the cognitive deficits of schizophrenia was confirmed by the inverse relationship between the level of inhibitory learning displayed and schizotypy. In addition, there was a positive relationship between increased conditioned inhibition and a measure of reward sensitivity, potentially relevant to our understanding of a wide range of disorders including TS. Moreover, TS often occurs together with cognitive symptoms of attention deficit and obsessional behaviours. These deficits indicate the potential for wider changes, also in the inhibition of S–S associations – that result in unwanted thoughts – as well as actions.

Notably, the Pavlovian phenomenon of latent inhibition, widely investigated in connection with schizophrenic attention deficit (Moran and Rouse, this volume), has been reported to be normal in TS (Swerdlow, Magulac, Filion, & Zinner, 1996). However, so-called latent inhibition refers to the reduction in associative learning produced by stimulus preexposure which establishes an otherwise effective CS as "irrelevant". This preexposure has been shown to be an effective bar to inhibitory as well as excitatory learning. Thus although so-called latent inhibition procedures retard later learning, they do not render the pre-exposed stimulus truly inhibitory: In other words, latent inhibition is a dissociable effect (Baker & Mackintosh, 1977).

Testing inhibition of S–S learning

We have recently adapted the task used by Migo et al. (2006) to make it more suitable for younger participants, including those with TS and ADHD. The stimuli to be conditioned are presented in the course of a "Mission to Mars": participants play the role of a starship commander travelling towards Mars with a fleet of spaceships, some of which explode en route. Participants are required to count the number of surviving spaceships and are asked to guess what might predict their survival.

In fact CSs are provided by planets displayed on screen. Additional smaller planets act as distractors [Figure 8.2(a)]. Because the goal is the success of the mission, presentation of an intact spaceship provides the US. The normal predictive relationship between the planet CSs and spaceship US does not hold when their presentation is preceded by a CI in the form of a discrete grey border on an otherwise the blank screen. On these trials the absence of the spaceship US is depicted by an exploded spaceship [Figure 8.2(b)].

During the testing sessions, participants are required to rate the likelihood of spaceship survival on a scale of 1 to 9 [Figure 8.2(b)]. When conditioned inhibition is shown, participants respond with a number less than 5 (the midpoint of uncertainty on the response scale). Critically, this procedure uses the summation test in that transfer of inhibition to a novel planet (novel stimulus, SN) and one not explicitly paired during training (transfer stimulus, CST), provides the key measure of conditioned inhibition. Figure 8.3 shows conditioned inhibition in normal participants as measured on the critical summation tests (Migo et al., 2006).

We have established that this "Mission to Mars" task is suitable for younger participants: they learn the discrimination in the modified variant readily and in fewer trials (Kantini, Cassaday, Hollis, & Jackson, 2011). This procedure was used to test the hypothesis that enhanced cortical inhibition in TS should enhance the discrimination between predicted and inhibited trials by selectively depressing spaceship expectancy on inhibited trials; thus to determine whether the enhanced cortical control demonstrated in tasks of executive function (Mueller et al., 2006, 2007) can

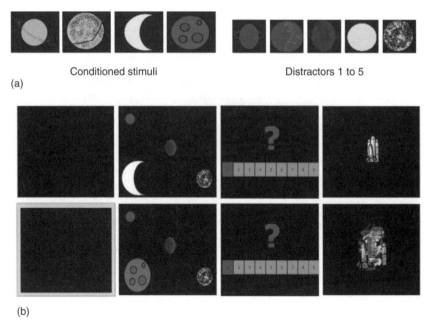

Conditioned stimuli   Distractors 1 to 5
(a)

(b)

Figure 8.2(a) The set of conditioned stimuli (CSs) and distractor stimuli used. (b) The top set of screens show the presentation of a planet CS (screen 2), followed by a spaceship US (unconditioned stimulus; screen 4). In the test phase participants are required to rate their confidence of spaceship survival (screen 3). The bottom set of screens show an inhibited transfer test trial. When the grey border has been presented (screen 1) the CS (screen 2) does not predict spaceship survival, as represented by the exploded spaceship (screen 4). As above, participants are required to rate their confidence of spaceship survival (screen 3). Procedures are based on Migo et al. (2006), see text for further details.

similarly improve performance in a Pavlovian procedure. We have yet to demonstrate significantly improved conditioned inhibition in TS. In the study conducted to date, TS participants showed overall normal inhibition of S–S associations in this task, and there was no correlation between inhibitory learning scores and symptom severity ratings measured using the Yale Global Tic Severity Scale. However, there was a clear reduction in the expression of conditioned inhibition in TS participants under medication with the noradrenergic alpha-2 agonist clonidine (Kantini et al., 2011). This finding has implications for the likely effectiveness of behavioural treatments in alleviating symptoms in cases of TS who are concurrently medicated. Through impaired conditioned inhibition, medication could impair potential cognitive control mechanisms for the suppression of tics (via an action on the associative chain that generates triggers). Thus impaired inhibition of S–S associations would leave TS sufferers potentially less able to inhibit the unwanted thoughts and premonitory associations that can lead to tics.

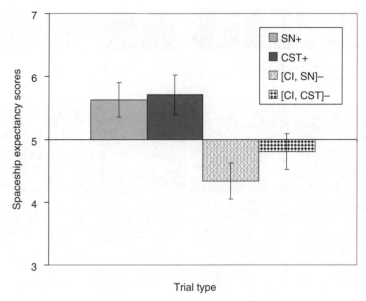

Figure 8.3 Overall expectancy scores (means and standard error bars, averaged over two experiments) for reinforced (predicted) and nonreinforced (inhibited) trials for the key summation test comparisons. A score of 5 represents the neutral point; scores above 5 reflect anticipation of the spaceship US (unconditioned stimulus); scores below 5 reflect inhibition of the planet CS (conditioned stimulus) and spaceship US association. SN = novel stimulus; CST = transfer stimulus; CI = conditioned inhibitor. Figure adapted from Migo et al. (2006), see text for further details.

Brain systems involved in Pavlovian conditioning

The majority of Pavlovian conditioning studies are concerned with excitatory (S–S) learning. Basic associative learning ability and Pavlovian inhibitory learning are inevitably confounded in the sense that prior learning is essential to the successful demonstration of conditioned inhibition. In other words it is necessary to learn that a US is expected before one can learn that a stimulus signals its absence. Thus the substrates identified for excitatory learning will be necessary, if not sufficient, for inhibitory learning also.

Although all Pavlovian conditioning follows general laws of associative learning, there are known to be differences in the specific neural circuitries involved depending on the type of conditioning in use. For example, eyeblink conditioning is known to be impaired by cerebellar lesions in humans as well as other animals (Daum et al., 1993) whilst an equally compelling body of evidence underscores the importance of the amygdala for normal fear conditioning (see Fanselow & Poulos, 2005; Kim & Jung, 2006, for review). Related to this issue, the nature of the conditioned responses that allow us to quantify the strength of associative learning varies from one task to the next. These conditioned response measures range from motor responses (in the case of eyeblink conditioning) to conditioned emotional responses that can show as response suppression (in fear conditioning). Thus differences in the nature of the learned response could (at least in part) account for differences in the underlying neural substrates.

The modulation of classical conditioning can depend on particular additional structures. For example, the hippocampus is required where associative learning must bridge a time gap between CS offset and UCS delivery, in both fear conditioning (McEchron, Tseng, & Disterhoft, 2000) and eyeblink trace procedures (Beylin et al., 2001). However, the role of hippocampus has yet to be demonstrated in appetitive trace procedures (Thibaudeau, Potvin, Allen, Doré, & Goulet, 2007). Therefore, the role of the hippocampus in bridging across temporal intervals, as distinct from a role in fear and eyeblink conditioning that may be accentuated under conditions that increase task difficulty, remains to be determined. Inhibition similarly presents as a process that should modulate normal excitatory learning, both in terms of expression (in summation tests) and acquisition (in retardation tests) (Rescorla, 1969).

However, the additional brain circuitry necessary for normal Pavlovian inhibition has yet to be firmly established. As seems to be the case in trace conditioning, this may vary depending on the conditioning procedure in use. Similarly, it has yet to be determined in what ways Pavlovian S–S associations – and the inhibition thereof – are dysfunctional in TS. However, encouragingly, what we do know about the substrates of inhibitory learning is fully consistent with the possibility that its dysfunction could contribute to the symptoms of TS. Specifically, in electrophysiological studies, DA neurons have been found to show opposite patterns of activity in inhibitory and excitatory conditioning: depression in firing when a CI was presented, whereas CSs that predicted reward increased firing in DA cells (Tobler, Dickinson, & Schultz, 2003). However, this dissociation in terms of the electrophysiological neuronal response was seen in functionally diverse brain regions.

Again consistent with an important role for the brain DA system, treatment with the indirect catecholamine agonist amphetamine enhanced the acquisition of conditioned inhibition (Harmer & Phillips, 1999). However, this was a study of the effects of chronic pre-treatment to produce sensitization: The acute, regionally localized, effects of more selective agonists might well be different. Moreover, amphetamine is also a noradrenalin (NA) agonist and a role for NA in conditioned inhibition is indicated by the effect of clonidine identified in our studies of TS participants (Kantini et al., 2011). The role of cortex in modulating the acquisition and expression of Pavlovian inhibitory learning has yet to be fully determined. Although much work has yet to be done, already the known role of catecholaminergic systems in both conditioned inhibition and TS supports the view that the deficits in this form of inhibition may be a contributing factor. Whether such deficits can arise in relation to TS *per se* or rather only in consequence of medication is yet to be established.

Related disorders

A syndrome such as TS refers to a set of symptoms perceived to "run together" in patients needing diagnosis. However, there can be overlap with related disorders, which should also be considered given that diagnostic boundaries are somewhat arbitrary and may be interpreted differently in different cultures. In the case of TS, there is a high level of comorbidity with ADHD (Comings & Comings, 1987; Gilbert et al., 2004; Ozonoff et al., 1998; Robertson, 2006; Sheppard et al., 1999; Spencer et al., 1998). In a study by Comings and Comings (1997), the authors found that TS patients were significantly different from controls with respect to DSM III symptoms of inattention, impulsivity, and hyperactivity. Moreover, they found that ADHD was diagnosed in 48.8 percent of the TS patients compared with 4.2 percent in the controls. Similarly, there is evidence for comorbidity between TS and OCD (Rankins, Bradshaw, & Georgiou-Karistianis, 2005; Swerdlow, 2001; Thibault et al., 2008) and there is evidence that participants who are comorbid for OCD perform worse on tests of inhibition than those with a diagnosis restricted to TS (Ozonoff et al., 1998; Gilbert et al., 2004). This means that studies which do not explicitly screen for comorbid illness could be argued to overestimate the level of impairment due to TS.

Superficially, TS, ADHD, and OCD present as quite different conditions. However, behavioural disinhibition is a feature of all these disorders (Ozonoff et al., 1998; Sheppard et al., 1999; Thibault et al., 2008), and both rely on the normal functioning of the DA system (Gilbert et al., 2004). Surprisingly then, relatively few studies have directly compared participants with TS and ADHD. Where this has been done, this has generally been in the context of studying comorbid groups rather than comparing separate groups.

As discussed earlier, Gilbert et al. (2004) investigated the relationship between motor cortex inhibition and tic severity using TMS. They found that the inverse association between tic severity and cortical inhibition was strongest in TS participants who were comorbid for ADHD. Indeed Gilbert et al. suggested that half of the variability in their index of cortical inhibition (SICI) was attributable to ADHD in participants with TS. Thus, hyperactivity and impulsive behaviours as well as the frequency of tics appear to be strongly linked with diminished motor cortex inhibition.

Similarly, returning to another study mentioned earlier in this chapter, whilst – as a whole – a large group of TS participants did not differ from controls, when this group was separated to distinguish those with "pure" TS and those comorbid for ADHD and/or OCD, the comorbid group were found to show an inhibition deficit as measured by negative priming (Ozonoff et al., 1998). Similarly, Thibault et al. (2008) investigated TS in OCD comorbid groups using specific event-related potentials and the "oddball" task. The oddball task requires participants to respond to unpredictable targets presented amongst a series of more predictable standard stimuli and shows a known association with the P300 component of the event-related potential. This association was reduced in patients with TS. However, this result only held in those comorbid for OCD (and the relationship between oddball performance and P300 was also reduced in OCD participants). Thus again where comorbidity is present, experimental outcomes can be attributable to the comorbid disorder rather than to TS.

Inevitably, comorbidity is typically confounded with reported symptom severity in TS. Ozonoff et al. (1998) found that when the combined TS group was divided by TS symptom severity according to standardized diagnostic measures, the group with highest symptom severity did in fact show reduced inhibition (as measured by the negative priming scores), both relative to TS participants with lower symptom severity and the matched controls. However, in cases such as the study by Ozonoff and colleagues where TS participants without comorbidity performed as well as controls this would seem to suggest that *TS* symptom severity is not key to the deficits at issue. However, dealing with comorbid illness is not straightforward as distinctions between related disorders are driven by diagnostic fashion and increasingly "translational" studies that seek to bridge human and animal studies are focused at the level of symptoms rather than syndromes.

Conclusions and implications

The fact that TS sufferers show problems with motor inhibition and S–R habits in a variety of experimental tasks is entirely consistent with their symptoms in that by definition they continue to tic and show other unwanted behaviours. The enhanced cortical control shown in switching tasks is paradoxical and consistent with functional compensation. Such compensation could plausibly be driven by sufferers' persistent attempts to suppress their tics. In terms of neural mediation of compensatory strategies, the frontal cortex is a likely substrate: task switching is an executive task likely to rely on frontal function; the development of the frontal cortex continues well into late adolescence. In some cases, TS behaviours would continue to persist because of the underlying dysfunction of the basal ganglia, in other cases cortical control might develop to the point where behavioural suppression is possible, in other words the basal ganglia dysfunction might be outweighed by the inhibition from frontal cortex. This model is consistent both with the fluctuating pattern of symptoms in TS and recovery in late adolescence in a high proportion of the cases who are motivated and able to control their symptoms. There is a general impression clinically that those with TS who are not also comorbid for ADHD are more successful at bringing their symptoms under control. This could be because comorbidity is confounded with severity or it could be that comorbid ADHD disrupts the ability to learn to suppress the unwanted TS behaviours.

A further consideration arises in that the response to show learning in tasks measuring S–S associations is generally less effortful than the response requirement to show S–R associations. Similarly, the conditioned responses that show learning of S–S associations are typically reflexive in any particular learning situation. In contrast, responses in instrumental tasks are voluntary, and to begin with somewhat arbitrary in form, though they can become highly automatic when S–R associations take over and habits are formed. Thus, whilst the level of learned responding in S–S and S–R tasks is generally taken to reflect the strength of the underlying association, other variables moderate the expression of learning through responding: (1) the level of motor requirement; (2) the level of automaticity with which the response is performed. These variables are both highly likely determinants of the role of motor versus cognitive inhibition required to suppress actions and thoughts. Such associative effects should be seen as modulating the expression of particular tics as associations are learned. Successful behavioural treatments to eliminate individual tics do not target the underlying neurological dysfunction responsible for the generation of tics. Thus (different kinds of) tics can and do reappear in cases of TS, in the same way an underlying anxiety disorder can result in different profiles of symptoms at different times.

We conclude that successful behavioural treatments will increasingly shift focus from the S–R association to target the S–S associations. In any chain of antecedent stimuli, the closest effective stimulus to the response will be cognitive, a perception or associated thought. Thus S–S associations provide the underlying mechanism whereby tics are triggered in particular contexts. Moreover, we have identified a potentially important role for conditioned inhibition that is susceptible to pharmacological manipulation.

Precisely because of the range and heterogeneity of disorders characterized by deficient inhibitory processes, as well as the confounded effects seen when these disorders co-occur in the same individual, and effects of medication that cannot always be clearly distinguished, human studies on their own will be insufficient to identify the neuropharmacological substrates of conditioned inhibition. Conditioned inhibition has long been established in animal research (Cole, Barnet, & Miller, 1997; Nicholson & Freeman, 2002; Rescorla & Holland, 1977), but the neural substrates have been little investigated to date. Thus further translational modelling will be necessary to pinpoint the key biological substrates of this important selective learning process and so identify its precise role in disorder. To date there is evidence for the likely role of DA and NA, but little if any direct evidence on where in the brain such effects are mediated.

Acknowledgements

We thank Simon Killcross, Georgina Jackson, and Steve Jackson for many helpful discussions about the psychological and neural basis of Tourette syndrome.

References

Adams, C. D. (1982). Variations in the sensitivity of instrumental responding to reinforcer devaluation. *Quarterly Journal of Experimental Psychology: Comparative and Physiological Psychology, 34B*, 77–98.

Adams, C. D., & Dickinson, A. (1981). Actions and habits: Variations in associative representations during instrumental learning. In R. R. Miller & N. E. Spear (Eds.), *Memory mechanisms in animal behavior* (pp. 143–165). Hillsdale, NJ: Lawrence Erlbaum Associates, Inc.

Albin, R. L., & Mink, J. W. (2006). Recent advances in Tourette syndrome research. *Trends in Neurosciences, 29*, 175–182.

Azrin, N. H., & Peterson, A. L. (1988). Habit reversal for the treatment of Tourette Syndrome. *Behaviour Research and Therapy, 26*, 347–351.

Baker, A. G., & Mackintosh, N. J. (1977). Excitatory and inhibitory conditioning following uncorrelated presentations of CS and UCS. *Animal Learning and Behavior, 5*, 315–319.

Beylin, A. V., Gandhi, C. C., Wood, G. E., Talk, A. C., Matzel, L. D., & Shors, T. J. (2001). The role of the hippocampus in trace conditioning: Temporal discontinuity or task difficulty? *Neurobiology of Learning and Memory, 76*, 447–461.

Canales, J. J. (2005). Stimulant-induced adaptations in neostriatal matrix and striosome systems: Transiting from instrumental responding to habitual behavior in drug addiction. *Neurobiology of Learning and Memory, 83*, 93–103.

Canales, J. J., & Graybiel, A. M. (2000). A measure of striatal function predicts motor stereotypy. *Nature Neuroscience, 3*, 377–383.

Chang, H. L., Tu, M. J., & Wang, H. S. (2004). Tourette's syndrome: Psychopathology in adolescents. *Psychiatry and Clinical Neurosciences, 58*, 353–358.

Cole, R. P., Barnet, R. C., & Miller, R. R. (1997). An evaluation of conditioned inhibition as defined by Rescorla's two-test strategy. *Learning and Motivation, 28*, 323–341.

Comings, D. E., & Comings, B. G. (1987). A controlled study of Tourette Syndrome. 1. Attention-deficit disorder, learning disorders, and school problems. *American Journal of Human Genetics, 41*, 701–741.

Conelea, C. A., & Woods, D. W. (2008). The influence of contextual factors on tic expression in Tourette's syndrome: A review. *Journal of Psychosomatic Research, 65*, 487–496.

Daum, I., Schugens, M. M., Ackermann, H., Lutzenberger, W., Dichgans, J., & Birbaumer, N. (1993). Classical conditioning after cerebellar lesions in humans. *Behavioral Neuroscience, 107*, 748–756.

Deckersbach, T., Rauch, S., Buhlmann, U., & Wilhelm, S. (2006). Habit reversal versus supportive psychotherapy in Tourette's Disorder: A randomized controlled trial and predictors of treatment response. *Behaviour, Research and Therapy, 44*, 1079–1090.

Eagle, D. M., & Robbins, T. W. (2003). Inhibitory control in rats performing a stop-signal reaction-time task: Effects of lesions of the medial striatum and d-amphetamine. *Behavioral Neuroscience, 117*, 1302–1317.

Fanselow, M. S., & Poulos, A. M. (2005). The neuroscience of mammalian associative learning. *Annual Review of Psychology, 56*, 207–234.

Faure, A., Haberland, U., Conde, F., & El Massioui, N. (2005). Lesion to the nigrostriatal dopamine system disrupts stimulus–response habit formation. *Journal of Neuroscience, 25*, 2771–2780.

Ferguson, E., & Cassaday H. J. (1999). The Gulf War and illness by association. *British Journal of Psychology, 90*, 459–475.

Gilbert, D. L., Bansal, A. S., Sethuraman, G., Sallee, F. R., Zhang, J., Lipps, T., et al. (2004). Association of cortical disinhibition with tic, ADHD, and OCD severity in Tourette syndrome. *Movement Disorders, 19*, 416–425.

Graybiel, A. M. (2008). Habits, rituals and the evaluative brain. *Annual Review of Neuroscience, 31*, 359–387.

Graybiel, A. M., Moratalla, R., & Robertson, H. A. (1990). Amphetamine and cocaine induce drug-specific activation of the c-fos gene in striosome-matrix compartments and limbic subdivisions of the striatum. *Proceedings of the National Academy of Sciences of the USA, 87*, 6912–6916.

Harmer, C. J., & Phillips, G. D. (1999). Enhanced conditioned inhibition following repeated pretreatment with d-amphetamine. *Psychopharmacology, 142*, 120–131.

Jankovic, J. (2001). Medical progress: Tourette's syndrome. *New England Journal of Medicine, 345*, 1184–1192.

Jog, M. S., Kubota, Y., Connolly, C. I., Hillegaart, V., & Graybiel, A. M. (1999). Building neural representations of habits. *Science, 286*(5445), 1745–1749.

Kantini, E., Cassaday, H. J., Hollis, C. P., & Jackson, G. M. (2011). The normal inhibition of associations is impaired by clonidine in Tourette Syndrome. *Journal of the Canadian Academy of Child and Adolescent Psychiatry, 20*, 96–106.

Kéri, S., Szlobodnyik, C., Benedek, G., Janka, Z., & Gádoros, J. (2002). Probabilistic classification learning in Tourette syndrome. *Neuropsychologia, 40*, 1356–1362.

Killcross, S., & Coutureau, E. (2003). Coordination of actions and habits in the medial prefrontal cortex of rats. *Cerebral Cortex, 13*, 400–408.

Kim, J. J., & Jung, M. W. (2006). Neural circuits and mechanisms involved in Pavlovian fear conditioning: A critical review. *Neuroscience & Biobehavioral Reviews, 30*, 188–202.

Leckman, J. F. (2003). Phenomenology of tics and natural history of tic disorders. *Brain and Development, 25*, S24–S28.

Leckman, J. F., Walker, D. E., & Cohen, D. J. (1993). Premonitory urges in Tourette's syndrome. *American Journal of Psychiatry, 150*, 98–102.

Leckman, J. F., & Riddle, M. (2000). Tourette's Syndrome: When habit forming systems form habits of their own? *Neuron, 28*, 349–354.

Lishman, W. A. (1987). *Organic psychiatry: The psychological consequences of cerebral disorder* (2nd ed.). Oxford, UK: Blackwell Science.

McEchron, M. D., Tseng, W., & Disterhoft, J. F. (2000). Neurotoxic lesions of the dorsal hippocampus disrupt auditory-cued trace heart rate (fear) conditioning in rabbits. *Hippocampus, 10*, 739–751.

Marsh, R., Alexander, G. M., Packard, M. G., Zhu, H., Wingard, J. C., Quackenbush, G., & Peterson, B. S. (2004). Habit learning in Tourette syndrome: A translational neuroscience approach to a developmental psychopathology. *Archives of General Psychiatry*, *61*, 1259–1268.

Marsh, R., Alexander, G. M., Packard, M. G., Zhu, H., & Peterson, B. S. (2005). Perceptual-motor skill learning in Gilles de la Tourette syndrome. Evidence for multiple procedural learning and memory systems. *Neuropsychologia*, *43*, 1456–1465.

Migo, E. M., Corbett, K., Graham, J., Smith, S., Tate, S., Moran, P. M., et al. (2006). A novel test of conditioned inhibition correlates with personality measures of schizotypy and reward sensitivity. *Behavioural Brain Research*, *168*, 299–306.

Mink, J. W. (2003). The basal ganglia and involuntary movements: Impaired inhibition of competing motor patterns. *Archives of Neurology*, *60*, 1365–1368.

Minzer, K., Lee, O., Hong, J. J., & Singer, H. S. (2004). Increased prefrontal D2 protein in Tourette syndrome: A postmortem analysis of frontal cortex and striatum. *Journal of the Neurological Sciences*, *219*, 55–61.

Mueller, S. C., Jackson, G. M., Dhalla, R., Datsopoulos, S., & Hollis, C. P. (2006). Enhanced cognitive control in young people with Tourette's syndrome. *Current Biology*, *16*, 570–573.

Mueller, S. C., Swainson, R., & Jackson, G. M. (2007). Behavioural and neuro-physiological correlates of bivalent and univalent responses during task switching. *Brain Research*, *1157*, 56–65.

Nelson, A., & Killcross, S. (2006). Amphetamine exposure enhances habit formation. *Journal of Neuroscience*, *26*, 3805–3812.

Nicholson, D. A., & Freeman, J. H. (2002). Neuronal correlates of conditioned inhibition of the eyeblink response in the anterior interpositus nucleus. *Behavioral Neuroscience*, *116*, 22–36.

Ozonoff, S., Strayer, D. L., McMahon, W. M., & Filloux, F. (1998). Inhibitory deficits in Tourette syndrome: A function of comorbidity and symptom severity. *Journal of Child Psychology and Psychiatry*, *39*, 1109–1118.

Packard, M. G., & Knowlton, B. J. (2002). Learning and memory functions of the basal ganglia. *Annual Review of Neuroscience*, *25*, 563–593.

Peterson, B. S., Skudlarski, P., Anderson, A. W., Zhang, H., Gatenby, J. C., Lacadie, C. M., et al. (1998). A functional magnetic resonance imaging study of tic suppression in Tourette syndrome. *Archives of General Psychiatry*, *55*, 326–333.

Prado, H. D., do Rosario, M. C., Lee, J., Hounie, A. G., Shavitt, R. G., & Miguel, E. C. (2008). Sensory phenomena in obsessive-compulsive disorder and tic disorders: A review of the literature. *CNS Spectrums*, *13*, 425–432.

Rankins, D., Bradshaw, J. L., & Georgiou-Karistianis, N. (2005). Local–global processing in obsessive-compulsive disorder and comorbid Tourette's syndrome. *Brain and Cognition*, *59*, 43–51.

Rescorla, R. A. (1969). Pavlovian conditioned inhibition. *Psychological Bulletin*, *72*, 77–94.

Rescorla, R. A., & Holland, P. C. (1977). Associations in Pavlovian conditioned inhibition. *Learning and Motivation*, *8*, 429–447.

Robbins, T. W. (2002). The 5-choice serial reaction time task: Behavioural pharmacology and functional neurochemistry. *Psychopharmacology*, *163*, 362–380.

Robertson, M. M. (2006). Attention deficit hyperactivity disorder, tics and Tourette syndrome: The relationship and treatment implications. A commentary. *European Child & Adolescent Psychiatry, 15*, 1–11.

Roessner, V., Albrecht, B., Dechent, P., Baudewig, J., & Rothenberger, A. (2008). Normal response inhibition in boys with Tourette syndrome. *Behavioural and Brain Functions, 4*, 29.

Saka, E., & Graybiel, M. A. (2003). Pathophysiology of Tourette's syndrome: Striatal pathways revisited. *Brain and Development*, Suppl. 1, S15–S19.

Serrien, D. J., Orth, M., Evans, A. H., Lees, A. J., & Brown, P. (2005). Motor inhibition in patients with Gilles de la Tourette syndrome: Functional activation patterns as revealed by EEG coherence. *Brain, 128*, 116–125.

Sheppard, D. M., Bradshaw, J. L., Purcell, R., & Pantelis, C. (1999). Tourette's and comorbid syndromes: Obsessive compulsive and attention deficit hyperactivity disorder. A common etiology? *Clinical Psychology Review, 19*, 531–552.

Siegel, S. (1977). Morphine tolerance acquisition as an associative process. *Journal of Experimental Psychology: Animal Behavior Processes, 3*, 1–13.

Singer, H. S. (2005). Tourette's syndrome: From behaviour to biology. *The Lancet Neurology, 4*, 149–159.

Singer, H. S., & Minzer, K. (2003). Neurobiology of Tourette's syndrome: Concepts of neuroanatomic localization and neurochemical abnormalities. *Brain and Development*, Suppl. 1, S70–S84.

Sowell, E. R., Thompson, P. M., Holmes, C. J., Jernigan, T. L., & Toga, A. W. (1999). In vivo evidence for post-adolescent brain maturation in frontal and striatal regions. *Nature Neuroscience, 2*, 859–861.

Spencer, T., Biederman, J., Harding, M., O'Donnell, D., Wilens, T., Faraone, S., et al. (1998). Disentangling the overlap between Tourette's disorder and ADHD. *Journal of Child Psychology and Psychiatry, 39*, 1037–1044.

Stewart J., de Wit H., & Eikelboom R. (1984). Role of unconditioned and conditioned drug effects in the self-administration of opiates and stimulants. *Psychological Review, 91*, 251–268.

Swerdlow, N. R. (2001). Obsessive-compulsive disorder and tic syndromes. *Medical Clinics of North America, 85*, 735–755.

Swerdlow, N. R., Magulac, M., Filion, D., & Zinner, S. (1996). Visuospatial priming and latent inhibition in children and adults with Tourette's disorder. *Neuropsychology, 10*, 485–494.

The Tourette Syndrome Classifications Study Group (1993). Definitions and classification of tic disorders. *Archives of Neurology, 50*, 1013–1016.

Thibaudeau, G., Potvin, O., Allen, K., Doré, F. Y., & Goulet, S. (2007). Dorsal, ventral, and complete excitotoxic lesions of the hippocampus in rats failed to impair appetitive trace conditioning. *Behavioural Brain Research, 185*, 9–20.

Thibault, G., Felezeu, M., O'Connor, K. P., Todorov, C., Stip, E., & Lavoie, M. E. (2008). Influence of comorbid obsessive-compulsive symptoms on brain event-related potentials in Gilles de la Tourette syndrome. *Progress in Neuro-Psychopharmacology and Biological Psychiatry, 32*, 803–815.

Tobler, P. N., Dickinson, A., & Schultz, W. (2003). Coding of predicted reward omission by dopamine neurons in a conditioned inhibition paradigm. *Journal of Neuroscience, 23*, 10402–10410.

Verdellen, C. W. J., Hoogduin, C. A. L., Kato, B. S., Keijsers, G. P. J., Cath, D. C., & Hoijtink, H. B. (2008). Habituation of premonitory sensations during exposure and response prevention treatment in Tourette syndrome. *Behavior Modification, 32*, 215–227.

Wang, L., Lee, D. Y., Bailey, E., Hartlein, J. M., Gado, M. H., Miller, M. I., et al. (2007). Validity of large-deformation high dimensional brain mapping of the basal ganglia in adults with Tourette syndrome. *Psychiatry Research: Neuroimaging, 154*, 181–190.

Watson, J. B. (1924). *Behaviorism*. New York: Norton.

Wilhelm, S., Deckersbach, T., Coffey, B. J., Bohne, A., Peterson, A. L., & Baer, L. (2003). Habit versus supportive psychotherapy for Tourette's disorder: A randomized controlled trial. *American Journal of Psychiatry, 160*, 1175–1177.

Woods, D. W., Walther, M. R., Bauer, C. C., Kemp, J. J., & Conelea, C. A. (2009). The development of stimulus control over tics: A potential explanation for contextually-based variability in the symptoms of Tourette syndrome. *Behaviour Research and Therapy, 47*, 41–47.

Yazgan, M. Y., Peterson, B., Wexler, B. E., & Leckman, J. F. (1995). Behavioral laterality in individuals with Gilles de la Tourette's syndrome and basal ganglia alterations: A preliminary report. *Biological Psychiatry, 38*, 386–390.

Yin, H. H., Knowlton, B. J., & Balleine, B. W. (2004). Lesions of dorsolateral striatum preserve outcome expectancy but disrupt habit formation in instrumental learning. *European Journal of Neuroscience, 19*, 181–189.

Yin, H. H., Knowlton, B. J., & Balleine, B. W. (2005). Blockade of NMDA receptors in the dorsomedial striatum prevents action–outcome learning in instrumental conditioning. *European Journal of Neuroscience, 22*, 505–512.

Yin, H. H., & Knowlton, B. J. (2006). The role of the basal ganglia in habit formation. *Nature Reviews Neuroscience, 7*, 464–476.

Yoon, D. Y., Gause, C. D., Leckman, J. F., & Singer, H. S. (2007). Frontal dopaminergic abnormality in Tourette syndrome: A postmortem analysis. *Journal of the Neurological Sciences, 255*, 50–56.

Glossary of basic learning theory terms

Blocking   The observation that little conditioning will be acquired to a conditioned stimulus (CS) when that CS is conditioned in compound with another CS that has already been conditioned.

Causal learning   The learning of a relationship between two neutral events. Distinguished from Pavlovian conditioning where the CS is neutral but the US is biologically significant.

Compound stimulus   Where two or more stimuli (e.g., a light and a tone) are presented together. The stimuli may be presented together at the same time (a simultaneous compound) or after one another (a serial compound).

Conditioned (or conditional) inhibitor   A CS that has received training that results in it being a predictor of the absence of the US.

Conditioned (or conditional) response (CR)   In classical conditioning, the response that is evoked by the conditioned stimulus, after conditioning.

Conditioned (or conditional) stimulus (CS)   In classical conditioning, an initially neutral stimulus that acquires the ability to evoke a response by being paired with a biologically significant stimulus.

Conditioning   A procedure in which a conditioned stimulus is scheduled to reliably predict the occurrence of an important biological event (unconditioned stimulus, for example, food), such that the conditioned stimulus comes to elicit a conditioned response.

Context   Background stimuli that are present during learning or recall. These stimuli may be extroceptive or introceptive.

Contingency   The statistical relationship between two events in the world (e.g., a CS and a US, or a response and a reward). Contingency can be positive (indicating that, for example, the reward is more likely given the presence of a response), negative (indicating that, for example, a reward is less likely given the presence of a response), or zero (for example, responding and reward are unrelated).

Counter-conditioning   A procedure in which the organism's response to a stimulus is reversed; for example, changing the appetitive response to CS first paired with food to a fear response by subsequently pairing the CS with a shock.

Exteroceptive stimulus   A stimulus originating outside of the body (e.g., a light or sound). Contrast with interoceptive.

Extinction   The loss of conditioned behaviour by a stimulus or a response brought about by presenting that stimulus in the absence of the unconditioned stimulus, or reinforcer.

Footshock   A painful electrical stimulus applied through the floor of the animals' experimental chamber.

Generalization   The transfer of learning from a trained CS to a similar CS.

Incentive value   The value of a reward or unconditioned stimulus (e.g., food, water) as a function of the motivational state (e.g., hungry/ satiated, thirsty/satiated) of the agent.

Instrumental conditioning (also operant conditioning)   The situation in which an organism experiences a relationship between their behaviour and its consequences. Such experience may result in goal-directed (response–outcome) learning or habit-based (stimulus–response) learning.

Interoceptive stimulus   A stimulus originating inside the body (e.g., hunger). Contrast with exteroceptive.

Latent inhibition   The retardation of learning by exposure to the conditioned stimulus prior to conditioning.

Overshadowing   A reduction in conditioned responding to a conditioned stimulus (CS) by conditioning that CS in compound with another, often more salient, CS.

Potentiation   An enhancement of conditioned responding to a conditioned stimulus (CS) by conditioning that CS in compound with another, often more salient, CS. Contrast with overshadowing.

Second-order conditioning   The acquisition of a conditioned response to a conditioned stimulus by pairing that conditioned stimulus with another stimulus that has been conditioned.

Unconditioned (or unconditional) response (UR)   In classical conditioning, the response that is evoked by the unconditioned stimulus.

Unconditioned (or unconditional) stimulus (US)   In classical conditioning, a, normally biologically significant, stimulus that can evoke a response before conditioning occurs.

Vicarious conditioning   Conditioning by observing the response evoked by another individual to a stimulus.

Author index

Subject index